A. M. Gibbs
June 1982

THE
HUT SIX STORY

THE HUT SIX STORY

BREAKING THE ENIGMA CODES

Gordon Welchman

McGRAW-HILL BOOK COMPANY
New York   St. Louis   San Francisco
Toronto   Hamburg   Mexico

1 2 3 4 5 6 7 8 9 D O D O 8 7 6 5 4 3 2

ISBN 0-07-069180-0

LIBRARY OF CONGRESS CATALOGING IN PUBLICATION DATA

Welchman, Gordon.
The Hut Six story.
1. World War, 1939–1945—Cryptography.   2. World War,
1939–1945—Secret service—Great Britain.   3. World War,
1939–1945—Personal narratives, English.   4. Welchman,
Gordon.   I. Title.
D810.C88W44   940.54'86'41   81-13657
ISBN 0-07-069180-0   AACR2

Book design by Stanley S. Drate

To Alastair Denniston, Marian Rejewski, Dilly Knox, and Edward Travis. To the many men and women whose varied talents and total dedication contributed to the success of Hut 6 in World War II. And to those among us who, seriously concerned with our national security, will see to it that the story of this success, no longer hidden, is fully utilized in our anticipation of future dangers.

Contents

PART FOUR

Today

List of Illustrations

Prologue

On a Sunday in the summer of 1974 my wife, Teeny, and I were staying in England with her godmother, whose son-in-law was reading the *Sunday Telegraph*. Finding an interesting article, he showed it to me. It was the second part of "Deepest Secret of the War" by F. W. Winterbotham, and it was a discussion of secret activities of World War II in which I myself had taken part. Fortunately the previous week's *Sunday Telegraph* had not been thrown away, and I was able to read the whole article there and then. It was a preview of Winterbotham's forthcoming book *The Ultra Secret*, which has since become familiar to readers throughout the world. For the first time it became public knowledge that two organizations of the British wartime Government Communications Headquarters (GCHQ) at Bletchley Park, known as Hut 6 and Hut 8, had succeeded in breaking the Enigma machine cipher that was used extensively by the Germans. Furthermore, Winterbotham had revealed that intelligence derived from these two sources, known by the code name Ultra, had been of immense value to the Allies.

I was tremendously excited. I had been the man primarily responsible, during the winter of 1939–1940, for building up the Hut 6 organization to a point at which it was ready for action when Hitler struck against Norway and France in April and May 1940. But in the years since World War II I had never felt at liberty even to hint at my own part in such activities. During the war it had sometimes been extremely difficult to distinguish between items of information that I had learned from Enigma decodes and those I had picked up from newspapers or radio broadcasts. The possibility that one might give away the secret in an unguarded moment was a continual nagging worry, so I had tried to avoid any discussion of the war except with people who were in the know. After the war I still avoided discussions of wartime events for fear that I might reveal information obtained from Ultra rather than from some published account. Indeed, I was careful in much of my subsequent work to avoid suggesting that many of my ideas were derived from wartime experience. Now, suddenly, what was indeed one of the best-kept secrets of the war had emerged into the light of day.

I felt that this turn of events released me from my wartime pledge of secrecy. I could at last talk to my friends, relatives, and colleagues about the activities of one of these two organizations, Hut 6, with which I was closely associated from the outset. I could even write my own account of what actually happened. I began to think of a book.

During the twenty-nine years from summer 1945 to summer 1974 I had thought very little about World War II events related to Hut 6, until I joined the MITRE Corporation* in 1962 and found myself involved in studying the information flow needed for coordination of ground and air forces in battle. In researching the optimum design of a communications system to meet the information needs of the future battlefield, I discovered that what I had learned from my work on the German system of World War II was still valid. Technology had changed tremendously, but the principles of handling the coded traffic were much the same.

Whereas years earlier I had been involved in breaking down the security of the German communications system, now my task was to protect the security, and also the survivability, of our new battlefield communications systems. The combination of these two experiences has strengthened my desire to discuss what we can learn

* The MITRE Corporation of Bedford, Massachusetts, and McLean, Virginia, is a non-profit, nonmanufacturing Federal Contract Research Center, providing services in systems analysis, systems engineering, and technical direction for U.S. Government Agencies and other public-interest organizations.

from the past that will help us to achieve national security in the future. Thus, in telling the story of Hut 6, I have emphasized those aspects of clandestine activities that are still relevant.

The foremost of these is that the way in which Hut 6 was able to break down the security of a major part of the German command communications of World War II contains valuable warnings to the many people—not just cryptographers—on whom the security of our future battlefield communications will depend. Second is that the study of cryptographic security must be widened to include survivability: making sure that communications will be available in working order to handle essential information in times of emergency. Third, that protection against various forms of "special means," such as sabotage, theft, infiltration of agents, jamming, spoofing, and so on is just as important, if not more important, than protection against enemy cryptanalysis. Fourth, because of continually changing world politics we need to be prepared for different kinds of military conflict in different environments. Fifth, that we must not neglect the nonmilitary means by which an enemy may seek to undermine our national will. And finally, that the really frightening pace at which technology is advancing introduces many new problems that are not yet being satisfactorily addressed. In thinking about security measures for a military communications system in the 1980s and 1990s, the near certainty that major technological advances will have occurred in the interval is a real worry. Will the security measures we plan today be adequate in the technological environment of tomorrow?

I am convinced that the Hut 6 story can contribute to this planning. The principle of the bombe, a completely new electromechanical device that we built to help us break the Enigma, should have been made known many years ago; it contains a clear warning, much needed today, that our confidence in cryptographic security should not depend solely on the number of possibilities an enemy cryptanalyst must examine to break a code, and on the assumption that he must examine each possibility individually.

My study of how the Germans made it possible for us to break a cipher machine that would have been unbreakable if properly used proves that if we are to achieve security, we must pay careful attention to the indoctrination, training, and monitoring of all personnel involved. The Hut 6 story also provides a striking example of the importance of close cooperation between different specialized activities in military action that requires coordinated operations. (We must consider an interdisciplinary approach to the planning of military capabilities and to the conduct of military operations.) We can also see that the German tactical communications system, apart from unknowingly allowing its Enigma to be broken, was an exceptionally effective tool of war. At present, however, our own tactical communications can only be regarded as a glaring weakness in our military defenses. Finally, an analysis of what was effective or ineffective in the exploitation of Hut 6 Ultra intelligence can hardly fail to be of value in planning how to handle intelligence on future battlefields.

PART
ONE

Backdrop to Hut Six

1

Britain Went to War

The Germans invaded Poland on September 1, 1939; Great Britain and France declared war on September 3. Most of us in England were pretty scared. We had attended first-aid classes in anticipation of bombing. The media had told us to expect immediate air attacks if war should come. We had also been told that about the safest place in the house was under the stairs. My first wife, Katharine, and I lived on the outskirts of the largely academic town of Cambridge where I was teaching mathematics at the university. Cambridge could hardly be regarded as a prime military target by anyone who had thought about war. Not having thought about war, however, we followed official advice. On that first night, when the air-raid sirens were sounded in Cambridge—a false alarm, incidentally—we crouched under the staircase with our one-and-a-half-year-old son, Nick. I must confess that Katharine saw the absurdity of the situation before I did.

This incident shows how poorly the British public was prepared for war. The country had been under the appeasement-minded government of Neville Chamberlain, who is remembered for the umbrella that he carried and for the monstrous "Munich Agreement" with Hitler of September 1938, which betrayed Czechoslovakia. Already, in March 1938, Austria had been invaded and annexed, yet most of us in England were far less concerned with the sinister trend of events than we should have been. We even welcomed the Munich Agreement, thinking mistakenly that the danger of war had been averted. After Munich, however, there were signs that the British government was taking the possibility of war seriously. We became increasingly alarmed, but were still abysmally ignorant of what to expect.

The general impression was that, from the outset of war, every town and village in Great Britain could expect to be bombed, and that after a few days there would be no more RAF pilots and the country would be defenseless. As I remember, I did once ask a guest, a senior Royal Air Force officer, a question to this effect: "If the Germans were to load all their aircraft with all the bombs they could carry, how large an area could they bomb in one raid?" But I could obtain no answer whatever. Our guest had evidently never considered the question of how much damage the Germans could actually cause.

As things turned out, even after the heaviest German bombing attacks, one could still drive around the English countryside and see few signs of damage. The area around Bletchley Park, where so much vital work was done on the breaking of the enemy's codes and ciphers, was never attacked, even though it also contained an important railway junction on one of the main lines to the north. In fact, the threat of countrywide German bombing had been grossly exaggerated.

For several years before the war, mercifully, many Britons who believed that Hitler could not and should not be appeased had been making preparations. One of these was the naval commander, Alastair Denniston, head of the Government Code and Cypher School, who had been one of the original cryptographers in Room 40 at the British Admiralty during World War I, first under Sir Alfred Ewing and then under the Director of Naval Intelligence, Captain William Reginald Hall, later Admiral Sir Reginald ("Blinker") Hall—whose nickname referred to a twitch that made one eye flash like a Navy signal lamp.

Between the wars, Denniston, seeing the strategic value of what he and his group were doing, had kept the Room 40 activity alive. In 1920 the name of the organization was changed to "Government Code and Cypher School" (GCCS), and it was transferred from the Navy to the Foreign Office. Alastair Denniston's son, Robin, was about twelve years old when World War II broke out. Today Robin is a leading member of the British book publishing establishment. Back in 1939, of course, he had no knowledge at all of what his father was doing, but he still has many significant memories.

Before the war, much of Alastair Denniston's social life consisted of sherry parties, golf matches, and other occasions attended by his colleagues of GCCS. In retrospect they seem to Robin to have been a very close, fiercely loyal, defensive, almost cozy group, perhaps under attack from other departments. He went to his father's office very seldom, but knew several of the group quite well, including Josh Cooper, Nigel de Grey, Dilly Knox, and John Tiltman; also Frank Birch, who had returned to Cambridge but kept in touch. All of these will appear in my story. Robin remembers many occasions when his father's colleagues gathered at his home. He feels that the interest they showed in his sister and himself reflected an admiration for their father.

Alastair Denniston planned for the coming war. Following the example of his World War I chiefs, he decided that the Universities of Oxford and Cambridge would be his first source of recruits. So he visited them and arranged for polite notes to be sent to many lecturers, including myself, asking whether we would be willing to serve our country in the event of war. He chose Bletchley, 47 miles from London, as a wartime home for GCCS because it was a railway junction on the main line to the north from London's Euston Station and lay about halfway between Oxford and Cambridge with good train service to both. He acquired Bletchley Park, a large Victorian Tudor-Gothic mansion with ample grounds. The house had been renovated by a prosperous merchant, who had introduced what Dilly Knox's niece, Penelope Fitzgerald, in her family memoir *The Knox Brothers*, was to call "majestic plumbing."

In the planning for the wartime Bletchley Park, Denniston's principal helpers, in Robin's recollection, were Josh Cooper, Nigel de Grey, John Tiltman, Admiral Sinclair's sister, and Sir Stuart Menzies. Edward Travis, whose later performance as successor to Alastair Denniston at Bletchley Park was so significant, must have been involved, but he was not one of the "family" team that dated back so many years. Robin believes that, before joining GCCS, Travis was involved in encipherment rather than codebreaking.

As preparatory work was being done, Denniston visited the site frequently, and made plans for construction of the numerous huts that would be needed in the anticipated wartime expansion of

GCCS activities. When war actually came, these wooden huts were constructed with amazing speed by a local building contractor, Captain Hubert Faulkner, who was also a keen horseman and would often appear on site in riding clothes.

The word "hut" has many meanings, so I had better explain that the Bletchley huts were single-story wooden structures of various shapes and sizes. Hut 6 was about 30 feet wide and 60 feet long. The inside walls and partitions were of plaster board. From a door at one end a central passage, with three small rooms on either side, led to two large rooms at the far end. There were no toilets; staff had to go to another building. The furniture consisted mostly of wooden trestle tables and wooden folding chairs, and the partitions were moved around in response to changing needs.

The final move of the GCCS organization to Bletchley was made in August 1939, only a few weeks before war was declared. As security cover the expedition, involving perhaps fifty people, was officially termed "Captain Ridley's Hunting Party," Captain Ridley being the man in charge of general administration. The name of the organization was changed from GCCS to "Government Communications Headquarters" or GCHQ.

The perimeter of the Bletchley Park grounds was wired, and guarded by the RAF regiment, whose NCOs warned the men that if they didn't look lively they would be sent "inside the Park," suggesting that it was now a kind of lunatic asylum.

Denniston was to remain in command until around June 1940, when hospitalization for a stone in his bladder forced him to undertake less exacting duties. After his recovery he returned to Bletchley for a time before moving to London in 1941 to work on diplomatic traffic. Travis, who had been head of the Naval Section of GCCS and second in command to Denniston, took his place and ran Bletchley Park for the rest of the war. In recognition of his achievements he became Sir Edward Travis in 1942.

In spite of his hospitalization, Denniston, on his own initiative, flew to America in 1941, made contact with leaders of the cryptological organizations, and laid the foundations for later cooperation. He established a close personal relationship with the great American cryptologist William Friedman, who visited him in England later. The air flights were dangerous. On Denniston's return journey a plane just ahead of his and one just behind were both shot down.

Denniston's daughter was nicknamed "Y," because she was an unknown quantity before her birth. Years later Friedman wrote a letter to her: "Your father was a great man in whose debt all English-speaking people will remain for a very long time, if not forever. That so few should know exactly what he did . . . is the sad part."

Not very long after the Munich Agreement of September 1938 I had answered "yes" to Denniston's polite note and had been called to London a little later for one or two weeks of preliminary indoctrination. It was a very informal affair. With several other new recruits I was introduced to the established manual methods of cryptography and cryptanalysis, and also to the various types of cipher machines that were in use at that time.

I did not see much of Denniston, but I remember that he had a very warm personality and a quiet but incisive manner of speaking. He was neat in appearance, and he must have had a somewhat distinctive gait because, though I could not possibly describe it, I recognized it in his son long afterward, when I met Robin. Denniston told me that, in the event of war, I was to report to him at Bletchley Park* in the town of Bletchley, Buckinghamshire.

I remember very little else about the preliminary indoctrination in London, except that I was very impressed by Oliver Strachey, a senior member of the GCCS staff, who during the coming war would head an organization known as Intelligence Services Oliver Strachey (ISOS). He seemed to be giving us an overview of the whole problem of deriving intelligence from enemy communications, and this may well have been a strong guiding influence on my wartime work. Our other instructors dealt with specific examples of manual cryptographic methodology. Dilly Knox, the GCCS expert on the Enigma machine, may have been there, but I do not remember meeting him on that occasion.

I have the distinct impression that the chances of ever being able to do anything with the German Enigma traffic were at the time considered minimal, at least until access to a machine could be achieved. The Enigma was one of a family of cipher machines that

* To the thousands of people who worked there, Bletchley Park will always be known as B.P. To any of those people who may read this book I apologize for not always referring to the place as B.P., but I feel that to the general reader the abbreviation will hardly have the same nostalgic appeal.

produced a highly variable "scramble" of the twenty-six letters of the alphabet by passing electric current through a set of movable rotors, each of which, by its internal electrical connections, contributed to the overall scramble. To discover the internal wiring of the rotors by purely cryptanalytical means appeared to be an insoluble problem.

In the interim between the preliminary indoctrination in London and the actual outbreak of war, I knew nothing of the GCCS activities. I was back in Cambridge, where I had been a mathematics scholar at Trinity College from 1925 to 1928, and a college lecturer in mathematics at Sidney Sussex College since 1929. I was working on a book, *Introduction to Algebraic Geometry*, for the Cambridge University Press. I had been writing it for about five years and was within a few months of having the manuscript ready for the publishers, but the war came just too soon. Publication was delayed until after the war.

The word "scholar" that I have just used, and will use again, needs explanation, because it has a very different meaning in America. In Cambridge, England, the scholars won their titles (major scholar, minor scholar, or exhibitioner) in a highly competitive examination before they entered the University. Being a scholar carried rights and responsibilities—for example, rooms in college as opposed to lodgings outside, and reading the lessons at early morning services in chapel. If a scholar needed financial assistance, he was entitled to generous amounts of money toward his tuition and other university expenses. Able boys, who did not need the money, took the scholarship exams simply to win the academic standing that the title implied.

On the morning after Britain declared war on Germany I drove from Cambridge to Bletchley and reported to Denniston, who sent me along to join Dilly Knox's Enigma group of about ten people in a building known as the "Cottage." In that small building in the stableyard I found that an event of immense importance had occurred very recently. I was not told very much about it, but the Poles had given us one or perhaps two replicas of the Enigma machine that had been issued to the German army and air force. We now knew all the electrical and mechanical details, and we also knew the procedures that were then being used for encoding and decoding. Furthermore the Poles had given us the full advantage of their brilliant work on Enigma. When I come to describe what happened at Bletchley Park it will become apparent that these gifts were of immense importance in getting us started on the road that led to Hut 6 Ultra.

At the time I did not bother about how the Poles had been able to make replicas of the German Enigma, or about how the machine had reached us. It didn't matter to me then, and even now I do not know which of several stories to believe. A point of general agreement is that a meeting was held in July 1939 at a hideout of the Polish Secret Service in the Pyry forest. At this meeting Colonel Gwido Langer, head of Poland's Cipher Bureau, astonished a British delegation, headed by Alastair Denniston and a French delegation headed by Captain Gustave Bertrand, by revealing that his team knew "everything about Enigma," and furthermore that two replicas of the machine were to be handed over, one for Britain and one for France. This much I have learned from Ronald Lewin's *Ultra Goes to War*, and I have not found any contradiction in other writings, though I must admit that I have not tried very hard.

But there are different stories about what led up to the meeting in the Pyry forest and what followed it. On the whole I like the story, told in *A Man Called Intrepid*, that in early 1939, when the new Enigmas were being delivered to frontier units, a German military truck containing one of them was ambushed. Polish agents removed the Enigma and put another machine in its place. They then made it appear that there had been an accident and that the truck had caught fire. Thus the Germans who examined the wreckage were led to believe that some charred bits of coils, springs, and rotors were the remains of their Enigma. For a reason that will appear immediately, I am inclined to believe that something of this sort must indeed have occurred.

There is a divergence of view as to how an Enigma reached England after the Pyry forest meeting. Stevenson, in *A Man Called Intrepid*, asserts that when Alastair Denniston, then in his fifties, stayed at the Bristol Hotel in Warsaw in August 1939, a large leather bag containing an Enigma machine, or its replica, was left beside a pile of luggage in the hotel's foyer. Denniston, carrying an identical bag containing some dirty shirts and some weighty but valueless books, casually exchanged the bags and returned to England with his prize. Robin Denniston believes this story of his father's exploit to be true, but cannot provide conclusive evidence. Another story, supported by Ronald Lewin in *Ultra Goes to War*, is that at the Pyry forest meeting two replicas of the Enigma were given to the Frenchman, Bertrand, and that he himself brought one of them to London, where he was met at Victoria Station by Menzies. Robin Denniston believes that this story too is true. And why not? In those dangerous times the Poles may well have decided to send us two Enigma replicas by different routes.

Anyway, what does it matter? The vital point is that the Poles managed to give us the details of the machine and the benefit of their expertise in time for us to exploit them early in the war. We would ultimately capture many Enigmas, but, as things turned out, everything was to depend on what we achieved in the first three months and later, in the very first year of the war. In fact, the Hut 6 balloon might never have gotten off the ground at all if I had taken six months instead of three to get things moving.

Just as this book was entering the final stages of publication, I received reliable information about the Polish contribution. In February of 1981, Monsieur Jean Stengers, Professor of History at the University of Brussels, sent me a copy of his article "La Guerre des Messages Codés (1930–1945)," which had just appeared in the magazine *L'Histoire*. The article contains a new account of Polish work on the Enigma, which fits exactly with what I know of the early days at Bletchley, and also with what I have guessed. I believe this account to be far more trustworthy than the many others that had previously appeared in print.

The story starts as early as 1930, when three mathematics graduates of the Polish University of Poznan, Marian Rejewski, Jerzy Rozycki, and Henryk Zygalski, were recruited by the Polish cipher bureau in Warsaw. In the autumn of 1932 Rejewski became aware of the Enigma problem. The Polish bureau had acquired a commercially available Enigma and knew that the German military were using a somewhat similar cipher machine. Rejewski, working alone, began an investigation that entitles him to be regarded as one of the greatest cryptanalysts of his day.*

In a few weeks Rejewski achieved a first breakthrough by estab-

* He died in Warsaw in February 1980.

lishing a mathematical approach that, in theory, would solve his problem. But the time required to reach a solution made his method impractical.

Then, on December 8, 1932, he was given what appeared to be authentic documents relating to the German military Enigma. Among them was a list of the keys used in the months of October and December 1931. These documents had been offered to the French intelligence bureau by a German named Hans-Thilo Schmidt. Captain Bertrand, later General Bertrand, the bureau's specialist on foreign ciphers, handled the contacts with Schmidt, who became known by the code name Asché. Having obtained the Enigma documents, Bertrand presented them to the cryptanalysts of his bureau, who were not interested. He then turned to the leaders of the Polish cipher bureau, with whom he had already established an excellent rapport. They were enthusiastic, and before long the documents appeared on Rejewski's desk.

Rejewski was now able to put his theory into practice.* After only a month of continuous and highly concentrated effort, he had worked out the electrical connections of the three wheels that were used at that time in the German Enigma. He was able to have a replica of the machine constructed. He began decoding German military messages in early 1933. He was then joined by Rozycki and Zygalski; these three men formed the team that, with the brilliant collaboration of Polish engineers, followed the changes in the German use of the Enigma during the following six years.

This team conceived and built two machines: the "Cyclometre," which consisted of two interconnected Enigmas, and the "Bomba," due primarily to Rejewski, which was a combination of six Enigmas. They developed a system of *feuilles perforées*, or perforated sheets, due primarily to Zygalski, who died in England in 1978. (Rozycki died in an accident in 1942.)

The reader of this book will recognize, when he comes to Chapter 4, that Zygalski's system of perforated sheets must have been the forerunner of the system developed in the Bletchley Cottage in the fall and winter of 1939/40. The testing machine used by Dilly Knox's team must have been based on the "Cyclometre." Rejewski's

---

* It seems that Dilly Knox in England may well have arrived at a comparable theory, but he did not have access to the Asché documents.

six-Enigma "Bomba" must have been the origin of the machine on which Turing was working in the fall of 1939. It must have used the idea of double-ended Enigma scramblers that I describe in the Appendix.

Rejewski and his team reached their peak of success in the first half of 1938, when they were decoding German Enigma messages almost every day. But this peak of success was followed by a staggering setback. On December 15, 1938, the Germans introduced two new wheels, making five in all, any three of which, in any order, could be employed in the Enigma machine. This resulted in the sixty alternative wheel orders with which the Cottage and Hut 6 were to be faced.

Even Jean Stenger's excellent article does not explain how Rejewski came to know the internal wiring of these two new wheels. That he did so is evident from what followed. But as an achievement of pure cryptanalysis it is hard to believe; it seems to me that the Poles must have obtained the new five-wheel Enigma by capture or some other nefarious means. Even then, however, the preparation and use of new perforated sheets would have demanded a far greater effort than the Polish team could provide. Finding themselves in deep trouble, the Poles sought first to find out whether the British or the French could help them. An international conference, organized in January 1939 by Bertrand, showed them that they were well ahead of their friends. They did not reveal their own success.

In July 1939, sensing the approach of war, the Poles decided to make all their achievements known to their counterparts in France and Great Britain. A conference near Warsaw, on July 25, 1939, was attended by a small French group, including Bertrand, and a small British group, including Dilly Knox. To the astonishment of their guests, the Poles explained and demonstrated all their remarkable achievements: their Enigma theory, the models of the German Enigma machines, their "Cyclometre," their "Bomba," their perforated sheets, and the decodes of German messages that they had produced when the Enigma machine had only three wheels. In August 1939, just in time, Polish models of the five-wheel German military Enigma were sent to France and England.

Jean Stengers appears to have been in close touch both with Rejewski and with Bertrand. He tells the story of what the Poles and the French were doing during the war. To my surprise, I now learn that an organization at Gretz in France was collaborating with Bletchley for a time. Later, in 1943 to 1945, Rejewski was in England, attached to the Polish army. He was still involved in cryptanalysis, but was not permitted to know how Hut 6 had carried on from the start that he had given them. Indeed, he did not know of the end result of his work until he read Winterbotham's book in 1974.

Professor Stengers expresses astonishment that, even now, he cannot complete his story with an account of how the British carried on. But he knows the reason for British reluctance to reveal the methods they developed. He has discovered that, after the war, Britain sold a considerable number of Enigma machines to certain countries, no doubt claiming that they were unbreakable. But, says Jean Stengers, British codebreakers had no trouble.

As I have made clear in this book, it is my firm conviction that what I have revealed should have been made available to our planners many years ago. The over-prolonged secrecy has, in my view, already been prejudicial to our future national security. The reason for the secrecy, made public at last, is hard to accept.*

---

* I, personally, have heard conflicting statements on this matter, but, on balance, I believe that Jean Stengers is correct.

2

Germany Prepared for War

German President von Hindenberg died on August 2, 1934. That same afternoon Hitler proclaimed himself Führer, and ordered the armed forces of Germany to swear an oath of unconditional obedience to him, stating that they would be ready, as brave soldiers, to risk their lives at any time. It was the old *Fahneneid*, or "flag oath," of the Teuton knights. The entire General Staff recited the oath. Soon afterward a plebiscite approved Hitler's assumption of the presidency and of sole executive power. Hitler, however, preferred to retain the title of "Der Führer." In March 1935 he startled the world by denouncing the clauses of the Versailles Treaty providing for German disarmament.

When in the years 1935 to 1940 Hitler was remaking Germany's military capabilities, he and his generals paid considerable attention to the writings of several Englishmen. In 1929 one of these Englishmen, Sir Basil Liddell Hart, had published a remarkable book, *The Remaking of Modern Armies*. Combining knowledge of the military technology of his day with a study of military history, particularly the history of cavalry tactics, Liddell Hart expounded a new theory of the proper use of tanks in battle that was put into practice by the Germans ten years later with stunning success. But Hitler and his generals improved on Liddell Hart's theory in two important areas: air support for ground forces, and battlefield communications.

The original theory was that tank strength should not be dispersed by assigning a relatively small number of tanks to each infantry division. Rather, tanks (*Panzers* in German) should be concentrated in panzer divisions and panzer armies capable of bursting through the enemy's defense line and wreaking havoc in his rear. The initial penetration of prepared defense lines might require well-coordinated cooperation with massed infantry and artillery, but if and when a breakthrough could be achieved, the panzer formations, accompanied by motorized infantry and self-propelled guns, should exploit the situation by operating on their own, well in advance of foot-mobile infantry and slower-moving artillery weapons.

The Germans under Hitler remade their army. They developed a branch of their air force, the dive-bombing Stukas, for the specific purpose of support for their armored ground forces. And they remade their military signaling capabilities to permit effective coordination of all their fast-moving forces. By doing these three things they achieved one of the greatest revolutionary changes in military history.

We will be primarily concerned with the developments in communications. The German planners had realized in good time that the successful conduct of their blitzkrieg would call for revolutionary radio communications capabilities. They developed such capabilities, and, to provide the main arteries of secure information flow, they trained a large, highly mobile signals organization equipped with the Enigma cipher machine. Indeed, if there was a single central idea underlying the concept of Hitler's blitzkrieg, it was "speed of attack through speed of communications." That this was so did not occur to me until I read William Stevenson's *A Man Called Intrepid*, which gives a brief account of Sir William Stephenson's prewar contacts with Hitler's Air Force chiefs.* At one conference Stephenson heard a description of "blitzkrieg." Dive bombers and tanks would spearhead each offensive, followed by troops in fast carriers. When he asked how their Air Force would get support so far ahead of the armies, General Erhard Milch, State Secretary for Air, replied:

---

* Note the confusion between Sir William Stephenson, who was called "Intrepid," and the book's author, William Stevenson.

The dive bombers will form a flying artillery, directed to work in harmony with ground forces through good radio communications. You, a radio expert, must appreciate that for the first time in history, this coordination of forces is possible. The Air Force will not require ground support, any more than the armored divisions will need repair units. Tanks and planes will be disposable. The real secret is speed—speed of attack through speed of communications.

At the start of World War II, as a result of this general principle, the Germans were overwhelmingly superior to the Allies in their radio communications for the speedy coordination of forces in battle. The Allies could not match the equipment illustrated in Figure 2.1, which shows the great German panzer general, Heinz Guderian, and his signals staff in a command vehicle. The general is standing with field glasses in hand. Next to him is a radio operator. And in the foreground, the man at the complicated-looking typewriter is operating an Enigma cipher machine.

It was common for the German regiment, division, and corps commanders to be accompanied everywhere by specially equipped radio command and control vehicles of this sort. So equipped, the German panzer generals were always well informed about the current situation and had means available to control their units, request air support, and keep in contact with their parent headquarters. An entire signal battalion was deployed with each panzer division to provide the necessary communications.

Such, then, was the German revolution in battlefield communications. It was not a major revolution in technology. Rather, it was a revolutionary attitude to what existing communications and cryptographic technology could contribute to the combined operations of fast-moving ground forces and their air support. It was a matter of organization, training, and scale of effort. Above all it was a matter of thinking out what problems had to be solved. Because the Germans had done such a good job, the problems with which we were faced were unprecedented. Never before had radio signaling and cryptography been employed on such a large scale to provide battlefield communications.

In thinking about the German preparations as they affected Hut 6, it will be worthwhile to look into some of the earlier developments both of signaling and of cryptography.

Figure 2.1   General Guderian's Command Vehicle

One of the pioneers of modern military signaling was an American, Albert James Myer. The U.S. Army had no Signal Corps at all before 1854. In that year Myer, then a young Army doctor, went on frontier duty in Texas and became interested in the problems of military signaling in the field. He invented the "wig-wag" system, which became sufficiently established to be used by both sides in the Civil War. Myer became the originator and first commander of the U.S. Army Signal Corps.

The invention of wig-wag stemmed directly from Myer's rediscovery of the work of a Greek historian, Polybius. Around 170 B.C. Polybius described methods of military signaling; in Chapter 46 of his tenth book of history he tells us:

> The last method that I shall mention was invented either by Cleoxenes or by Democritus, but perfected by myself. This method is precise, and capable of signifying everything that happens with the greatest accuracy. A very exact attention, however, is required in using it.

I shall have occasion to echo the last sentence.

The Polybius method was an alphabetic signaling system. First the letters of the alphabet were arranged in a square matrix or checkerboard, with five numbered rows and five numbered columns. This provided positions for twenty-five letters, enough for the Greek alphabet. For our twenty-six-letter alphabet we could combine two letters, say I and J, and form a Polybius square thus:

	1	2	3	4	5
1	A	B	C	D	E
2	F	G	H	I/J	K
3	L	M	N	O	P
4	Q	R	S	T	U
5	V	W	X	Y	Z

In this matrix any letter can be represented, rather as in a map reference, by a combination of two numerals—the numbers of the horizontal row and the vertical column in which the letter occurs.

To transmit a message consisting of a series of letters, it was necessary to send a sequence of signals that would identify ordered pairings of the numerals 1 to 5. For example, the letter R is in row 4 and column 2 and is therefore represented by the combination 4,2; the letter P by 3,5. The pairs of numerals are "ordered" in the sense that the pair 2,4 does not have the same meaning as the pair 4,2, though they consist of the same numerals.

In the Polybius system a signaling station, probably on the top of a hill, would have two walls side by side, facing the remote station with which communication is to be established. Each wall was about 10 feet long and a little less than the height of a man. Along the top of each wall were five sockets in which torches could be placed. To signal a letter, say H, the operator referred to his Polybius square and found that H was in row 2 and column 3. He set torches in two of the holes on the left-hand wall, and in three of the holes in the right-hand wall. The distant observer saw first the two torches, then a little to their left, the three torches. He referred to the second row and third column of his Polybius square, and saw that the letter signaled to him was H. And so on until the laborious process of message transmission was completed.

This method triggered Myer's imagination and, with remarkably few additional inventions, led to the alphabetic signaling technology that was to be available to Hitler's planners. Myer retained the Polybius square, but discarded the walls and torches. In their place he introduced a lightweight signal staff with a maximum length of about 16 feet, which could be disassembled into 4-foot lengths for easy portability. During daylight a flag was attached to the top of the signal staff; at night its place could be taken by a torch.

To transmit a message a signalman would stand facing the signal station that was to receive it. He would hold his signal staff in a "neutral" position, pointing straight up. Then, to transmit the letter H, represented by 2,3, he would simply "wig" his staff by dipping it twice to his left, and then "wag" it by dipping it three times to his right. The receiving operator would count the wigs and the wags and so recover the letter H.

In principle Myer's system was beautifully simple, and the necessary equipment was very easily portable by an individual signaler. However, as Polybius pointed out, a very exact attention was required in using it. Strict adherence to standard operating procedures was essential. For example, the transmitting signalman would have to make sure that the distant signalman was ready to receive; he would have to indicate, probably by dipping his staff forward, whenever he was about to transmit a letter; he might have to wait for an acknowledgment signal before transmitting another letter; and he would need to indicate when a message transmission had been completed.

After the American Civil War, Myer's wig-wag signaling system was adopted by the British army, and by military establishments throughout Europe. However, one very important change was made. The Polybius square was replaced by the more versatile Morse code, which had been developed for the electric telegraph in 1843, and used combinations of "dots" and "dashes" to represent the twenty-six letters of our alphabet, the ten decimal digits 0 to 9, and a few other things. Any combination of dots and dashes could be transmitted by the wig-wag system, using a wig for a dot and a wag for a dash.

The electric telegraph depended on the transmission of pulses of electrical current along a wire circuit connecting two terminals. A pulse was transmitted from one terminal by tapping a key connecting the circuit to a source of electric current. At the other terminal the pulse would produce an audible sound, whose duration would depend on the length of time the key had been held down. Thus the operation of the key, or "keying," could transmit any Morse character as a sequence of short pulses (dots) and long pulses (dashes, which were about three times as long as the dots). At the receiving terminal the characters would be recognized aurally. Operating speeds varied from a hundred to two hundred Morse characters a minute, depending on the experience of the operators. On long circuits relay stations were needed to amplify signals before they became too weak.

The development of radio, or wireless, introduced a new feature. The signals from an electric telegraph station could only be picked up at places connected to that station by wire circuit. A radio transmitter, however, could be omnidirectional; the reception of its signals depended solely on range and signal strength.

This feature of omnidirectional transmission led to the simplex radio net, which was to be used extensively in Hitler's command communications system to handle Enigma messages in Morse code.

The term "net" implies that several subscribing stations would be communicating with each other. The term "simplex" means that all these stations would use the same radio frequency both for transmitting and for receiving. Thus a transmission from any one station of the net could be picked up by all the other stations.

The Polybius dictum on the need for "a very exact attention" remained valid for radio nets. Standard operating procedures had to be developed and rigidly observed. Strict control was needed to ensure, in particular, that no two stations of the net would transmit at the same time. But this control could be exercised as necessary by any station of the net, and could be passed from one station to another. Furthermore, military units using the net could be mobile, and could join or leave the net at any time. All these features would be vitally important for Hitler's far-ranging blitzkrieg.

I will have to discuss the operating procedures of the German radio nets in some detail, for they were at the heart of the Hut 6 story. Of what went before I need only say that there were very few revolutionary changes in technology between the "perfected signaling method" of Polybius and the German radio nets that were the concern of Hut 6. Torches on walls to Myer's signal staff to radio transmission. Polybius square to Morse code. That was all! Indeed, Myer's wig-wag system was still in use in World War II, as a means of training our intercept operators in reading Morse code signals.

One of the pioneers of modern military cryptography was Auguste Kerckhoffs, who was born at Nuth, Holland, but spent most of his life in France. In 1883 he published *La Cryptographie Militaire*, which is still considered one of the fundamental books on the subject. In laying down basic principles for selecting usable field ciphers, Kerckhoffs sought to solve the problems that were being introduced by new conditions. David Kahn quotes him as saying "it is necessary to distinguish carefully between a system of encipherment envisioned for a momentary exchange of letters between several isolated people and a method of cryptography intended to govern the correspondence between different army chiefs for an unlimited time." In laying down fundamental principles, Kerckhoffs was the first to make the basic distinction between the general system and the specific "key." He foresaw that if a general system were to be used by too many individuals it would inevitably be compromised, and that secrecy should reside solely in the particular key, which could be changed at will. Thus Kerckhoffs introduced, nearly a century ago, what nowadays is sometimes called the fundamental assumption of military cryptography: that the enemy knows the general system.

As to what Kerckhoffs meant by the general system and the key, he was thinking of the manual methods of his day, which I do not intend to discuss. But his meaning will become very clear when we come to the principles of the Enigma machine. The performance of this could be varied in several ways in accordance with instructions that constituted the key. Ability to decode an encoded message depended on knowing this key. Possession of the machine would not be sufficient.

Kerckhoffs' teachings are highly relevant to the cryptographic aspects of our story. We and the Germans were dealing with a great volume of radio correspondence taking place over an extended period of time. The Germans did put their trust in keys rather than in the Enigma machine, but they failed to recognize the danger of use by too large a number of individuals.

During World War II we were somewhat careless over our terminology, regarding codebreaking as part of cryptography. As early as 1920, however, a distinguished American exponent of the art, William Frederick Friedman, had introduced the new term "cryptanalysis" to mean the methods of breaking codes and ciphers. He used "cryptography" to mean the methods by which a message is rendered unintelligible to outsiders by various transformations of the plain text employing "codes" and ciphers. "Cryptology" was to be the name of the science that embraces both cryptography and cryptanalysis. In my narrative I propose to use Friedman's terminology, since it is widely accepted today. It should be noted, however, that Friedman allowed the term "codebreaking" to include the breaking of ciphers, and that I will talk about "decoding" Enigma messages, even though the Enigma was a cipher machine.

There is no clearly defined distinction between codes and ciphers, but for our purposes we can regard a "cipher" as a method of transforming a text in order to conceal its meaning. A "code," on the other hand, is a system in which groups of symbols are used to represent a variety of things, such as letters, numerals, words, complete phrases, and so on.

In the United States there are "zip codes" in which a group of five decimal digits represents a postal delivery zone, and we have already talked of the Morse code for signaling, which uses groups of dots and dashes. In commercial communications many codes have been developed in which thousands of groups of letters or decimal digits are used to represent anything from an individual letter to a commonly used phrase. In sending a cablegram, it is possible to save a good deal of transmission time, and cost, by using a single code group to represent a frequently used form of birthday salutation. Thus, unlike ciphers, codes are not always associated with secrecy. But if the "code book" that sets out the meanings of the code groups is kept secret, the content of a message may be concealed. Such were the codes with which the British Code and Cipher School was dealing, as were similar organizations all over the world. Breaking a code implied discovering the meanings of the individual code groups. Moreover, a message that had been encoded by means of a code book could then be enciphered by a cipher system, a process known as "superencipherment."

David Kahn, writing in 1967, said that the First World War marked the great turning point in the history of cryptology, the direct cause being the vast increase in radio communications. Commanders soon found that radio was a speedy, convenient means of communication during military operations. The volume of messages soared, interception capabilities grew, and cryptanalysis flourished. Cipher key after cipher key, code after code, were betrayed by needless mistakes, stupidities, or outright rule violations. This was because so large a volume of messages had to be handled by so many untrained men. In Kahn's view the great practical lesson of World War I cryptology was the necessity of enforcing an iron discipline on the cryptographic personnel. This lesson had been forgotten when World War II came. It could be forgotten again.

During the First World War, because the volume of communications traffic had increased so enormously, all the manual enciphering methods that offered a high degree of security had proved unacceptedly slow and cumbersome. After the war, therefore, inventors turned their attention to the design of cipher machines. A German, Arthur Scherbius, produced the original version of the Enigma machine and tried unsuccessfully during the 1920s to promote it as a commercial product. (The commercial version was the one originally acquired by the Poles.) In the 1930s the German high command became interested. They decided that the Scherbius machine was well suited to the type of communications system needed for the coordination of their forces in their blitzkrieg, so they designed their own portable, battery-operated version and put it into large-scale production.

PART
TWO

The First Year

3

Cottage and School

September and October 1939

When I turned up at Bletchley Park in September 1939 I knew nothing about all this historical "backdrop" of communications, cryptology, and German preparations for war. I was absolutely green, and I simply tried to learn what I needed to know as quickly as possible. I was interested in finding out what the problem was, not in how it had arisen.

The Victorian mansion of Bletchley Park incorporated samples of a wide variety of architectural styles, as will be evident from the photograph, Figure 3.1. The stableyard was behind the mansion and a little to the right. Further to the rear was a small building known as Elmers School, or simply "the School." When I reported for duty on September 4, 1939, I found that the bow window of Alastair Denniston's office on the ground floor looked out across a wide lawn to a pond, with attractively landscaped banks. There were rose beds near the mansion and near the pond. Before long the landscaping would be impaired, as rose beds and lawn were sacrificed to the much-needed wooden huts.

Denniston, who was extremely busy, received me cordially and sent me to join Dilly Knox, the man in charge of work on the German Enigma cipher machine. Knox and his staff occupied a building in the stableyard, the former residence, I suppose, of the coachman. It had already become known as the Cottage. Alan Turing, from Kings College, Cambridge, was already there, and had

Figure 3.1 Bletchley Park

been working with Dilly for some time. John Jeffreys, whom I knew well, arrived from Downing College, Cambridge. Jeffreys, with Knox and Turing, all now dead, were three key characters in what was to happen.

I was to see very little of Dilly. Our paths would diverge within two weeks or so and would not come together again except on one brief occasion. What I know of his achievements I did not learn until 1979, when I read Ronald Lewin's *Ultra Goes to War* and *The Knox Brothers* by Dilly's niece, Penelope Fitzgerald. Robin Denniston tells me that his father loved Dilly and admired his work. Before discussing my own exploits, I will give a brief account of him, because it sheds light both on his achievements and on the friction between him and myself, which until recently has puzzled me.

Dillwyn Knox went up to Kings College, Cambridge, as an undergraduate in 1903, three years before I was born. By 1910 he was a fellow, studying Greek literature. When the First World War broke out, since he owned a much-loved motor bicycle, he tried to enlist as a military dispatch rider. But he was called to London instead as part of the expansion of the original cryptanalytic effort in I.D. 25, a department of naval intelligence that became better known as Room 40.

Dilly did outstanding work in I.D. 25, particularly in a solo performance on the "Flag Code" used by the Commander in Chief of the German Navy. He married in July 1920, at a time when the Room 40 of World War I was in the process of being transferred to the Foreign Office as the Government Code and Cypher School, or GCCS.

Then, in 1931, he had the motor bicycle accident that had been long expected by those who knew him well. His leg was badly broken, and thereafter he always walked with a limp. He wore horn-rimmed spectacles, and was helpless without them. His health was not good. He had persistent stomach trouble. By 1938 cancer was suspected, and he had a preliminary operation. Earlier he had been tempted to return to his research in Kings College, but in 1936 GCCS was faced with the Enigma problem, and Dilly chose to stay on to tackle it.

At the outbreak of war his old stomach trouble was bothering him, and he never felt well. He slept in the office, returning to his home only once a week. After I lost touch with him, according to

Penelope Fitzgerald, he did brilliant and important work on the ciphers of the Italian fleet and the Abwehr (German spy organization), both of which used variations of the Enigma differing from the machine with which Hut 6 was dealing. After hospitalization in 1942 he was unable to return to Bletchley Park, but continued to work at home on a difficulty in the Italian cipher until his death on February 27, 1943.

Dilly was neither an organization man nor a technical man. He was, essentially, an idea-struck man. He was not interested, as I was, in the administration and automatic routine needed to handle the enormous volume of Enigma traffic generated by the German army and air force. Also, apart from a few lifelong friends, by and large Dilly seems to have disliked most of the men with whom he came in contact.

Certainly during my first week or two at Bletchley I got the impression that he didn't like me. I don't remember what I learned in the Cottage, but after a week or so he gave me some sort of test and appeared to be, if anything, annoyed that I passed.

Basically, I suppose, my problems were to be far simpler than those that interested Dilly. What I needed to know about Enigma could have been explained to me in less than an hour, and will, I believe, be easily understood by every reader. Anyway, very soon after my arrival I was turned out of the Cottage and sent to Elmers School, where I was to study "callsigns and discriminants," groups of letters and figures which were a regular feature in the preambles of the German Enigma messages. Alex Kendrick, a civilian member of Dilly's prewar staff, was sent along to get me started. He was fairhaired, walked with a stick as a result of a paralyzed leg, and was noted for the holes burnt in his trousers by a cigarette, or possibly by ash from a pipe. We occupied a fairly large room with bare walls and no view from the windows; its only furniture was a long table and a few wooden chairs. Nobody else was working in the School, so Kendrick and I felt a bit lonely.

In those early days the whole GCHQ staff met at lunch in the dining room of the mansion. Also any trace of loneliness was relieved for me every evening, for I had been assigned a billet, with two other new arrivals, at an excellent pub, the Duncombe Arms, in the hills to the south of Bletchley. Our host made us extremely comfortable, and his billiards and darts room became a social club for Bletchley Park personnel who were billeted nearby. The company was very enjoyable. Dilly's great friend Frank Birch was the central figure. James Passant, a close friend of mine and the history fellow of Sidney Sussex College, often joined us. So did Dennis Babbage, another close Cambridge friend from Magdalene College, who would join Hut 6 later on. I remember his skill on the billiard table, particularly with strokes played behind his back; before the war he had repeatedly defeated me at squash and tennis.

When we started work in the School, Kendrick and I were given two collections of Enigma traffic to analyze. And, as things turned out, my banishment from the Cottage to the School proved to be the real start of the Hut 6 organization that was to develop.

At that time almost all the British-intercepted Enigma messages that I was to study were being plucked out of the ether by the experienced operators at an Army station on a hill at Chatham, on the Thames estuary. Hidden behind the ramparts of an old fort, this highly efficient and highly secret organization had been producing a little-used output for some time. Each day's accumulation of messages had been regularly bundled up and sent to Bletchley Park together with a report on the day's traffic. Now these bundles and daily reports were made available to Kendrick and me.

Colonel Tiltman, in charge of Army operations at Bletchley Park, instructed his sergeant in charge of records to give me all possible assistance. The sergeant did so; in fact, it was probably he who first told me something about the function of the callsigns that I was to study, and about how the Germans operated their radio nets. He also gave me a large collection of intercepts, traffic reports, and other material that had been received from the French but had not yet been studied.

The composition of a typical intercepted Enigma message of those days is indicated in Figure 3.2. There was an unenciphered preamble followed by an enciphered text arranged in five-letter groups. The preamble, as transmitted by a German operator, contained six items of information:

1. The callsigns of the radio stations involved: first the sending station, then the destination(s).
2. The time of origin of the message.
3. The number of letters in the text.

4. An indication whether the message was complete, or was a specified part of a multi-part message (for example, the second part of a four-part message).
5. A three-letter group, the discriminant, which distinguished among different types of Enigma traffic.
6. A second three-letter group, which I will call the "indicator setting." This was related to the procedure for encoding and decoding the text of the message.

INTERCEPT OPERATOR'S ADDITIONS

a. Frequency 4760 Kilocycles
b. Time of Interception 11:10

UNENCIPHERED PREAMBLE

1. Call Signs: P7J to SF9 and 5KQ
2. Time of Origin: 10:30
3. Number of letters: 114
4. Single or Multi-part: Part 2 of 4 parts.
5. Discriminant: QXT
6. Indicator Setting: VIN

ENCIPHERED TEXT

```
W Q S E U    P M P I Z    T L J J U    W Q E H G    L R B I D

F E W B O    J I E P D    J A Z H T    T B J R O    A H H Y O

J Y G S F    H Y K T N    T D B P H    U L K O H    U N T I M

O F A R L    B P A P M    X K Z Z X    D T S X L    Q W H V L

R A G U Z    Z T S G G    Y I J V
```

Figure 3.2 Composition of a Typical Enigma Message

Before this information in the preamble, the intercept operator would include two more items:

a. The radio frequency used for transmission.
b. The time of interception.

Note that the British intercept operator would have warning that a message was about to be transmitted, because the control station of the radio net would have been making the necessary arrangements. Thus he would often be able to enter the frequency and time of interception, and perhaps the callsigns too, before the German operator had gotten started on the preamble and the text.

The messages from Chatham were handwritten, exactly as taken down by the intercept operator. Sometimes our intercept operator would be uncertain of the correct interpretation of a Morse character, in which case he would give alternatives. Sometimes the signal would be garbled, and he would miss part of it, in which case he would give an estimate of the number of five-letter groups he had missed.

Kendrick started to work on the large collection of material from Chatham, and set me a good example by beginning to analyze its characteristics in a methodical manner. His approach was reminiscent of the period some five to ten years earlier when I had been doing research in algebraic geometry and had often been faced with the problem of thinking of something to think about. In those earlier days I had found that the best approach to this problem was to force myself to start writing, and here was Kendrick dealing with the same problem in the same way. I followed suit. We simply started making lists of this and that, and gradually we came across things that seemed of some interest. Soon, however, Kendrick was transferred to another job. I had to carry on alone.

It was about then that Josh Cooper, in charge of Air Force operations at Bletchley Park, gave me what was at that time our one and only collection of decoded German Enigma messages. It did not amount to much: decodes of at most two or three days of intercepted traffic. At the time I did not know how the collection had been obtained.

When I started to delve into those few decoded German Enigma messages, I had little idea of what I would find. However, the fact that Josh Cooper was able to hand them to me at that time was to have far-reaching consequences, for I believe it was the study of these decodes that gave me my first glimpse of what my job was all about.

Previously I suppose I had absorbed the common view that cryptanalysis was a matter of dealing with individual messages, of solving intricate puzzles, and of working in a secluded back room, with little contact with the outside world. As I studied that first collection of decodes, however, I began to see, somewhat dimly, that I was involved in something very different. We were dealing with an entire communications system that would serve the needs of the German ground and air forces. The callsigns came alive as representing elements of those forces, whose commanders at various echelons would have to send messages to each other. The use of different keys for different purposes, which was known to be the reason for the discriminants, suggested different command structures for the various aspects of military operations.

Even more important, perhaps, was the impression I got from the messages themselves. Although my knowledge of German was very limited, I could see that the people involved were talking to each other in a highly disciplined manner. They were very polite to each other, in that the originator of a message would be careful to give the full title of the officer or organization to which the message was to be sent. Furthermore, in the signature that came at the end of the message, the originator would be careful to give his own title in full. These early impressions proved to be of immense importance later on, and it was fortunate that I had this period of secluded work.

Before I can explain the early development of traffic analysis in the School, I must say a little about the Enigma machine and how it was used. I must beg the reader not to be misled by descriptions of the machine that have appeared in the literature, and I must also ask for patience. For, if I am to explain the weaknesses in the machine and in its usage that were so helpful to us, I must discuss its anatomy with some care.

We are concerned with the portable battery-operated machine that appears in General Guderian's command vehicle (Figure 2.1). One can see that this machine has a keyboard of twenty-six keys, corresponding to the letters of the alphabet. Behind the keyboard is a lampboard. When a key, say a letter P, is pressed, some other letter, say Q, lit up on the lampboard, will be the encode of letter P. But, if the same letter P is pressed repeatedly, the encoded letters lit up on the lampboard will appear to be a random sequence. This is because the substitution of letters is produced by electrical connections through the wheels of a "scrambler" at the back of the machine, whose setting is varied as each letter of a message is encoded by pressing a key on the keyboard. How it was arranged that an authorized recipient could decode a message will appear shortly.

The Germans had adopted the principle that the security of their communications must rest not on the machine itself, but rather on a "key" that would determine how the machine was to be set up for a particular purpose. Moreover, they were concerned with both external and internal security. They wanted to prevent their enemies from reading their messages and also to prevent their own units from reading messages that were not intended for them. For example, three of the many different types of Enigma traffic were messages between operational units of the regular army and air force; messages between units of Hitler's private army, the SS or Schutzstaffel; and messages involved in the training exercises of new signals battalions. All three kinds of messages were enciphered on identical Enigma machines, but the regular army and air force units were not to be allowed to read the texts of SS messages. Nor were the trainees to be permitted to read the texts of the other two types of traffic. Consequently, different keys were issued for different types of traffic. This, however, did not quite solve the problem, because messages of different types were often transmitted on the same radio net. It was therefore necessary to provide means by which a receiving unit's operator would know what type of clear text was hidden behind the enciphered text, and whether he had the necessary key to read it.

The Germans chose to solve this problem by using a three-letter "discriminant" transmitted in the unenciphered message preamble. Let me emphasize: This discriminant was not part of a key. Its purpose was simply to indicate which of many keys was being used. A cipher clerk would examine the discriminant of each incoming message to determine whether he had been issued the key used for its text encipherment. If he did have the key, he could set up his Enigma and decode the message. If not, he couldn't.

To understand what follows, we must become fully acquainted with the machine that appears in Guderian's command vehicle, Figure 2.1. The basic components are the keyboard, lampboard, scrambler unit, and steckerboard. The keyboard appears at the end nearest to the cipher clerk who is operating the machine. It has twenty-six letter-keys arranged as follows:

Q W E R T Z U I O

A S D F G H J K

P Y X C V B N M L

The lampboard, which appears behind the keyboard (from the operator's viewpoint) is a similar arrangement of letters on small glass windows, any one of which can be illuminated from below by a lamp.*

On looking at the keyboard in Figure 2.1, one might think that it must be like a typewriter keyboard—but one would be wrong.

For one thing, the alphabet keys are arranged a little differently. Then again, a typewriter keyboard has about twice as many keys, including ten for the numerals 0 through 9 and functional keys such as the shift, space, backspace, and carriage return. Because the Enigma keyboard has only twenty-six keys, corresponding to the capital letters A through Z, numerals in message texts had to be spelled out in full. Also, pressing a typewriter key causes mechanical motions that may or may not include the printing of a symbol, while the Enigma had no printing mechanism. Pressing its letter-keys caused only one type of mechanical motion, that of the scrambler, of which more in due course.

Figure 3.3 shows the commercially available Enigma machine that the Polish cipher bureau had already acquired when Marian Rejewski began his studies in 1932. The heart of this Scherbius Enigma was its scrambler unit, built around a set of four movable wheels, or rotors. Protruding flanges of the wheels appear behind the keyboard and lampboard. Comparing Figure 3.3 with Figure 2.1, we see that the military version of the Enigma, developed by the Germans for widespread use in World War II, has a scrambler in which there are only three movable wheels. However, the military version, with which we are concerned, had five different wheels, numbered 1 through 5, only three of which were placed in the scrambler unit at a time.

* Or "glowlamp." Hence the name "Glowlamp Machine" by which the German Enigma was called.

Figure 3.3 Enigma with Wheel Cover Listed.

To the right of the scrambler's three movable wheels is a fixed commutator, a shallow cylinder containing a circle of twenty-six flat terminals with which twenty-six spring-loaded pin terminals of the right-hand wheel can make contact. The flat terminals of the commutator will be called the "in-out scrambler terminals." They correspond to the letters A to Z in alphabetic order. Each of the three movable wheels in the scrambler has a circle of spring-loaded pin terminals on the right, numbered 1 through 26, which are cross-connected to a circle of flat terminals on its left-hand side. (The five wheels, numbered 1 through 5, have different internal cross-connections.) To the left of the three movable wheels, in a fixed cylindrical mounting, is a circle of spring-loaded pin terminals, 1 through 26, which are interconnected in pairs. This fixed cylinder at the left-hand end of the scrambler is called the "turn-around wheel," or, in German, *umkehrwalze*.

Each of the protruding flanges of Figure 2.1 has twenty-six rounded identations into which a spring-loaded bar at the back of the machine is pressed. This bar holds each wheel in one of twenty-six discrete positions to ensure that good electrical contact will be made between the pin terminals and flat terminals of adjacent wheels. But the operator can rotate a wheel to any desired position by finger pressure on the protruding part of the flange. The position of each wheel is indicated by a letter on an alphabet ring, which shows through a window to the left of the flange. These alphabet rings, however, are not fixed to the wheels. On each wheel the ring can be rotated and held in position by a spring clip so that any chosen letter, say K, will be opposite a fixed "zero" position of the wheel. This chosen letter is called the ring setting.

Thus the scrambler unit is a package consisting of the in-out terminals A to Z of the commutator, the three movable wheels with their internal cross-wirings, and the fixed interconnections of the turn-around wheel, or *umkehrwalze*. Electric current entering at one of the in-out commutator terminals on the right will flow from right to left through the internal connections of the three wheels to the *umkehrwalze*, which will turn the current around and send it back by a different route through the three wheels to an in-out terminal different from the one where the current entered. In fact the whole effect of the scrambler, in any one position of its wheels, is to interconnect pairs of its in-out terminals. Any such electrical inter-connection will work both ways. Thus if current put in at in-out terminal G comes back to in-out terminal Q, current put in at Q will come back to G.

To understand how we broke the Enigma codes it is important to make a clear distinction between the scrambler and the whole Enigma machine. This distinction was, in fact, at the bottom of our success. An Enigma machine had a keyboard, a lampboard, and a steckerboard as well as a scrambler unit. The scrambler consisted only of in-out terminals, three moving wheels, a fixed turn-around wheel, or *umkehrwalze*, and a drive mechanism, which I will de-scribe later. When I talk about a scrambler I will mean just that.

The steckerboard or "cross-plugging board" appears in Figure 3.4, in which the front flap of the Enigma is folded down, revealing an array of twenty-six pairs of sockets. These correspond to the letters of the alphabet arranged in the same pattern as the keyboard. The purpose of the steckerboard is to vary the interconnections between the in-out terminals of the scrambler unit and the letter-keys and lamps. If there is no plug in a particular pair of sockets, say the pair corresponding to letter A, then input-output terminal A of the scrambler is connected to letter-key A and lamp A. In this case we say that letter A is steckered to itself. On the other hand, if one of the two-wire cables shown in Figure 3.4 is used to provide cross-plugging between socket-pair B and some other socket-pair, say G, the result is that in-out scrambler terminal B is connected to letter-key G and lamp G, while in-out scrambler terminal G is connected to letter-key B and lamp B. We say that B is steckered to G, or B/G.

For each type of traffic, keys were issued for a month at a time to authorized units. Each key was valid for twenty-four hours, and was changed at midnight. A complete Enigma key consisted of three items:

1. The order of the three wheels that were to be placed in the scrambler unit. Example: 413.
2. The ring settings of the left-hand, middle, and right-hand wheels in the scrambler. Example: OUB.

Figure 3.4 Enigma with Steckerboard Uncovered

3. Cross-pluggings on the steckerboard. Actually only eleven cross-pluggings were specified, leaving four letters steckered to themselves. For example:

K/Y, T/O, Z/L, B/U, W/D, C/X,
I/J, G/A, P/H, N/R, and F/M,

leaving E, Q, S, and V self-steckered.

When two Enigma machines are set to the same key and their three wheels are in the same positions, the electrical connections through their steckerboards and scramblers will produce the same thirteen pairings of the twenty-six letters of the alphabet. Moreover the resulting letter substitution is reversible, since electric current can flow in either direction along the path that results in each pairing. Thus, if pressing letter-key K on one of the machines causes lamp P to be lit, then pressing letter-key P on the other machine will cause lamp K to be lit. This is the basic principle of encoding and decoding on the Enigma. Once it is fully understood the rest is easy.

When the text of a message was to be encoded, the originating cipher clerk was allowed to choose the wheel setting, say RCM, at which he would start the encoding process. I will call this the "text setting" for the message. With his Enigma set up to the appropriate key, he would use the flanges to turn the wheels until the letters R, C, and M appeared in the windows. He would then press the keyboard keys corresponding to the successive letters of clear text, writing down the sequence of letters lit up on the lampboard to obtain the enciphered text. As the keys are pressed, the wheels go through a cyclic series of positions. The right-hand wheel moves on one position every time a key is pressed. When the right-hand wheel reaches one particular position, known as its "turnover position," the left-hand wheel also moves ahead one position. In due course the middle and right-hand wheels may both be in their turnover positions, at which time pressing a letter-key will cause all three wheels to move.* Each time a key is pressed, encipherment takes place when the wheels have reached their new position.

---

* The three wheels would have to go through a cycle of $26 \times 26 \times 26 = 17,576$ successive positions before they would return to their starting position, RCM.

A receiving cipher clerk, with his Enigma set to the same key, would turn his scrambler wheels to the text setting RCM, and tap out the successive letters of the enciphered text he received. The wheels of his scrambler unit would follow the same cycle of positions as those of the encoding Enigma, so that the original clear text would be recovered letter by letter. But for this to happen—and this is vital—the decoding operator would have to be told the wheel setting, RCM, that had been chosen. How this was done introduced yet a further level of obscurity through which a cryptanalyst would have to fight his way. Fortunately, when I arrived at the Cottage on September 4, 1939, we already knew the procedure that the Germans were using.

Before encoding the clear text, the originating cipher clerk carried out a preliminary procedure. He chose a wheel setting at random, say VIN, which we will call the "indicator setting." He then set his scrambler wheels to VIN and encoded his chosen text setting *twice over*, tapping out the letter sequence RCMRCM on the keyboard and noting the sequence of letters, say WQSEUP, appearing on the lampboard. This sequence, which is the encode of RCMRCM with starting position VIN, we will call the "indicator." Having obtained his indicator in this manner, the encoding operator turned his scrambler wheels to his chosen text setting, RCM, and proceeded to encode his plain text message letter by letter. When the encoded message was transmitted on a radio net, the indicator setting VIN was sent at the end of the unenciphered preamble, and the six letters of the indicator, WQSEUP, appeared at the beginning of the message text, constituting the first five-letter group and the first letter of the second group (Figure 3.2). The encipherment of the clear text started with the second letter of the second group. A decoding cipher clerk with his Enigma set up to the same key turned his wheels to the indicator setting, VIN, that he found in the preamble. He then pressed letter-keys WQSEUP in turn, and saw the letters RCMRCM appearing successively on his lampboard. He knew from this that the text setting chosen by the originating cipher clerk was RCM; he could proceed to decode the message by setting his wheels to positions R, C, M, tapping out the successive letters of the encoded text, and writing down the letters that appeared on the lampboard.

Note that the process of encipherment on an Enigma machine was not directly related to the transmission of the enciphered message. In fact the Enigma was what is known as an off-line cipher machine. Getting an Enigma message on the air involved three people: the originator, a cipher clerk, and a radio operator. The originator would prepare the clear text on a standard form, at the top of which he would note such things as the addresses, the time of origin, and, if necessary, the Enigma key to be used. A cipher clerk would then go through the encoding process I have described, preparing a message text and a preamble that would include a discriminant and an indicator setting. The preamble and message text would be handed to a radio operator for transmission in manually keyed Morse code. Long messages would be handled in two or more parts, each encoded separately with its own text setting, indicator setting, and indicator.

What I have said about the Enigma machine, the keys, and the procedure for encoding and decoding should be sufficient to prepare the reader to understand the ideas that arose in the School and led to the establishment of Hut 6. However, a few additional comments, combined with recapitulation of important points, may prove helpful.

The effect of the scrambler unit in any particular position is to interconnect the twenty-six in-out terminals in thirteen pairs. The combination of scrambler and steckerboard has the effect of interconnecting the letter-keys and lamps in pairs. Current can flow in either direction between each of the latter thirteen pairs, so if any letter-key, say A, is pressed, the lamp representing some other letter, say H, will be lit up. If letter-key H had been pressed, lampboard letter A would have been illuminated. Typical letter substitutions produced by the Enigma in six successive positions of its scrambler wheels are shown in Figure 3.5. For each position, the top row represents the letters of the keyboard. The bottom row indicates what letter of the lampboard would be lit by pressing a letter key.

The property of reversibility illustrated by the letter substitutions of Figure 3.5 can be used to explain the principle of encoding and decoding. Suppose that the letters TARGET are enciphered

POSITION

1	A	B	C	D	E	F	G	H	I	J	K	L	M	N	O	P	Q	R	S	T	U	V	W	X	Y	Z
	H	I	U	L	O	S	Q	A	B	T	Z	D	X	Y	E	V	G	W	F	J	C	P	R	M	N	K

2	A	B	C	D	E	F	G	H	I	J	K	L	M	N	O	P	Q	R	S	T	U	V	W	X	Y	Z
	F	V	L	G	M	A	D	Y	P	N	S	C	E	J	U	I	T	Z	K	Q	O	B	X	W	H	R

3	A	B	C	D	E	F	G	H	I	J	K	L	M	N	O	P	Q	R	S	T	U	V	W	X	Y	Z
	N	W	S	E	D	X	H	G	Z	K	J	M	L	A	Y	R	V	P	C	U	T	Q	B	F	O	I

4	A	B	C	D	E	F	G	H	I	J	K	L	M	N	O	P	Q	R	S	T	U	V	W	X	Y	Z
	G	U	V	I	H	T	A	E	D	L	X	J	W	Y	R	Z	S	O	Q	F	B	C	M	K	N	P

5	A	B	C	D	E	F	G	H	I	J	K	L	M	N	O	P	Q	R	S	T	U	V	W	X	Y	Z
	Q	Z	S	M	P	T	O	L	X	K	J	H	D	V	G	E	A	U	C	F	R	N	Y	I	W	B

6	A	B	C	D	E	F	G	H	I	J	K	L	M	N	O	P	Q	R	S	T	U	V	W	X	Y	Z
	S	E	O	K	B	T	R	V	J	I	D	U	W	Z	C	Y	X	G	A	F	L	H	M	Q	P	N

Figure 3.5 Letter Substitutions in Six Successive Positions of the Enigma

successively in the six positions. In the first position J is substituted for T, in the second F for A, and so on. Thus pressing letter keys T, A, R, G, E, and T in turn will light up lamps J, F, P, A, P, and F. In fact JFPAPF is the encode of TARGET. Now suppose that some other cipher clerk, receiving JFPAPF, can set his Enigma to produce the same sequence of substitutions. Then, as Figure 3.5 shows, in the first position pressing letter-key J will light up letter T, in the second F gives A, and so on. Thus the second clerk recovers the original clear text word, TARGET. However, let me repeat that in order to get the same sequence of substitutions, the receiving cipher clerk would have to know two things—the key to which he must set up his Enigma and the setting of the wheels that the originating cipher clerk has chosen to use to encode TARGET. The receiving clerk would have been given the key ahead of time, but the originating clerk would have to give him the wheel setting.

When an Enigma machine is being assembled for use, the three chosen wheels are placed in order on a spindle. The left-hand end of this spindle fits into the center of the *umkehrwalze*, the right-hand end into a central sleeve attached to the commutator containing the in-out terminals. A lever-operated mechanism then pushes the in-out terminal commutator toward the *umkehrwalze* so that good contact is established between the circles of pin terminals to the right of the *umkehrwalze* and the three wheels, and the circles of flat terminals on the wheels and the commutator against which they are pressed. When this has been done, electric current entering the scrambler at any in-out terminal, say G, will flow through the three wheels from right to left, be turned around by the *umkehrwalze* to flow back through the wheels from left to right, and will emerge at an input-output terminal.

The whole arrangement of lampboard, keyboard, steckerboard, and scrambler unit is shown diagramatically in Figure 3.6, which may help clarify what I have said about the machine. The letter keys Q through L and lamps Q through L are connected electrically to the corresponding upper sockets of the steckerboard. The lower sockets are connected to a set of twenty-six terminals, which I will call the in-out steckerboard terminals. These terminals, in alphabetic sequence A through Z, are connected to the circle of scrambler in-out terminals A through Z by a twenty-six-way connector cable.

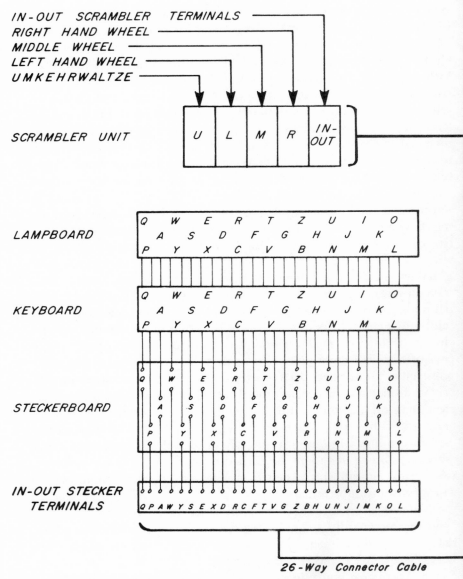

Figure 3.6 Electrical Connections Between Lampboard,
Keyboard, Steckerboard and Scrambler

When any letter-key is pressed down, the circuit to the corresponding lamp is broken and contact is established between an electric battery and the corresponding upper socket of the steckerboard. Current flows from this upper socket either to the corresponding lower socket or through a cross-connection to one of the other lower sockets, reaches an in-out steckerboard terminal, and is passed on to the corresponding in-out terminal of the scrambler. Pressing the letter-key will also have caused the scrambler wheels to move to a new position in which the scrambler will produce a return current to another of its in-out terminals. After passing through the steckerboard, this return current will light up a letter on the lampboard.

With five wheels to choose from, the three wheels to be used in the scrambler can be selected in ten ways, and for each such selection the three wheels can be arranged in six different ways. Thus, if wheels numbered 1, 3, and 4 are chosen, the six arrangements are: 134, 143, 314, 341, 413, 431. In all, therefore, there are $10 \times 6 = 60$ possible wheel orders to choose from.

I have noted that the alphabet ring on each wheel is movable, and can be set to any one of twenty-six positions, by means of a spring clip, which holds a selected letter of the ring opposite a fixed "zero" position on the wheel. This means that the position of a movable wheel in relation to the fixed in-out commutator is not determined by the letter of the alphabet ring appearing in the window, unless the ring setting too is known. Thus the setup of the scrambler that is to be specified by a key involves $26 \times 26 \times 26 = 17{,}576$ possible combinations of ring settings on top of the 60 possible wheel orders. Altogether there are $60 \times 17{,}576 = 1{,}054{,}560$ possible ways of setting up the scrambler, any one of which can be specified in a key by a set of three numerals, say 413, determining the wheel order, and a set of three letters, say OUB, determining the ring settings.

If the creator of keys had chosen to specify thirteen stecker pairs the number of possible cross-pluggings of the steckerboard would have been $25 \times 23 \times 21 \times 19 \times 17 \times 15 \times 13 \times 11 \times 9 \times 7 \times 5 \times 3$, or almost 8,000,000,000,000, a formidable number. Surprisingly, by leaving four letters unsteckered he increased the possibilities by a factor of 26, giving more than 200,000,000,000,000 (two hundred trillion) possibilities, an even more formidable number. As we have seen, the wheel order and ring settings provide more than a million variations, so the total number of possible keys is more than 200 quintillion (or two hundred million million million).*

Even when the key is known, a message cannot be decoded without an additional item of information—the three-letter text setting chosen by the originating cipher clerk as a starting point for encoding. This text setting could be chosen in $26 \times 26 \times 26 = 17,576$ ways. Thus the Enigma, though simple in principle and primitive in many ways, presented the cryptanalyst with a dazzling number of possibilities.

When I went from Cottage to School in September 1939, with instructions from Dilly Knox to study callsigns and discriminants, I had been told about the operation of an Enigma machine and about the composition of an Enigma key. I also knew that, associated with each such key, there would be four three-letter groups called "discriminants," such as: KQV, LMY, GJR, and ABO.

These discriminants, as I have said, were not part of the key. One of the four would be included in the unenciphered preamble of any message whose text had been enciphered with an Enigma set up to this particular key. The order of letters in a discriminant could be varied. For example, QVK or VKQ could be used instead of KQV. I don't know why the Germans chose to use four discriminants at that time, and it doesn't matter. What does matter is the purpose of the discriminant that appeared in the preamble of an Enigma message. This was simply to tell a receiving cipher clerk which, if any, of the keys issued to him had been used to encipher the text. This much had been explained to me, and someone, I don't remember who, must have told me a little about the operation of the radio nets of those days and the use of callsigns, for I had known nothing about such matters when I arrived at Bletchley Park.

The Germans, in their concept of a blitzkrieg, reckoned that many groups of fast-moving fighting, command, support, and staff elements would need effective communication among themselves wherever they might be, and furthermore that the activities of these

---

* After all these years I am not quite certain that the number of self-steckered letters was four. It could have been six, in which case the total number of stecker combinations would have been around 150 trillion rather than a little over 200 trillion. This, however, does not affect the story that I am telling.

groups would have to be tied into the higher command system. The elements of each cooperating group were to be served by signals detachments operating a "radio net" on an assigned radio frequency. Under ideal conditions any message transmitted by any radio station operating in the net on the assigned frequency would be heard by all the other stations. One station of the net would act as control, to ensure that no two stations would cause interference by transmitting at the same time. There were to be many such nets, and a station could operate in two or more nets, so that messages originating at any point could be relayed to any other point.

The callsigns were simply the means of identifying the individual elements that were participating in this overall radio communications system. When messages were passing between elements within a single radio net, the preamble would contain the callsigns of the originator and intended recipient(s) of each message. When a message was to be forwarded to other elements, their identifying callsigns would also be included in the message preamble. Thus, by studying callsigns, we had an opportunity to learn something about the structure of the enemy's forces. As the callsigns were changed every day, however, the detective work had to begin anew every twenty-four hours.

Our intercept operators listened to the Enigma messages and their preambles, writing them out by hand on standard message forms. The main part of the form was used for the succession of five-letter groups, or "words," which constituted the indicator and text of a message enciphered on an Enigma machine. At the top of the form was a space in which the intercept operator entered the preamble that the German radio operator had transmitted ahead of the message. Indeed the form used by our intercept operators must have been very similar to the form used by the German cipher clerks. The intercept operator, however, also entered the radio frequency on which he was listening and the time of intercept (see Figure 3.2).

When I started to study my working material I simply followed Kendrick's example of painstakingly making lists and charts in the hope that something interesting might turn up. As no one else at Bletchley Park, so far as I could tell, had studied any of the material at all thoroughly I was soon breaking new ground. The enciphered texts of the intercepted messages from Chatham were of course incomprehensible, and anyway of no interest to me at the time, but I took note of the radio frequencies and the times of interception, as well as the discriminants, the callsigns, and the times of origin that appeared in the message preambles. I charted each day's traffic by radio frequency and time of intercept. When I had succeeded in grouping the discriminants of the day in sets of four that were used with the same key, I marked the entries on the chart by underlining them in different colors according to their keys. At first it was usually possible to identify three different keys, for which I used red, blue, and green pencils. As it turned out I had, out of necessity, designed a format that remained virtually unchanged for half the war. Even the color names stuck—particularly "Red."

As part of their daily reports the traffic analysts at Chatham gave the groupings of discriminants, and they sometimes got them wrong. The reason was that they did not fully understand the working of the Enigma machine and the purpose of the discriminants. Since I had come to understand this purpose in the terms I have described, it was obvious to me that the successive parts of a multi-part message, since they would be going to the same addressee(s), would be encoded with the same key, and hence that the discriminants in the preambles of all the parts must belong to the same set of four. Thus in analyzing a day's traffic I would start by looking for multi-part messages. Fortunately the Germans nearly always used different discriminants in the successive parts, which often made it very easy for me to establish a group of four. Indeed, one four-part message would ordinarily do the job for me.

I knew very little about the "Green" traffic that appeared sporadically in the Chatham intercepts until I studied French intercepts and reports, which told me that this traffic came from the administrative network of the German army. It was not at all easy to intercept at Chatham, as most of it was on frequencies in the medium frequency range and did not carry far. Consequently the French intercept stations did a lot better than Chatham, and their intercepts gave me a good deal of Green traffic over quite a long period. When I analyzed the callsigns of earlier Green traffic I found that they were repeating from month to month, so I was soon in a position to give Chatham a forecast of callsigns that might be expected on the Green network each day.

These two matters of the correct grouping of discriminants and the repetition of callsigns may seem trivial, but in the end they proved important. In those early days, their greatest value to me was that they gave me a sufficient excuse for my first venture into the outside world: a visit to the army's radio intercept station at Chatham. I immediately made friends with the officer in charge, Commander Ellingworth, who taught me many things I badly needed to know, and who was to be a tower of strength throughout the war. He gave me a very friendly welcome, introduced me to his staff, took me around the station, and let me watch the operators at work.

We had a lot to talk about. Because of security regulations I could not yet tell him about the small collection of decodes that Josh Cooper had given me, but I did talk about my study of discriminants and the French intercepts. For his part, he began to give me a picture of how the German radio nets operated, and informed me about the problems of interception. The reader may well wonder what these things have to do with cryptanalysis, but the fact that I learned about them so early in the game was important for the ultimate success of Hut 6, which was to depend largely on the close coordination of our activities with those of our intercept stations.

Ellingworth told me a little about the characteristics of shortwave radio transmissions and the problems involved in intercepting weak signals in Morse code from distant transmitters. I find that some people today who listen only to AM and FM radio find it hard to believe that we in England could pick up German radio signals from places as far distant as Stalingrad and the borders of Egypt. The point, of course, is that for radio transmissions in the AM and FM ranges there is no reflection from the upper atmosphere. Strong shortwave transmissions, on the other hand, can sometimes bounce back and forth between ground and upper atmosphere several times, permitting reception at extremely long distances. Marconi sent the first messages ever transmitted by wireless from England to Australia on September 22, 1918, using this phenomenon.

Ellingworth went on to explain that radio frequency measurements were not exact. The actual transmitting frequency of a German radio station could drift quite a bit from its nominal value, so that intercept operators might well record different frequencies on messages from the same radio net. This drifting had its effect both on the intercept operators and on my analysis. At my end, it was sometimes difficult to distinguish on my frequency/time-of-day charts between different nets using nearby frequencies. At the intercept station an operator might be in difficulty if he were asked to take messages from a net operating on a specified frequency. He would have to hunt around, and could easily pick up a station on another net operating on a nearby frequency.

I also learned that a great deal depended on the individual intercept operator. His effectiveness rested partly on experience in listening to the German radio nets and in getting to know their individual characteristics, and also on acquired arts, such as that of picking up a weak signal that no ordinary operator would hear at all. And these were individual talents. Some of the old hands at Chatham were quite phenomenal. The extraordinary human combination of brain and hearing made it possible to pick up signals that would have been missed by any automatic method of reception.

By the end of the day Ellingworth and I had agreed on what was to prove a basic procedure throughout the war—that a register of all intercepted Enigma traffic would be sent to Bletchley. The traffic analysts at Chatham had other tasks and could not attempt the sort of analysis that I had initiated, but they could use my results if they could get them quickly enough.

For my analysis I did not need the full text of each intercepted message. All I needed was the information that the intercept operator had entered at the top of the message form: the frequency and time of intercept; the preamble, containing discriminant, indicator setting, time of origin, callsigns, and so forth; and the first two five-letter groups of the message text, which contained the indicator. Ellingworth agreed to send me this information by teleprinter as the messages were intercepted, waiting only for the accumulation of enough items to make a transmission worthwhile. This was our "traffic register."

It was agreed that I would telephone each day as soon as I had identified sets of discriminants. I would provide all available predictions of callsigns, and in general I would make suggestions about what traffic seemed to me to be of particular interest. Thus was born a system of cooperation between Bletchley Park and the intercept stations, the critical importance of which will become fully apparent in later chapters.

It must have been soon after my visit to Chatham that I acquired my first assistant, Patricia Newman. She took over the job of making entries on the day's frequency/time chart as each page of the traffic register arrived by teleprinter from Chatham. Between us we improved the organization of the enormous daily chart, which was about the size of a desktop. When I had identified the Red, Blue, and Green discriminants for the day, and had telephoned them to Chatham, we were able to mark the message entries on the chart accordingly, using colored pencils.

With Patricia doing a lot of the work, I was able to investigate the messages that had discriminants other than those of the Red, Blue, and Green traffic. The Chatham people had tended to follow the radio nets that they knew, so this other traffic appeared only sporadically. However, by frequent telephone calls, Ellingworth and I were able to direct interceptor attention to this "other traffic," and soon could investigate it more thoroughly. As I remember, it was not long before we were following Brown and Orange traffic as well as Red, Blue, and Green. Thus we were distinguishing among several different groupings of elements in the German military force structure, all of them using the same Enigma machine, but with different keys.

As our work developed, Patricia Newman was joined by Peggy Taylor, and the empty room in the Bletchley Park Schoolhouse, with its long table and bare walls and no view from its windows, became less lonely than it had been. Nobody else seemed much interested in what we were doing except Josh Cooper and Colonel Tiltman. Cooper and Tiltman were not only heads of expanding sections, they were both distinguished cryptanalysts. I was far too wrapped up in my own work on Enigma to know about the breaking of other codes and ciphers under the direction of these two experts. I remember, however, being told by Josh Cooper that his work was an almost intolerable strain. Success so often depended on flashes of inspiration for which he would be searching day and night, with the clock always running against him. My worries would be of a different nature.

In my own work, as I have said, I was quick to realize that my problem was not that of classical cryptanalysis, in which brilliant experts struggled with individual messages. The classical crypt-analyst would have paid little attention to the communications system involved, yet for us it was essential first to understand the German radio nets in detail, and to be able to distinguish among types of traffic. It was lucky that, as soon as I went from Cottage to School, I began to analyze intercepted Enigma traffic simply as traffic—worrying about the structure of the communications system rather than the unknown content of the messages that it carried. I was working almost alone at the start, and the progress that I was able to make was small in comparison with the later achievements of others. It was enough, however, to get things moving in the right direction.

It must be emphasized here that in building up the organization that was to become Hut 6 to the point at which it could produce decodes of Enigma messages I was dealing with only part of the Enigma material. The Germans employed Enigma cipher machines for many different purposes. There were thus several different categories of Ultra, derived from the decoded Enigma traffic of different users, such as the army, navy and air force, and the spy organization. For this reason I have introduced the term "Hut 6 Ultra" to denote the intelligence that was derived from Enigma traffic decoded by Hut 6, which was mostly army and air force traffic. (Enigma traffic was also decoded elsewhere with keys provided by Hut 6.) The immense task of analyzing this and squeezing from it the last drops of intelligence about enemy capabilities, intentions, etc., was to be performed by our sister organization, known throughout the war as Hut 3. From my close association with Hut 3, I am qualified to say a little about what they did, and I intend to do so in the proper place. However, I am definitely not qualified to talk about, for example, Hut 8's decodes of the German navy's Enigma traffic, nor about the production of Hut 8 Ultra intelligence. As Ronald Lewin points out, Bletchley Park activities were highly compartmentalized, largely because of the high level of security involved. Few of us knew, or wanted to know, anything about what was going on outside our own bailiwick.

Ideas and Plans

October and November 1939

While I was still working in isolation in the School, during the second and third months of the war, I made two somewhat startling breakthroughs.

People have asked how these breakthroughs came to me, and it is really very hard to explain. Basically the answer goes back to a memory from childhood; that of being lucky enough, with no purposeful effort on my part, to find myself opposite the vacant chair when the music stopped.

In this chapter, however, I will attempt to give a lucid account of something that I find difficult even to understand myself: just how the two important advances came into my mind so soon after my arrival at Bletchley Park. If obscurity creeps in from time to time, it will hardly be surprising. I can only hope that I will be able to satisfy those readers who will want to know how my thinking developed, without infuriating others. If anything is certain, it is that the breakthroughs came to me a lot more rapidly and easily than the explanation I am about to write. But the fact that these advances did actually occur in October and November of 1939 is so important that it must be tackled here. The "fun" part of my story, which will be told in due course, did not start until early 1940.

The first of my two ideas had to do with the indicator setting and indicator of an Enigma message. I can identify ten successive steps in my thought process. The reader should not be disturbed if some of them seem trivial. The final results, and some of the intermediate steps, were very exciting.

As I have already explained, a three-letter indicator setting, say VIN, appeared in the unenciphered preamble of an Enigma message, and a six-letter indicator, say WQSEUP, appeared at the start of the enciphered message text. I had been told that this indicator setting and indicator were the means by which an originating cipher clerk informed a distant cipher clerk that he had chosen a particular wheel setting, say RCM, as a text setting—the setup of the three wheels of the scrambler at which he had started to encode his message text. Moreover I had also been told that the letter sequence WQSEUP was obtained by enciphering RCMRCM with starting position VIN. From this I knew that the letters W and E in the first and fourth places of the indicator were the encodes of the same letter. Similarly Q and U were the encodes of the same letter. So were S and P in the third and sixth places. This was real solid information. Could we use it?

Getting to the point of asking myself this question was Step 1. Having reached this starting point, I proceeded to think, largely by chance, about indicators in which the same letter would appear in places 1 and 4, or 2 and 5, or 3 and 6. For a reason that will soon appear, indicators of these three types came to be known as "females." To distinguish between the types, I will refer to them as 1-4 females, 2-5 females, and 3-6 females.

For example the following combinations of indicator setting and indicator might occur:

KIE	SPESNT	(Letter S in places 1 and 4)
LTS	VBYQGY	(Letter Y in places 3 and 6)
EGP	OHAOCM	(Letter O in places 1 and 4)
RYM	XWNPWV	(Letter W in places 2 and 5)
XXY	ZDFJDA	(Letter D in places 2 and 5)

In the first example, a 1-4 female, letter S in places 1 and 4 must have been the encode of the same unknown letter. Thus the Enigma, by means of its steckerboard connections and scrambler, had been able to pair the same two letters of the alphabet in two machine positions that were three places apart in the machine cycle.

Next I must have come to wonder whether this was always possible. This was Step 2.

The reader can appreciate my growing excitement at this stage of the thought process by going back to Figure 3.5, in which I showed typical reversible alphabet substitutions that might have been produced by an Enigma in six successive positions of its scrambler wheels. In positions 1 and 4 there is one pair of letters, N and Y, that appears in both letter substitutions. In positions 2 and 5 no letter pairing is repeated. Positions 3 and 6 have no letter pairing in common. Thus it was *not* always possible for the Enigma to produce the same letter pairing in two positions three places apart in its cycle. *This was the germ, seed, or whatnot from which the success of Hut 6 was to grow.* It was Step 3, but I still had a long way to go in my thinking before the ultimate answer dawned.

I must have wondered about the probability that two different positions of the Enigma would produce the same letter pairing. Although I had been a professional mathematician before the war, probability was never one of my strong points. Later in the war I was to depend on others, notably Hugh Alexander and Alan Turing, for answers to the many questions of probability that arose. But in October 1939 Hugh Alexander, the British chess champion, had not yet joined the staff, and I hardly knew Alan Turing, who was working with Dilly Knox in the Cottage. I suppose I must have solved the problem myself. Fortunately it was an easy one. In each of the two positions, the Enigma would produce a reversible scramble of the alphabet, one in which if A goes to B then B goes to A. Suppose that the first position produces the scramble

A B C D E F G H I J K L M N O P Q R S T U V W X Y Z
R G L Y P Z B U W T S C O Q M E N A K J H X I V D F

(The reversible feature is illustrated by the fact that A goes to R and R to A, B to G and G to B, and so on. The scramble involves thirteen letter pairings: AR, BG, etc.) In a second reversible scramble, letter A is equally likely to be paired with each of the other 25 letters, so the chance that it will be paired with R is 1 in 25. Similarly the chance that *any* particular letter pairing of the first scramble will recur in the second scramble is 1 in 25. Since there are 13 pairings in the first scramble, the chance that one of them will appear in the second scramble is 13 in 25, or approximately 1 in 2.

Let us take this a little further and calculate the chance that the same letter will actually be repeated in the first and fourth positions of the six-letter indicator of an Enigma message. And let us use Figure 3.5 as an illustration of successive letter substitutions, or scrambles, that might occur in the six successive positions of the Enigma in which the three letters of the text setting are twice encoded. The mere possibility that the letter repetition could occur depends on whether the two scrambles have a letter pairing in common. We have just seen that the chance of this is 13 in 25. However, assuming that we have hit on a pair of Enigma positions that would permit the same letter to appear in the first and fourth positions of the indicator, we still have to consider that, if this phenomenon is to occur, the first letter of the three-letter text setting must have been one of the two letters that are paired in both positions of the Enigma. The probability of this is 1 in 13.*

Thus the chance that the same letter will be repeated in positions 1 and 4 of an indicator will be 13 in 25 multiplied by 1 in 13, or 1 in 25. The chance that the same letter will be repeated in positions 1 and 4, *or* 2 and 5, *or* 3 and 6 is 3 times as good, namely 3 in 25, or approximately 1 in 8. In other words, we could confidently expect that around 1 message in 8 would have an indicator with a repeated letter in either the first and fourth, or the second and fifth, or the third and sixth positions.

Thus we have established two properties of the females. First, only about half of the 17,576 choices of indicator setting VIN can offer the possibility of a 1-4 female, and the same applies to 2-5 and 3-6 females. Second, we could expect to find females of one of the

---

* In the example of positions 1 and 4 in Figure 3.5, in which there is a common letter pairing, the first letter of the text setting would have had to be either N or Y, in which case the repeated letter in the indicator would have been Y or N. If the first letter of the text setting had been N, the letters appearing in positions 1 and 4 of the indicator would have been Y and Y.

three types at the rate of about 1 in 8 messages. These conclusions represent Step 4 in the thought process.

Next came the remarkable discovery that I could ignore all those steckerboard cross-pluggings. Up to now I have been talking about the whole Enigma, with its vast number of possible cross-pluggings. But the question of whether or not the same letter pairing can occur in two positions of the Enigma is a property of the scrambler unit that is completely unaffected by different choices of steckerboard interconnections. This is an extremely important point. If, with the added complexity of the fixed steckerboard cross-pluggings, the Enigma can produce the same letter pairing in positions that are three places apart in its cycle, then the same must be true of the scrambler unit by itself, and vice versa. For, if two keyboard letters are electrically interconnected through steckerboard and scrambler, the letters to which they are steckered must be interconnected through the scrambler alone. The reverse is also true, in that if a pair of letters are interconnected through the scrambler, then the keyboard letters to which they are steckered are interconnected through the whole Enigma. Thus, because we are talking about whether or not the same letter pairing can occur in two different positions of the machine, we can completely ignore the more than 200 trillion (200,000,000,000,000) steckerboard cross-pluggings, which are specified in the Enigma key for the day, and concentrate on the effects of the cyclic motion of the scrambler on the repetition of letter pairings. With only the 60 wheel orders and 17,576 ring settings to worry about, we are down to around a million possibilities. In fact we have reduced the odds against us by a factor of around 200 trillion. This was Step 5, and quite a gain!

Let us return to the five typical females:

KIE	SPESNT	(1-4 female)
LTS	VBYQGY	(3-6 female)
EGP	OHAOCM	(1-4 female)
RYM	XWNPWV	(2-5 female)
XXY	ZDFJDA	(2-5 female)

Not knowing the ring settings of the key in use, we would not know the actual wheel settings of the scrambler represented by the indicator settings KIE, LTS, etc. Nor would we know the wheel order. But suppose we try all possible combinations of wheel order and ring settings in turn. For each such combination, and there are about a million of them, we could set up a scrambler to KIE and determine the letter substitutions, similar to those of Figure 3.5, that would be produced in the first and fourth positions of the scrambler following position KIE. About half the combinations of wheel order and ring settings will give letter substitutions with a common letter pairing. The others can be ruled out because they could not produce the female KIE SPESNT.

Thus this one female rules out about half the combinations. Similarly the next female, LTS VBYQGY, rules out about half the remaining combinations. Together, the five females listed above would divide the number of possible combinations by a factor of 32. If we could find twelve females among the messages encoded on the same Enigma key, we would be able to divide by a factor of 4,096, leaving only about 250 possible combinations, or a little more than 4 possible ring settings for each of the 60 wheel orders.

We could expect one female in every eight messages, so, in order to find twelve females enciphered on the same key, we would have to intercept about a hundred messages. At that time, October 1939, we could already expect to obtain this volume of traffic on the two keys that I was calling Red and Blue. Each of the 250 combinations of wheel orders and ring settings that could not be ruled out by the twelve females would have to be examined more closely to determine whether it might be the true combination, but the work involved in doing this 250 times did not seem unreasonable, and represented the outcome of Step 6.

What did seem horrendous was the prospect of trying each of the million-odd combinations in turn to see whether it could be ruled out by one of the twelve females.

The starting point for the last four steps in the thought process must have been the realization that the testing for the possibility of a female need not be repeated for each new key. It need only be done once. For each of the 60 wheel orders and each of the 17,576 starting positions of the three wheels it could be determined whether or not a 1-4 female, or a 2-5 female, or a 3-6 female could be produced. The yes-or-no answers could be permanently recorded for easy access. But how? In asking myself this question I was getting hot.

Let us first consider the 1-4 females for a particular wheel order, say 413, and let us assume that the ring setting of each of the scrambler wheels is Z. We can represent all possible starting positions of the three wheels by individual squares in twenty-six rectangular matrices on separate thin cardboard sheets, each having twenty-six columns and twenty-six rows. Each sheet will represent one of the twenty-six positions of the left-hand wheel. The columns on each sheet represent positions of the middle wheel, the rows those of the right-hand wheel. A typical sheet is illustrated in Figure 4.1. It is called sheet K (1,4) for wheel order 413 because it records the possibility of 1-4 females occurring when the left-hand wheel is set to letter K with ring setting Z. A circle in a square of the matrix indicates that a 1-4 female could occur with the wheels at the corresponding starting position and ring settings Z,Z. Absence of a circle means that a 1-4 female cannot occur. Thus to test the 1-4 female KIE SPESNT we look at square IE, the intersection of column I and row E. We see that there is no circle, so we have ruled out the possibility that this female could occur with wheel order 413 and ring settings ZZZ. A minor achievement, perhaps, but we are at Step 7, and well on the way.

Let us consider what the other squares of sheet K (1-4) will tell us about the female KIE SPESNT. The square JE for instance, which is immediately to the right of IE, tells us whether or not a 1-4 female can occur with starting position KJE and ring settings ZZZ. But this is the same as position KIE with ring settings ZYZ.* Similarly, squares KE, LE, ME, etc., will represent starting position KIE with ring settings ZXZ, ZWZ, ZVZ, etc. Going upward from square IE, we see that squares IF, IG, IH, II, etc., represent starting position KIE with ring settings ZZY, ZZX, ZZW, ZZV, etc. In fact the squares of sheet K (1,4) will tell us whether our female

---

* To see this, imagine that the middle wheel is held in position J while the ring setting is moved back from Z to Y. The letter showing in the aperture will change from J to I. And don't worry if this does not seem obvious. It took me quite a long time to figure out which way the letter in the aperture would go.

		A	B	C	D	E	F	G	H	I	J	K	L	M	N	O	P	Q	R	S	T	U	V	W	X	Y	Z	
R	Z	o	o		o	o	o		o	o	o	o	o	o	o					o			o	o	o		o	Z
I	Y				o	o			o	o	o			o			o	o			o	o						Y
G	X	o	o	o		o	o	o	o	o	o		o	o	o		o			o		o	o	o				X
H	W	o	o	o					o	o	o			o			o	o		o	o	o		o				W
T	V	o			o	o	o	o				o							o	o		o			o	o		V
	U		o		o			o	o			o		o				o	o			o	o	o	o	o	o	U
H	T	o				o	o						o			o				o	o	o	o	o	o	o		T
A	S	o						o		o	o	o												o	o	o		S
N	R	o	o	o		o	o	o			o			o	o			o		o	o	o				o	o	R
D	Q									o			o	o	o	o		o	o	o					o		o	Q
	P		o	o	o		o		o	o	o					o		o	o	o			o					P
W	O	o		o				o	o	o	o				o			o	o	o	o			o				O
H	N		o		o	o		o	o			o		o						o			o	o				N
E	M		o	o	o			o	o			o	o			o	o		o	o	o	o						M
E	L		o		o					o	o	o					o	o	o			o		o				L
L	K	o					o		o	o					o				o		o	o	o			o	o	K
	J	o	o		o		o					o	o	o			o		o		o	o	o		o			J
P	I		o	o			o	o				o	o	o		o	o	o	o		o	o	o	o	o	o	o	I
O	H	o	o	o		o	o	o	o		o	o	o		o		o			o		o		o				H
S	G	o	o	o	o	o	o	o	o	o	o				o			o	o	o					o	o	o	G
I	F		o	o		o				o	o	o	o	o	o		o			o			o	o	o	o	o	F
T	E			o		o				o		o		o				o				o			o		o	E
I	D		o		o	o				o	o			o	o					o	o	o			o		o	D
O	C	o	o	o		o		o				o	o	o	o		o	o	o	o	o			o		o	o	C
N	B		o			o	o		o			o	o	o	o	o	o		o		o	o			o			B
S	A	o	o		o				o	o	o	o	o	o	o		o	o	o							o		A
		A	B	C	D	E	F	G	H	I	J	K	L	M	N	O	P	Q	R	S	T	U	V	W	X	Y	Z	

MIDDLE WHEEL POSITIONS

Figure 4.1 Sheet K(1,4) for Wheel Order 413.
Left-hand wheel in position K. Ring
Settings ZZZ. Circles indicate possibility
of a 1-4 female.

could or could not occur for all possible ring settings of the middle and right-hand wheels, with the left-hand wheel at ring setting Z.

We have now taken Step 8 and we are very near the denouement, the ultimate inspiration, the last piece in the jigsaw puzzle, or whatever. Let us look at Figure 4.2, which shows the area that would be occupied by a sheet like that of Figure 4.1, except that columns ABCDE are repeated on the right, and rows ABCDE are repeated at the top. Figure 4.2 shows the positions in different and separate sheets of five sub-matrices that would be used to investigate our five females.

F-1	KIE	SPESNT	(1,4)
F-2	LTS	VBYQGY	(3,6)
F-3	EGP	OHAOCM	(1,4)
F-4	RYM	XWNPWV	(2,5)
F-5	XXY	ZDFJDA	(2,5)

At bottom left is a portion of sheet K (1,4) that would be used to study female F-1. It runs from column I to column M, from row E to row I. The letters in the squares indicate the ring settings of the middle and right-hand wheels that they represent, when used to test the possible occurrences of female F-1.

To test the same twenty-five ring settings for female F-2 we would use sheet L (3-6), and the appropriate squares would be in a different part of the sheet, as is shown in Figure 4.2. Similarly the examination of females F-3, F-4, and F-5 would involve sheets E (1,4), R (2,5), and X (2,5). Figure 4.2 shows the positions on the sheets in which the twenty-five ring settings are represented. Note that for females F-4 and F-5 we would not have been able to represent the twenty-five ring settings neatly in a 5 × 5 sub-matrix if we had not repeated columns ABC and rows ABC. Note also that, having done this, we could stack the five sheets on top of each other in staggered positions so that the 5 × 5 sub-matrices of Figure 4.2 would be on top of one another. Then, if we used a punched hole to record the possibility of a female, light would only be able to penetrate all five sheets in positions representing ring settings that would permit the occurrence of all five females. We would be able to test

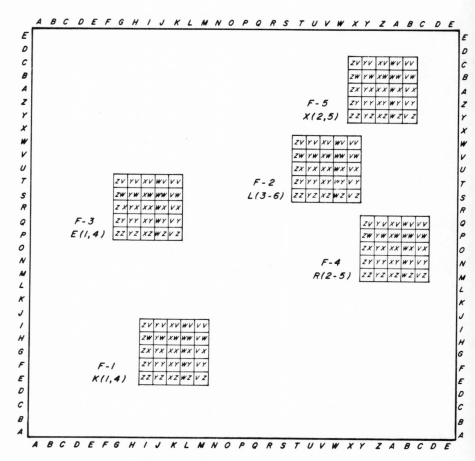

Figure 4.2 Portions of Five Sheets

all twenty-five ring settings at once. If we extended our sheets to represent the whole alphabet twice, we would obtain square sub-matrices representing all ring settings of the middle and right-hand wheels from Z to A, and we could stack the appropriate sheets so that relevant 26 × 26 sub-matrices would be on top of each other. We would be able to test all 676 ring settings in one fell swoop!

This was it! What we had to do was now clear. Our sheets would have fifty-two columns and fifty-two rows, representing letters A to Z twice over. On any particular sheet, say K (1-4) for wheel order 413, there will be two P columns and two Q rows, intersecting in four PQ squares. Holes will be punched in all four PQ squares if and only if a test has shown that a 1-4 female could occur with wheel order 413, ring settings ZZZ, and starting position KPQ. The same will be done for all columns and rows.

To use the sheets we will need a table with a window the size of a 26 × 26 matrix. This window will be illuminated from below, and sheets representing the twelve females will be stacked in such a manner that the appropriate 26 × 26 sub-matrices are above the window.

The relative positions of the five 26 × 26 sub-matrices that we are talking about are shown schematically, and at half scale, in Figure 4.3. To deal with the first of our twelve females, KIE SPESNT, we take sheet K (1,4) and place it on the table so that the 26 × 26 sub-matrix in the position that I have labeled F-1, K (1,4) will be exactly over the window. Then, to deal with F-2, we take another sheet, L (3,6), and lay it on the table so that its sub-matrix, in the position that I have labeled F-2, L (3,6) in Figure 4.3, will be exactly over the window. Similarly, to deal with the third female, F-3, we take a third sheet, E (1,4), and lay it on the table in a staggered position that will put its 26 × 26 sub-matrix over the window. And so on. The crucial point is that squares that are on top of each other will represent the same assumption of ring settings for the middle and right-hand wheels. Thus, as I said before, we can test 26 × 26 = 676 ring settings in one fell swoop. As each sheet is placed on the stack, the absence of a hole will block the light in about half the places in which it has not already been blocked. If at any stage we find that no light gets through anywhere, we have ruled out the ring setting of the left-hand wheel that we are investigating, and we move on to another ring setting of that wheel. On

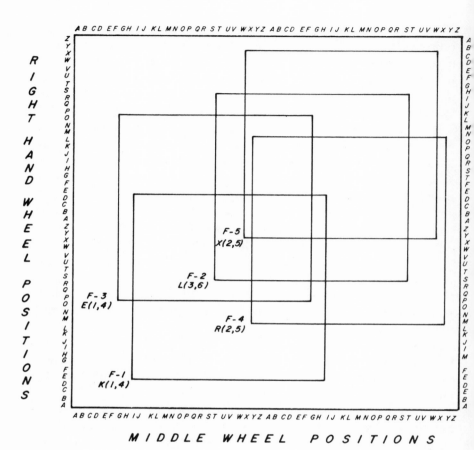

Figure 4.3 The Relative Positions in their Sheets of Matrices that are to be Stacked Over an Illuminated Window in a table

the other hand, if we do find that light shines through all twelve sheets at some particular place, this will be reported to Machine Room experts who will determine whether or not the indicated ring settings and wheel order could possibly be the correct ones.

So ended Step 9. The final step in my thought process was the realization that I had hit on a thoroughly practical method of breaking some of the German Enigma traffic. At that time I don't think that I worried over much about the massive task of testing and punching. Nor did I think much about how the experts would do their job. It just seemed to me that the testing and punching could be accomplished in months, and that the sheet stacking and wizardry involved in breaking a key for which we had intercepted twelve females could be accomplished in less than half a day. In which case the decoding of Enigma traffic, which was our entire purpose, was only a matter of months away!

Of the twenty-six stackings of selected sheets for any one wheel order, about four would result in light showing through somewhere, indicating that a particular set of ring settings had not been ruled out by the twelve females. This would be reported to the experts. When the correct combination, giving the key for the day, was discovered, the stackings would be discontinued and decoding of the day's traffic could begin. Thus, if we could do the testing and get the cardboard sheets punched, and could find twelve females on the Red or Blue key for a particular day, we could confidently expect to discover that key after an average of 780 stackings. And we could be sure of success provided that nothing had gone wrong. We could be foiled if we had inadvertently used a female that had been encoded on a different key, or if there had been an error in the transmission or interception of the critical nine letters. But we could hope to guard against such gremlins, and the prospect seemed extremely good. So in great excitement I hurried from School to Cottage to tell Dilly about it.

Dilly was furious. What I was suggesting was precisely what he was already doing, and the necessary sheets were being punched under the direction of my Cambridge friend and colleague John Jeffreys. Dilly reminded me that I had been told to study discriminants and callsigns, not methods of breaking the Enigma. He sent me back to the School without telling me how the testing and sheet punching were being done. Indeed I never did know whether Jeffreys designed his sheets in the way that had occurred to me. It is entirely possible that there may have been errors in my thinking at that time, or in my attempt now, forty years later, to reconstruct my sequence of thought processes. But this did not matter then and does not matter now. What did matter was that a sheet-stacking process similar to the one I had suggested was being developed. From my association with Jeffreys before the war, I had a very high opinion of his abilities and felt quite sure that he would do a good job.

In fact I was confident that the scheme was going to work. The sheet-stacking process would reduce the possible assumptions of wheel order and ring settings to a manageable number, indicated by positions in which light would shine through a stack. Each of these not-ruled-out assumptions would be called a "drop"* and would require cryptanalytical examination by experts, whom I will call "wizards" with affectionate regard for their many skills. They did the actual breaking of the Enigma keys, but they also performed other functions that can hardly be regarded as cryptanalytical ones. I was not told how it was proposed that the wizards would test drops and achieve breaks. One thing I did learn, however, was that the term "female," that I have used in my discussion, had become established in the Cottage. The reason, no doubt, was the analogy between a punched hole, through which light can shine, and a female socket into which a plug can be inserted to make an electrical connection.

The reader may find it hard to believe that I had not been made aware of so important a development. Dilly was notorious for not telling anyone anything, though he often thought that he had done so. Moreover Bletchley Park as a whole must have been pretty chaotic in October 1939 and for many months after that. Huts were being built all over the place by the energetic, likable horse-riding Captain Faulkner. Sections were being formed and expanded to handle the many areas of work. The reader should not bother about

* The term "drop" was probably derived from information retrieval systems using a stack of edge-punched cards. A search for desired information was conducted by sticking long pins through appropriate holes in the stack and shaking. Cards that might contain what was wanted would drop out.

the purposes for which Huts 1, 2, 3, 4, etc., were built, or what went on in them. It would be too confusing. The numbers attached to the actual wooden structures kept being changed so that a section could continue to be known by the same hut number when it moved to new quarters. But with growing pains such as these, it was unlikely that there would be an organized flow of information.

As for the strange reaction of Dilly Knox, an explanation of this outburst has recently occurred to me. It is possible that Dilly did not know about the Germans' double encipherment of their text settings until the meeting in the Pyry forest in July 1939 at which the Poles had revealed that they knew "everything about Enigma." It seems probable that, at the same meeting, Dilly had been told about the identical method of breaking the Enigma that would occur to me a few months later in the School. If this was so, Dilly would not have had a chance to think up the idea for himself. It would have been infuriating for him to find that a newcomer, and one whom he had kicked off his Cottage team, had come up with an idea he had not thought of.

This first of my two breakthroughs proved to be a lead balloon—in that others, almost certainly the Poles, had already had the same idea. But it proved extremely important that the idea had come to me, too, and so early in the game. The planning for exploitation that I am about to describe was based on the confident expectation that we were going to be able to decode Enigma traffic, and I might not have known this for months if I had not thought of the idea myself. And we didn't have months to spare. The planning for exploitation might have started too late.

It may seem odd, but I have no memory of being particularly irritated by Dilly's behavior, or of feeling frustrated by the fact that my idea was not new. Any such feelings must have been submerged in my delight at finding that the Cottage people believed, as I did, that the idea would work and that we were going to break into the Enigma traffic. Back in the School, however, as I mulled over the implications of this exciting development, I had the uneasy feeling that it was regarded in the Cottage as primarily a cryptological success. No one seemed to be thinking about the activities outside Bletchley Park that would be needed to exploit the break to the full. I started to think about that problem on my own.

In the autumn of 1939 we were in the period of the "Phony War," and nothing much was happening. Even in this period of relative quiet, however, we did not have enough operators to intercept all the German Enigma traffic. For only two types of traffic, the Red and the Blue, did we have a hope of sufficient volume to make the Jeffreys apparatus effective when it became available.

Furthermore, as a result of my traffic analysis and my contact with Ellingworth at Chatham, I was very conscious of the fact that accuracy of interception was vital and presented a very real problem, because many of the intercepted signals were weak. Added to the problem of poor signal strength was the fact that several pairs of letters, such as U and V, are easily confused when transmitted in Morse. Our intercept operators often had to write down alternate letters to indicate their uncertainty about some of the Morse code characters they received.

Even more evident, perhaps, was the need for maximum coverage of the German radio nets so that, if we were able to break a given day's key, we could provide the intelligence people with decodes of as many messages as possible. And, since the war might suddenly become hot again, we must be ready for a lot more radio traffic, and probably more keys too. To exploit our technique to the full we would need many more intercept operators. It would also be highly desirable to establish intercept stations in widely separated locations, so that a signal too weak for reliable interception at one station might come in strongly at another.

Furthermore, our chances of success would be enhanced if we could use only those sets of nine letters (indicator setting and female indicator) which could be confirmed by two or more intercept operators. To satisfy both cryptanalytic and intelligence needs to the fullest extent possible with inevitably limited intercept resources, there would be a need for coordination from Bletchley Park. At that time I myself was the only coordinator, and self-appointed at that, and I was dealing with only one intercept station, Chatham.

The traffic analysis that I had initiated in the Schoolhouse would also need considerable expansion to meet the requirements of hot war and to handle the output of the more extensive interception capabilities I hoped for. The work would have to be highly accurate, because any attempt to break a particular key could be wrecked if a message enciphered on a different key were mistakenly used. Moreover the sheer volume of the registration effort would be far greater. The much larger number of German radio nets we could expect under hot war conditions would, I was sure, require many frequency/time charts for each day's traffic, by contrast with the single chart that had sufficed for my own early traffic analysis. In addition to all this, it was clear that we would have to operate around the clock. With my staff of two young women I could not possibly cope with the needs of traffic analysis and coordination of interception.

On the cryptanalytic side of the picture the situation was equally unsatisfactory. It was obvious that we would need a considerable staff to carry out the sheet-stacking routine within an acceptable time after a sufficient number of females on the same key had been intercepted with adequate confirmation. We would also need a staff of Enigma experts who would work on the drops thrown up by the routine sheet stacking. Starting every midnight, when keys were changed, this staff of wizards would keep a close eye on the traffic registers coming in by teleprinter from the intercept stations, and on expanded traffic analysis charts similar to those that I had brought into use during the low-traffic period. They would decide when their collection of females was good enough to start a sheet-stacking attempt to break a particular key. At the time I am talking about we had very few people to staff the sheet-stacking operation, and very few qualified Enigma experts. Around-the-clock activity would have been impossible.

Finally, on the assumption that we were going to achieve breaks, we would need a decoding room equipped with British cipher machines, which would have to be adapted to operate like German Enigma machines.* We would need enough decoding personnel on duty at any time of the day or night to start decoding all intercepted messages on a broken key as soon as the break could be achieved, and to get the decodes to intelligence people within an acceptably short time. Remember that the same key would usually have been used for the encoding of more than a hundred messages, all of which would be decodable as soon as we had discovered the key.

---

* Fortunately, though I did not know it at the time, the British Type-X cipher machines that were already in production could be adapted without much trouble. Thus there was no need to design, develop, and manufacture duplicates of the German Enigma.

With considerations such as these in mind, I formulated an organizational plan and took it to Commander Edward Travis, deputy director, under Alastair Denniston, of all Bletchley Park activities. Travis was a broad-shouldered man of heavy build. His spectacles gave him a curious expression, which I found disconcerting until I knew him better. I think they were of a kind that was unusual in those days, a narrow lens for reading with a flat-topped metal rim over which he could scrutinize distant objects and people to whom he talked.

I explained to him that, as soon as Jeffreys and his team had completed the punching of sheets in the Cottage, we would have a golden opportunity that we were very ill-equipped to exploit. We had reason to believe that we could break into a significant part of the German Enigma traffic, even during the quiescent period of the Phony War. If we were to exploit our opportunity under hot war conditions, a lot had to be done in a hurry. Within the Bletchley Park complex we had to build up a completely new twenty-four-hour operation of five closely coordinated departments: a Registration Room to perform a continuous traffic analysis of Enigma messages based on traffic registers received by teleprinter from the intercept stations; an Intercept Control Room, which would keep in continuous touch with the intercept stations, helping them concentrate on the most valuable traffic; a Machine Room handling the cryptanalytic aspects in close collaboration with the Registration Room and the Intercept Control Room; a Sheet-Stacking Room, which would be called into action by the Machine Room whenever the traffic of a particular day on a particular key merited an attempt at a break; and finally a Decoding Room to handle the messages on any key that might be broken. We had not yet even begun to acquire any such capabilities within our organization.

Outside Bletchley Park we were going to need a major expansion of intercept facilities. In particular, in view of the possibility that the Army station at Chatham might be required to concentrate on German army traffic, it seemed very important to have a station operated by the Royal Air Force and dedicated to the interception of enemy air force Enigma traffic.

Travis' response was all I could have hoped for. He immediately saw the urgent need for a buildup, approved the plan in full—and wasted no time. He quickly obtained official agreement to the establishment of a new section in the Bletchley Park complex to handle this possibility of Enigma breaks on an interservice basis. Denniston, the head of Bletchley Park; Tiltman, head of the Army section; and Cooper, head of the Air Force section, all gave their full support to the plan.

It was a time for me of great excitement and great challenge, and in winning approval of this plan at so early a date I probably made my biggest single contribution to the war effort. I had come to Bletchley Park as a green recruit only a short time before and yet, because of the work that Dilly Knox had asked me to do in the School, I had had the luck to stumble on some important aspects of the command communications system that the Germans had developed for their blitzkrieg. I had had a vision of how the Jeffreys apparatus, then being developed in the Cottage under Dilly's direction, could be fully exploited. And I had been able to convince my superiors that a radically new situation called for an entirely new organization. That the necessary organization could be built up speedily, and was ready for action when the Jeffreys apparatus became available, was tremendously important—how important will become apparent as we go on.

The second breakthrough that I was able to make before the war was three months old had to do with the design of electromechanical machines called "bombes," which played an important part in the Hut 6 story. The name "bombe" seems to have been attached by the Poles to an earlier concept, but it was also applied to the machines that we actually used. The term "bombe" is simply the French for "bomb"; the connection with our machine is not clear to me, but it may have had to do with the idea of a mechanism that will go on ticking until it reaches a combination that will cause it to produce an output—in our case not an explosive one. Our bombes were said to make a noise like a battery of knitting needles.

One of the basic ideas behind our bombe was to move a battery of Enigma scrambler units in synchronism through all possible positions. A group of Polish experts had come to Bletchley and worked with Knox and Turing on the concept of such a machine for a time before going to France. Now Turing was working on the exploitation of their machine; my contribution to its development was to add the principle of the "diagonal board," which greatly increased its power. The fact that the idea came to me so early proved to be extremely fortunate, and again, for those readers who may be interested, I will attempt to reconstruct my mental processes.

I was certainly influenced by those precious decodes that Josh Cooper had given me when I started work in the School. As I explained in Chapter 3, I had noticed that stereotyped addresses and signatures appeared in the texts of this small sample of decodes. Now I began to wonder if this gave us the possibility of using these as cribs to break Enigma keys.

The notion of a "crib" may need a little explanation. Several definitions of the word will be found in the dictionary, including "a device used for cheating in an examination."* Cryptologically speaking, however, one has a "crib" to a cipher text if one can guess the clear text from which some specific portion of the cipher text was obtained. As my analysis of the Enigma traffic began to reveal certain routine characteristics in the preambles of individual messages, I realized that, if we could somehow determine to whom they were addressed, or by whom they had been sent, we might be able to guess a portion of the clear text either at the beginning or at the end of each of the messages, and so have cribs.

To illustrate what I had in mind, let us consider the imaginary crib shown at the top of Figure 4.4. Somehow it has been possible to guess that the thirty-one letters CQNZP through UFLNZ at the start of a message have been obtained by enciphering the plain text address TO THE PRESIDENT OF THE UNITED STATES. The numbers 1 through 31 refer to the successive positions of the Enigma's scrambler unit at which the letters of the plain text were encoded. These 31 positions are consecutive ones somewhere in the scrambler cycle of 17,576 positions.†

I have explained that the idea of the Jeffreys sheets rested on the fact that it was not always possible for the same pair of letters to be

---

* "And they found in his palms . . . what is common in palms, namely dates."

† Remember that a scrambler position involves three wheel positions, and that each wheel has twenty-six positions, of which one is a turnover position. In the scrambler cycle the right-hand wheel always advances one notch with the encoding of each letter. The middle wheel advances only when the right-hand wheel is in its turnover position, which will occur once in every twenty-six consecutive scrambler positions. The left-hand wheel advances only when both the right-hand and middle wheels are in their turnover positions, which will occur once in every 676 consecutive scrambler positions.

Crib

C	Q	N	Z	P	V	L	I	L	P	E	U	I	K	T	E	D	C	G	L	O	V	W	V	G	T	U	F	L	N	Z
T	O	T	H	E	P	R	E	S	I	D	E	N	T	O	F	T	H	E	U	N	I	T	E	D	S	T	A	T	E	S
1	2	3	4	5	6	7	8	9	10	11	12	13	14	15	16	17	18	19	20	21	22	23	24	25	26	27	28	29	30	31

Diagrams

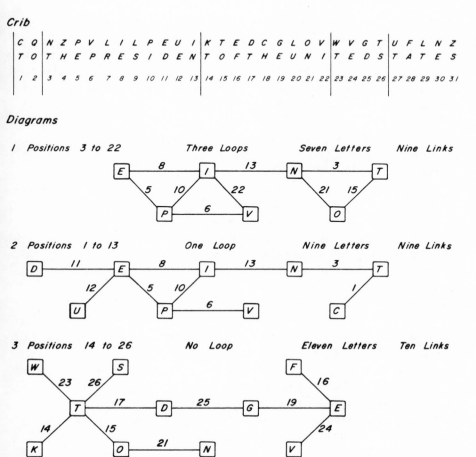

1 Positions 3 to 22   Three Loops   Seven Letters   Nine Links

2 Positions 1 to 13   One Loop   Nine Letters   Nine Links

3 Positions 14 to 26   No Loop   Eleven Letters   Ten Links

Figure 4.4 Diagrams Derived From a Crib

the encodes of each other in scrambler positions three places apart in the cycle of machine positions. The principle of the bombe on which Turing was working may be regarded as a more complex version of the same idea. Turing, however, was now concerned with patterns formed by several letter pairings of a crib, rather than with the occurrence of females, and by the fact that patterns of certain types could not always be produced by a set of scramblers in the relative positions in the machine cycle indicated by the places in the crib in which the letter pairings occurred. Turing intended to use a battery of Enigma scramblers set at relative positions corresponding to a set of letter pairings in a crib that he would select for study. The whole battery of scramblers would be moved in synchronism through all $26 \times 26 \times 26$ positions of each scrambler. In each position of the battery an automatic test would be applied to determine whether his selected set of letter pairings could occur. In this way, as in the case of stacking Jeffreys sheets, he could hope to achieve a major reduction in the possibilities requiring serious cryptanalytical study.

On examining the crib in Figure 4.4 we see that the encode of E in position 5 is P, that the encode of E in position 8 is I, and that the encode of I in position 10 is P, the letter from which we started. This closure of the loop—P to E to I to P—is an example of the type of pattern that Turing intended to use.

Figure 4.4 shows three diagrams that can be derived from the letter pairings of the crib. In the first diagram the loop that I have just discussed is represented on the left. A line numbered 8 links two boxes containing letters E and I. This is a convenient way of indicating that the letters E and I are the encodes of each other through a scrambler in position 8 of the sequence 1 through 31; in fact the line or link between letters E and I represents this scrambler. Similarly the letters E and P are the encodes of each other in position 5, letters I and P in position 10, and so on. The diagram involves three closed loops, seven letters, and nine links indicating scramblers in positions ranging from 3 to 22. The bombe, as it was being developed by Turing from Polish ideas, depended entirely on being able to construct a diagram, similar to the first diagram of Figure 4.4, containing three closed loops.

The idea that flashed into my mind in the School was that, by interconnecting the scramblers in a completely new way, one could increase the effectiveness of the automatic test by a very large factor. I saw that we need not depend on obtaining three closed loops. Instead a bombe could be constructed that would make use of configurations such as those shown in the second and third diagrams of Figure 4.4, involving one loop or no loops at all.

When this new method of interconnecting the scramblers of a bombe came to me, I couldn't believe it. But I sat down with a few colored pencils, drew a simple wiring diagram, and convinced myself that the idea would indeed work. Armed with this diagram I hurried once again to the Cottage, this time to talk to Turing. On this occasion I had a better reception than I had received from Dilly. Turing was incredulous at first, as I had been, but when he had studied my diagram he agreed that the idea would work, and became as excited about it as I was. He agreed that the improvement over the type of bombe that he had been considering was spectacular.

With Turing's support it was not difficult to convince Travis that the development of the improved bombe was urgently important for handling the Enigma traffic of the German army and air force, and the naval Enigma traffic as well. Again Travis wasted no time. Although I did not realize it then, Harold "Doc" Keen of the British Tabulating Machine Company, which was associated with IBM in America, must already have started on the design of the Turing bombe. Travis asked me to work closely with Keen, and this started what was to become both a close collaboration and a close friendship. Keen soon grasped the new idea and set to work on two prototype bombes incorporating the diagonal board. The design proved to be extremely flexible, quite adaptable to changes as they became necessary. This was no doubt due to Keen's long experience with punched-card equipment, which was always being called upon to perform tasks that no one had thought of when specifications were being prepared.

As is often the case with revolutionary ideas, mine, after it had occurred to me, proved extremely simple. It involved interconnecting a battery of scrambler units through what came to be known as a diagonal board. But practical realization in the form of a workable

bombe required several other ideas.* Furthermore, the exploitation
of the bombes in Hut 6 called for a kind of cryptanalytical wizardry
that had not yet been developed. Thus the bombe in its final realization was not the brainchild of any one person; and we thought very
little, in those hectic days, of who should take credit for what.

It will become clear that the purpose of a bombe run was to
determine whether, for one of the 60 possible wheel orders, a certain
pattern of letter pairings derived from a crib could occur with a set
of scramblers in relative positions corresponding to the positions of
the letter pairings in the crib. The automatic test, of which I have
talked, involved trying to prove that no combination of stecker
pairings could allow the pattern to occur. It was accomplished in
one fell swoop by electric current flowing to and fro between the
battery of scramblers and the diagonal board. Thus the vast number
of stecker combinations (around 200 trillion) on which the German
cryptographers probably pinned their faith was of no avail against
the bombe. In essence our automatic test could examine all possible
stecker combinations in less than a thousandth of a second.

As in the case of the sheet-stacking idea, I believe it to be very
significant that an idea as important as that of the diagonal board
came to a complete novice within three months of his exposure to
the characteristics and operating procedures of the Enigma. I do not
know what types of expertise contributed to the design of the German Enigma system that was in use at the outbreak of World War
II, but it must have been a carefully considered design. Yet I, a
completely inexperienced recruit from Cambridge University, having been told how the system worked, very soon came up with two
complementary methods of breaking the Enigma traffic.

What do we learn from this? It seems to imply that professional
cryptographers, however good they are, may fail to see how a mind
with a different background might find a way of defeating them.
And the lesson seems to be that, even against the threat of pure
cryptanalysis—by no means the greatest threat to the security of
our communications in the 1980s and 1990s—it would be dangerous to depend only on the expertise of professional cryptologists

---

* In the Appendix "The Bombe with a Diagonal Board" I will go into greater detail,
explaining the use of double-ended scramblers, how my bombe differed from the Turing
bombe, and why the introduction of the diagonal board was so important.

who operate under the protective cover of super-high-level secrecy. Whatever systems these professionals may design should be subjected, under stringent conditions of secrecy, to close scrutiny by nonprofessionals who may possibly come up with new ideas.

For example, as I see it, the security of our cryptographic systems seems too often to be reckoned by the number of possibilities that an enemy computer would have to examine one by one. In the bombe, however, particularly with my addition of the diagonal board, we were able to examine an enormous number of possibilities in one fell swoop. Thus the mere number of possibilities proved to be invalid as a measure of system security. It could happen again.

Noncryptological threats to the security of our future communications systems might also be detected by someone other than the experts who devise the cryptographic systems. This possibility will become more apparent later on, as we see how the security of the German Enigma was undermined by the errors of its users rather than by those of its designers. Should we not subject our cryptographic systems to close scrutiny by many different minds before they are accepted, and to thorough monitoring when they are in use? Furthermore, as I will be better able to argue toward the end of this book, we should make sure that the noncryptanalytic threats to the security and survivability of our communications are very thoroughly examined from *many* points of view. In failure to do so lies the greatest danger.

Thus ends my discussion of the first three months. We can now move on to the remaining nine months of the first year, up to the time when Hitler abandoned his plans to invade England and decided to deploy his forces to other theaters.

5

Early Days

December 1939 to May 1940

Recruiting for Hut 6 went fast. Travis produced a scientist, John Colman, to take charge of the Intercept Control Room, which was to maintain close contact with the intercept stations. Colman was soon joined by another scientist, George Crawford, a former schoolmate of mine at Marlborough College. Travis also persuaded London banks to send us some of their brightest young men to handle the continuous interchange of information with intercept stations. Thus, very soon, we had an intercept control team large enough to operate round the clock. They quickly established close and very friendly relations with the duty officers at Chatham.

For my part, I quite shamelessly recruited friends and former students. Stuart Milner-Barry had been in my year at Trinity College, Cambridge, studying classics while I studied mathematics. He was not enjoying being a stockbroker, and was persuaded to join me at Bletchley Park. He arrived around January 1940, when the Hut 6 organization was about thirty strong, bringing with him the largest pipes I have ever seen smoked. Stuart in turn recruited his friend, Hugh Alexander, who had been a mathematician at Kings College, Cambridge, and was then Director of Research in the John Lewis Partnership, a large group of department stores. They brought us unusual distinction in chess: Alexander was the British Chess Champion, while Milner-Barry had often played for England and was chess correspondent for the London *Times*. Two other friends from Cambridge undergraduate days joined me later: Harold Fletcher, top mathematician in the college entrance scholarship exams in 1925, and Houston Wallace, who had become a Chartered Accountant.

Another mathematical friend from Cambridge, Dennis Babbage, had come to Bletchley in the early days as an Army officer and, after working with Dilly Knox in the Cottage, became one of the original wizards of the Hut 6 team. He and I had been members of a group of geometers known as Professor Baker's "Tea Party," who met once a week to discuss the areas of research in which we were all interested.

Before the war, when I was College Lecturer in Mathematics at Sidney Sussex College, Cambridge, John Jeffreys had been a Research Fellow in Mathematics at Downing College. For two years or so he had been helping me supervise the studies of my math students. We had become close friends, and were both considered pretty good math supervisors. Consequently we found it not too difficult to persuade some of our best students to join us, including three very good young mathematicians, David Rees, John Herivel, and John Chamberlain. Other nonmathematical Sidney men, Howard Smith and Asa Briggs, joined the team and distinguished themselves.

Nor did I stop at the university level in my forays for bright young men. Before going to Trinity College, Cambridge, in 1925, I had studied at Marlborough College under an outstanding math teacher, A. Robson. I had kept in touch with him, and we had spent summer vacations together in the English Lake District collaborating on mathematics textbooks. So I now appealed to him to send me his best young mathematicians. This produced another influx of very good people, including John Manisty. At the same time other men were being recruited, mostly, I believe, on the basis of personal contacts such as those I was exploiting. Probably this was inevitable. Recruits could not be told what kind of job they were going to do, so they needed assurance from someone they could trust that what they were being asked to do was really worthwhile. Aitken, the chess champion of Scotland, was one man acquired by this means; another was David Gaunt, a very able young classics scholar from Cheltenham College.

This kind of piracy was to be curtailed in 1941. The government decided that the use of the best young brains in the country should be regulated. C. P. Snow, of Christs College, Cambridge, whom I had known before the war (and now a celebrated author), was put in charge of allocation of all scientists and mathematicians, and from then on I had to recruit my male staff through him. I could not tell him what we were doing in Hut 6, and I do not know to this day what, if anything, he had been told about our operation. Nevertheless he was extremely cooperative, and sent me some very good men. Perhaps it was another fortunate accident that Snow happened to know me fairly well and believed what I said about the importance of our work.

One problem that arose later should perhaps be mentioned now. Some of the young men who were sent to Hut 6 because of their brains found themselves trapped there by the demands of security. They longed for active service in the air force, the navy, or the army, but they knew too much about our success with the Enigma for their capture by the enemy to be risked. They were doing an exhausting job, and it was obviously helping the war effort, but many of them longed to play an active part in the fighting. There was, too, the inevitable feeling that not being at the front was somehow dishonorable; one young man received a scathing letter from his old headmaster accusing him of being a disgrace to his school.

Recruitment of young women went on even more rapidly than that of men. We needed more of them to staff the Registration Room, the Sheet-Stacking Room, and the Decoding Room. As with the men, I believe that the early recruiting was largely on a personal-acquaintance basis, but with the whole of Bletchley Park looking for qualified women, we got a great many recruits of high caliber.

I was very little involved in the recruitment of the important female component of the Hut 6 staff, but I may perhaps venture one anecdote. I had been married in 1937, and my wife, Katharine, and son, Nick, were still in Cambridge, so I returned there as often as I could. While there I hunted around for staff for Hut 6. I recruited June Canney, the daughter of a doctor, and in due course drove her from Cambridge to Bletchley. On the way she remarked that she had been wondering why I had asked at our initial interview if she were colorblind. When she arrived in Hut 6 she could see for herself: We depended on color discrimination. My original key colors, red, blue, green, brown, and orange, had been added to. Indeed, before long the British supply of colored pencils ran out, and we had to appeal to America for the supplies we needed for our Registration Room. It may seem absurd, but those colors really helped, and we could never think of an adequate substitute. Men from the Machine Room and the Intercept Control Room would keep wandering into the Registration Room to examine the traffic charts, and the identification of keys by color was a great help to them. June Canney's color vision was fine, but she didn't stay long in the Registration Room. She became my secretary, and did much to help me in running Hut 6 and making it a happy organization as well as an efficient one.

In the very early days, of course, we had nothing to decode, but we managed to acquire a staff for the Decoding Room who had learned to operate our modified Type-X machines as if they were German Enigmas. Thus while we were waiting for the completion of the "Jeffreys apparatus," we assembled a strong supporting staff, and developed an organization that would be ready to go into action as soon as codebreaking became possible.

In fact the punching of the Jeffreys sheets was near completion, so we did not have much time, and the buildup of our intercept control capabilities was particularly urgent. When Travis brought in Colman he had hoped that, even before we could start breaking the German Enigma traffic, a scientific analysis of message volume might yield valuable intelligence. Colman's most important function at that time was to establish the closest possible cooperation with intercept stations, but he gave Travis' idea a good try.

He concentrated on the Red and Blue traffic, because at that time no other Enigma keys were offering a volume of messages that would give the Jeffreys apparatus a chance. Colman and his staff found out how to use naval intercept facilities for direction finding (D/F). From close contact with Chatham they were able to get the naval D/F stations onto specific Enigma messages, with the intention of determining the locations of the transmitting stations.

By now Colman was also getting help from the RAF intercept station at Cheadle. He found that, whereas transmitters of Red traffic were pretty widespread, those of the Blue traffic were concentrated in the northwest of Germany, an area from which military operations might be expected to originate. Consequently Colman concentrated his attention on Blue traffic, analyzing its fluctuations, which were considerable. On several occasions an unusual peak in Blue caused us to believe that an outbreak of hot war was imminent. We got quite excited about it. However, when the Jeffreys apparatus became available and we finally broke the Blue traffic, we found that it was nothing more than training exercises. The Germans, with their phenomenal planning, foresight, and thoroughness, were busily training the Enigma-equipped signals detachments that were to accompany German ground and air forces on their fast-moving rampages throughout Europe and northern Africa. Of course, when we discovered that the Blue traffic was only an exercise for the German signals organization, we concentrated on the Red, which at that time was genuine Luftwaffe traffic. As we were to discover, the Red traffic became the operational traffic of the German ground and air forces as soon as the war became hot.

During the Phony War, the combat units of the German army had no need for radio communications. They could, and no doubt did, use established telephone-type communications. But as soon as they moved out of their homeland, the German army needed radio communications among their own mobile units and with those of their air force. They used the Red key, which was intended for this purpose.

The fact that the Red key was being used for army–air coordination must have been apparent during Hitler's invasion of Norway. It certainly became obvious during the invasion of France. Yet the myth that Red was an air force key has persisted; even Ronald Lewin in his excellent *Ultra Goes to War* still accepts it. But I am guilty too. The myth was not dispelled from my own mind until I argued with Ronald about the tactical army–air messages that we decoded during the Battle of France—messages that gave a picture of what was going on at the combat level, rather than at the higher command level. In the picture of Guderian's command vehicle shown in Lewin's book and reproduced here (Figure 2.1), there is an Enigma that must have been used for messages on the Red key. But neither Guderian himself, nor his cipher clerk and Enigma operator, were air force personnel. Furthermore, many of the crucial messages at the higher command level that are discussed by Winterbotham and Lewin were quite definitely army messages (for example, orders from the German Commander in Chief, von Brauchitsch, to van Bock's Army Group B and to von Kluge's 4th Army). Surely an Enigma key that was used to encode such messages cannot be regarded as an air force key. But let us get back to our "Early Days."

In anticipation of the advent of the Jeffreys apparatus, it was necessary to introduce a three-shift schedule in other sections as well as in Colman's Intercept Control Room to cover the twenty-four hours of each day. At the time, this was a novelty in Bletchley Park, and in addition to organizational problems, it created an unexpected problem concerning "proper" behavior. In the early days of three-shift operation, my night staff would consist of one man in the Intercept Control Room with one girl assistant, and perhaps two or three girls in the Registration Room. This situation was considered highly improper by the Foreign Office administration of Bletchley Park! Fortunately, the problem did not come to a head in time to hamper our operation; we were able to keep going until the advent of the Jeffreys apparatus called for more people on night shift and therefore, perhaps, safety in numbers. We did not have to wait long.

While I was busy building up the Hut 6 organization and working with Doc Keen on the functional design of the bombes, John Jeffreys and his team were patiently performing a monumental task in the Cottage. I was not a participant myself, but I have already given a broad picture of what must have been involved. I do know that the Cottage people had a very simple manually operated testing machine that would determine in a matter of seconds whether a particular assumption of wheel order and starting position could or could not produce a 1-4 female, a 2-5 female, or a 3-6 female.

Though each test was simple, there were $3 \times 17,576$ tests to be made for each of the 60 possible wheel orders, and the result of each test had to be recorded by punching or not punching a hole in one of the Jeffreys sheets. It was a great achievement by the Cottage staff. Once the sheets were punched, however, we had a permanent record that could be applied in the breaking of any daily Enigma key.

As I have already explained, the actual breaking of a key would depend on skilled work by the experts in the Machine Room. The sheet-stacking did no more than reduce the number of possibilities that had to be investigated. In the School days I did not attack this problem seriously. I was not told how Jeffreys proposed to solve it. When Hut 6 became operational, Jeffreys was in charge of Sheet-Stacking and Machine Room activities, while I worried about Registration, Intercept Control, Decoding, and relations with the intelligence people in Hut 3. I can see how the breaks might have been achieved, but will not discuss the matter. The important fact is that the breaks were actually achieved by John Jeffreys and his team.

Thanks to our early planning and recruiting, and the establishment of twenty-four-hour shift operations, we achieved a workable routine as soon as the Jeffreys sheets were ready for use. From midnight on, three copies of the teleprinted sheets of the traffic register from Chatham were studied in the Registration Room, in the Intercept Control Room, and in the Machine Room. The staff of the Registration Room would start the day's traffic sheets, determining the sets of discriminants that identified the various keys. The Intercept Control Room Staff, using the charts in the Registration Room, would be trying to concentrate our interception resources on the traffic that we wanted most. The Machine Room personnel would decide when enough suitably confirmed females had been found on one key to justify an attempt to break that key for the day. The Red key, rather than the Blue, would have priority.

Once the Machine Room had found a satisfactory set of Red females, the people in the Sheet-Stacking Room would begin their routine. From time to time they would obtain a "drop," which would be tested by the Machine Room staff. Most of these drops would prove false; indeed, the Machine Room decision to attempt a break was based on a calculation of the number of false drops that could be expected from the data it had given to the Sheet-Stacking Room.

With luck the sheet stacking would at last produce a true drop that would enable the Machine Room to determine the Red key for the day. When this happened, a shout of triumph would be heard, and the Decoding Room staff would be activated. As an indication of how long all this might take, the shout of triumph for the key of a day's Red traffic would usually be heard in the early hours of the next morning.

Soon after the Jeffreys sheets came into use, I invited Commander Ellingworth of Chatham to spend a night with me. In the evening he watched what was going on in the Sheet-Stacking Room, and then we settled down in my office to discuss the operation in general. At about one in the morning we heard the shout, and hurried along the corridor to the Decoding Room. Soon Ellingworth was seeing the first decodes of the previous day's messages as they came out of the Type-X machines.

That night together in Hut 6 was a great help to us both. Ellingworth got a clear picture of our activities, and we were able to talk realistically about the problems of handling Enigma traffic. For example, there was the question of message texts. The teleprinted traffic register, which had been initiated after my first visit to Chatham, contained all the information that we could use in breaking an Enigma key—preamble, with discriminant and indicator setting, and the first two text groups containing the twice-enciphered text setting, or indicator. Once the key was broken, however, we needed the message texts for decoding. These texts were recorded by intercept operators on standard forms and bundled together for dispatch to us. Until we started breaking, nobody had had any use for these bundles, but now there was suddenly an urgent need to get them to Bletchley Park in a hurry. During that night Ellingworth and I discussed how the bundles of messages could be transported to Hut 6 in time for instant decoding whenever a key was broken. Our teleprinter facilities were utterly inadequate to handle so much volume, so we had to continue to depend on dispatch riders. The debt that we owe to these riders, who faced all kinds of weather on their motorcycles, has never, to my knowledge, been properly recognized.

There was also the question of giving certain messages priority, and for that we did use the teleprinter. The problem became a great deal more complicated later on, but I believe that the idea of the "Welchman Special" was born that night. Even in those early days it had become apparent that we in Hut 6, by studying the teleprinted traffic register, could often identify messages that would be of particular interest from the point of view of the intelligence experts.* In such cases, Ellingworth and I agreed, Colman's people would telephone the intercept station to ask that the anticipated

---

* For example, messages on a particular radio net, appearing each day with the same time of origin, might have been found, by previous decodes, to be daily reports or daily commands of considerable significance.

messages be given special treatment, whereupon the Chatham people would immediately transmit them by teleprinter. The term "Welchman Special" was introduced at Chatham shortly after Ellingworth's visit to Hut 6.

The idea of "Welchman Specials" was to be helpful to us in many ways in the later phases of the Hut 6 activities. However, let us first think of the importance of the idea for intelligence. Wonder has been expressed at the speed with which information from Hut 6 decodes could sometimes reach Allied commanders. It has even been said that on some occasions these commanders would actually receive information before the German addressees did.

Readers of Winterbotham's *The Ultra Secret* will know that one of his tasks in World War II was to pass to Winston Churchill those decoded messages that Churchill would regard as highly significant. It seems probable that these messages would usually have been to or from high-level German commanders, in which case they would have been messages that we would have identified as potentially important from our analysis of the teleprinted traffic registers. Thus a high proportion of the decodes mentioned in Winterbotham's book as having been passed to Churchill had reached him earlier than would otherwise have been possible because they had been handled as "Welchman Specials." The same applies to many of the sensational decodes whose sanitized content is now known to have been passed to commanders in the field.*

After September 1940 the "Welchman Special" technique was used to speed up the breaking of keys as well as the decoding of important messages; but much needs to be explained before this becomes fully intelligible. The name "Welchman Special" was coined at Chatham to denote messages that were given special handling as a result of descriptions provided in advance by Hut 6. The use of my name resulted from the happy personal relationship that I had established with Chatham in October 1939. But the exploitation of this procedure was always a routine matter, handled by the Hut 6 staff. A more appropriate name would have been "Bletchley

---

* The word "sanitized" may need explanation. If the exact translation of a decode had been sent, and had somehow been read by the enemy, it might have revealed the fact that the information could only have been obtained by decoding, thus revealing our highly secret capability. Consequently the information derived from a decode had to be presented accurately, but in a manner that would not obviously relate it to an Enigma message.

Special," or "Hut 6 Special." What is of significance is that this important procedure was originated when Commander Ellingworth of Chatham visited Hut 6 early in 1940.

I was continually bothered by the possibility that this "Welchman Special" procedure might be a dangerous breach of security. If we in Bletchley Park could tell an intercept station that a particular message was of special importance, the clear implication was that we could decipher that message. My concern was not so much that the telephone wires might be tapped—one worried less about that in those days—but that the special attention to certain messages might reveal to the intercept operators that the traffic was being broken. I discovered, however, that the intercept operators believed that all their intercepts were decoded. The protection of our secret depended on the fact that the intercept operators had sworn not to tell anyone anything about what they were doing, not even the fact that they were intercepting enemy radio signals.

In those early days of Hut 6 some important related activities were beginning to develop elsewhere. All will be discussed more fully in later chapters, but they bear some mention now as part of the context of our early operations. One such activity was the now famous one known as Hut 3.

Even before the Jeffreys apparatus became available it was confidently anticipated that Hut 6 would start breaking Enigma traffic. Therefore it was necessary to have intelligence analysts, with an intimate understanding of the German language, ready to begin working on our decodes.* Arrangements were made for a small Foreign Office intelligence group to occupy a tiny hut between Hut 6 and the main building, then designated as Hut 3. This group, headed by Commander Malcolm Saunders and with an early membership that included two Cambridge dons, F. L. Lucas and Harold Knight, went into action as soon as Hut 6 started to produce. In the early days Winterbotham introduced an air intelligence section under Wing Commander Humphreys. My early contacts with intelligence, however, were with Saunders and his group of civilians. I understand that there was an organizational change early in 1942, after which Commander Saunders was definitely in charge for a

* I do not believe that anyone in Hut 6 had more than a smattering of German.

time. At some point the intelligence effort moved to a larger hut, adjacent to Hut 6, which was again named Hut 3. Very confusing!

As Winterbotham has noted, the content of the early decodes was not very exciting, because it was still a "phony" war. The German ground forces were not on the move, and much of their traffic was probably going by landlines. However, the mere fact that we had begun to "crack" Enigma keys was realized to be of great significance. As Winterbotham recalls, his boss, Colonel Menzies, soon to become Chief of the British Secret Service, was enthusiastic. Menzies and Winterbotham put a great deal of thought into plans for the dissemination of Ultra intelligence.

This was not my concern. What was of immense importance to the future of Hut 6 was the fact that, thanks very largely to Winterbotham, official enthusiasm was sufficient to convince the British Army and Royal Air Force to establish a joint intelligence unit at Bletchley Park. Thus began an extremely close relationship. Throughout the war the Hut 6/Hut 3 complex operated as an interservice organization under Foreign Office administration.

For the moment I am concerned with what happened in the first year, but let me mention that much later in the war Saunders was asked by Travis to undertake another important pioneering job: making all necessary preparations for the operation of the many bombes that were to come. In this job Saunders was assisted by Harold Fletcher of Hut 6.

Another important activity was starting up in London in the Military Intelligence organization, MI8. A small group of analysts was beginning to study the German radio nets that were being intercepted at Chatham. Their objectives were very different from mine: While I was concerned with our hopes for breaking the Enigma traffic, they had started with the assumption that the Enigma traffic was unbreakable. Their objective instead was to derive intelligence from a detailed study of the operation of the German radio nets.

I will return to this matter in Chapter 9; for now it is enough to say that, to avoid simultaneous transmissions and to counter the problem of drifting frequencies, German radio nets depended for their proper functioning on continuous coded conversation between the control station and the subscriber stations. This chitchat permitted frequency settings to be constantly readjusted. Our intercept operators logged this German chitchat, and the new MI8 group in London proposed to study all the logs of all the Chatham intercept operators. By doing so they had a good chance of discovering all the callsigns used on each net on a particular day.

As one of its objectives, this log-reading organization set out bravely on the task of breaking the new annual callsign books of the German army and air force. These books contained sequences of callsigns, one of which would be assigned to each unit that would originate or receive radio transmissions. Each sequence provided a different callsign for every day in the year; thus a full year of log reading would be needed before callsign recurrences would help to identify enemy units by their radio transmissions.

In the early days I saw very little of this log-reading group. By June 1941 my principal contact was the author Edward Crankshaw. Subsequent expansion was headed by Hamish Blair-Cunynghame, and the senior liaison man at Bletchley Park was a Colonel Harry Sayer. My close relationship with these three men helped resolve problems that might have impeded the development of the Hut 6/Hut 3 partnership.

Thus early in 1940 the plan that had originated in the School was being implemented, and important relationships with associated efforts outside Hut 6 were being developed. The sheets that had been designed and produced in the Cottage were working well, and when the war became hot again, with Hitler's invasion of Denmark and Norway on April 9, 1940, we were able to intercept and decode a good deal of the German operational command traffic. We were in close touch with the people in Hut 3 who were translating our decodes, and the messages we read were disheartening. They gave a picture of the efficiency of the small German forces involved, and of the inept coordination of the British efforts. I remember being particularly impressed by the speed with which the Germans established their battlefield communications. Apparently the well-trained Enigma-equipped signals teams accompanied the first assault troops wherever they went.

During the Battle of France in May 1940 the decoded messages were equally disheartening. We were reading a great deal of the operational traffic being exchanged among the German field commanders, as well as their reports to the higher command and the directives they received. For example, when any one of their armored units was held up by an Allied defensive position, we would probably decode an Enigma message from the unit's commander requesting air support. A little later we would hear that an attack by dive-bombing Stukas had been effective, and that the armored unit had resumed its advance. At intervals all the major Panzer commanders would report their progress and their assessments of Allied capabilities.

We in Hut 6 would pass the decoded messages to the intelligence officers of Hut 3, providing them with a clear overall picture of events on the battlefield, as well as a detailed picture of each sector. The intelligence derived from this flood of Hut 6 decodes could have had little if any effect on the course of the Battle of France—for one thing, as part of the overall Allied unpreparedness, the use of such a prolific source of intelligence had not been worked out in advance—yet it seems to me that in this campaign, Hut 6 Ultra achieved its first major success, albeit a negative one. Our decodes must have given early warning that the military situation was utterly hopeless. This mass of combat intelligence can hardly have failed to speed the organization of the extraordinary fleet of miscellaneous boats that brought so many men back from the beaches of Dunkirk. Indeed, it seems probable to me that assembly of this fleet was initiated in England by senior commanders with access to Hut 6 Ultra before the commander of the British Expeditionary Force, Lord Gort, announced his decision to evacuate. The true story has yet to be told.

Be that as it may, the days of the Jeffreys apparatus were numbered. By a simple change in procedure, the Germans had already dealt us a blow that could well have been fatal. The exact date of this blow eluded me until Jean Stengers sent me his article in the February 1981 issue of *L'Histoire,* to which I have already referred. From my own memory it seemed that the blow must have fallen in May 1940. It now appears that the Germans made their procedural change on May 10, 1940, the day of their invasion of France. This, indeed, would have been good cryptographic strategy. Let us see what was involved and how, miraculously, we were able to break the Enigma during the Battle of France.

6

Silly Days

May to September 1940

On May 10, 1940, with no warning whatever, our traffic registers showed a change in the preambles of all messages. It was a small change that might have seemed unimportant to anyone not intimately familiar with the encoding procedure of the German Enigma operators. It was just an additional three-letter group in each preamble, but to our Machine Room staff this change was shattering. We guessed at once that the Germans had dropped the double encipherment of the message setting. This was soon verified, and it meant that the Jeffreys apparatus had suddenly become useless.

To explain what had happened, let me recapitulate the procedure, described in Chapter 3, that had been followed before the change. The operator originating an Enigma message on a particular key would choose an indicator setting, say VIN, and a text setting, say RCM. With the wheels set at VIN he would encode RCMRCM and obtain six letters, say WQSEUP. The letters VIN would be transmitted in the preamble, and WQSEUP would be the first six letters of the message text. The receiving operator, with his Enigma set up to the same key, would set his wheels to VIN, press the WQSEUP keys, and recover the RCMRCM sequence.

Now, however, the originating operator would set his wheels to VIN as before, but he would encipher RCM once only, obtaining WQS. He would then put the two three-letter groups VIN and WQS in the message preamble. Our "females" were lost to us.

Nor could our preparations for the arrival of the bombes offer us any immediate help. When the Jeffreys apparatus began to work I had asked Milner-Barry to make a careful study of decodes. I wanted him to develop an intimate knowledge of the people who were communicating with each other on the German radio nets as this might enable us to find cribs, and cribs, with the bombes to help us, could lead to breaks.

Milner-Barry had indeed acquired an intimate knowledge of the traffic, and he had found that the addresses and signatures were often both lengthy and stereotyped. Thus, by the time the change came, he was well able to produce cribs. But the two prototype bombes would not come into action for many months, and the cribs were no use without the bombes.

Fortunately, with the help of German procedural errors that had already been discovered, we were able to improvise new methods of breaking right away. Some of our people had been studying the habits of the German Enigma operators from a very different point of view, and had found some remarkable quirks. The two astonishingly bad habits that now enabled us to go on breaking Enigma even without females were dubbed the "Herivel Tip" and the "Sillies." The first often enabled us to guess the ring setting of each wheel to within two or three letters; the second often allowed us to guess text settings. Both had to do with the lazy habits of the German operators.

Herivel's attention was drawn to a quirk in machine setup practice. When an Enigma operator was changing the setup of his machine to a new key, he had to choose the correct set of three wheels out of the five available, set the alphabet ring on each wheel, insert the wheels in the machine in the correct order, and close the cover. To set an alphabet ring on a wheel, he would probably hold the wheel in one hand so that the clip position was facing him, and then rotate the ring until the correct letter was opposite the clip position. There the clip would engage. Herivel's contribution was to realize that, when the operator inserted the wheel into the machine, the letter determining the ring setting would probably still be facing him, and when he closed the cover it was quite likely that the three letters appearing in the apertures would be pretty close to the ring settings of the new key. Indeed, if the operator was lazy he might leave the wheels in their initial position when he encoded the text setting for his first message of the day. If so, the letters of the indicator setting in the preamble of this message would be pretty close to the ring settings in the new key.

To exploit this habit, the midnight-to-eight-A.M. Machine Room watch, working on the traffic registers, would first identify the discriminants of the Red traffic for the new day. They would then look for the first message on the new key originating from any radio transmitter. The indicator settings of these messages would be entered on a "Herivel Square," Figure 6.1. Indicators HDR, TKZ, JFW, etc., would be entered by writing the letter R in the square in column H and row D, Z in square TK, W in square JF, and so on. Before too long a cluster would appear somewhere in the square. In Figure 6.1, the cluster consists of the entries GRI, HSK, GTK, and FRJ. The Machine Room would then hazard a guess that the ring settings of the three wheels must be:

Left-hand wheel	F, G, or H
Middle wheel	R, S, or T
Right-hand wheel	I, J, or K

From previous experience they might reckon that the most likely guesses, to be tried first on test runs, were GRK, GSK, GRJ, GSJ, GRI, GSI. It was as simple as that. The 17,576 possible ring settings had been reduced to 6 probables.

Now for the "Sillies."* Suppose the traffic register showed a three-part message whose indicator settings and indicators were:

First part	QAY MPR
Second part	EDC LIY
Third part	TGB VEA

Having observed the habits of Enigma operators in the traffic that we had decoded, it was not hard to guess what the operator had done, from the arrangement of the Enigma keyboard:

---

* I have no idea how the term arose.

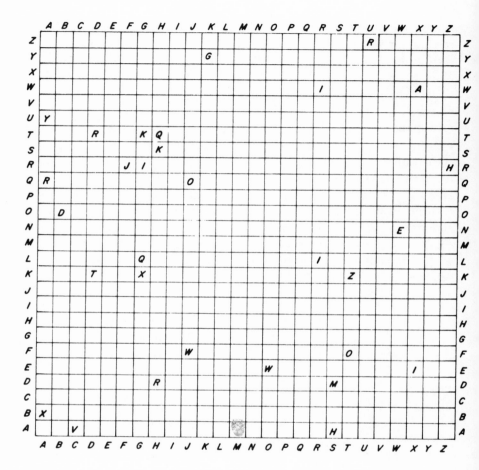

HDR   TKZ   JFW   AQR   GRI   BOD

DKT   TFO   RLI   HTQ   WNE   ABX

HSK   ZRH   KYG   OEW   AUY   SAH

JQO   GKX   GTK   GLQ   XWA   FRJ

XEI   CAV   DTR   RWI   SDM   UZR

Figure 6.1 A Herivel Square, with Entries Representing 30
Indicator Settings

```
Q  W  E  R  T  Z  U  I  O
   A  S  D  F  G  H  J  K
P  Y  X  C  V  B  N  M  L
```

He had obviously chosen as his indicator settings the alternate keyboard diagonals QAY, EDC, and TGB. We would conclude that his text settings would be the alternating diagonals: WSX, RFV, and ZHN. If the text setting of the first part of the message was WSX, we knew that, with wheels set to QAY, MPR was the encode of WSX. Similarly at setting EDC, LIY was the encode of RFV, and at setting TGB, VEA was the encode of ZHN. Thus this set of three "Sillies" gave us nine letter pairings. We knew that, at the wheel setting following QAY in the scrambler cycle, M and W were paired, that at the next wheel setting P and S were paired, and so on. It was, in fact, a form of crib.

Suppose that, in addition to this three-part message, we could find on the traffic register two single-part messages with indicator settings QWE and QAP. Looking at the keyboard with an eye to pattern and the known habits of individuals, we might well guess that the corresponding message settings were ASD and OKL. This would give us six more letter pairings which, combined with the Herivel tip, would probably enable us to break the Red key for the day. Unbelievable! Yet it actually happened, and it went on happening until the bombes came, many months later. Indeed, though I cannot remember when the two prototype bombes arrived, it seems to me that we must have been entirely dependent on Herivel tips and Sillies from the invasion of France to the end of the Battle of Britain, right up to the final crunch on "Eagle Day," September 15, 1940. By then the RAF was nearly exhausted, and it appears that Hitler was not prepared to invade until his Luftwaffe had completely knocked them out. Therefore Goering planned a conclusive triumph. Hut 6 Ultra revealed his plans for that critical day, and helped the RAF to make the best use of its remaining capabilities. Goering's attempt to knock out the RAF failed, thanks in part to Hut 6 Ultra. Two days later a Hitler directive, received via Hut 6, made it clear to the intelligence staff at Bletchley that invasion plans had been abandoned.

What I have called "Eagle Day" should perhaps be called "The Last Eagle Day." Reg Jones, the author of *The Wizard War*, tells me that the Germans had mounted an earlier Eagle Day (*Adler Tag*) on August 13, 1940, when they flew 1,485 sorties. Later, on August 15, 1940, they are said to have mounted 1,786 sorties. The objective on each occasion was elimination of the RAF as a force that could oppose an invasion. The last "Eagle Day" attack, on September 15, involved fewer than a thousand German aircraft sorties, and the British claimed 185 enemy aircraft shot down. But this was the day when Churchill was told that the RAF had no reserves.

There were other types of Sillies that sometimes allowed us to guess a message setting. Occasionally, for example, a lazy operator would get in the habit of using the same three letters both for the indicator setting and for the text setting. This would mean that, having encoded his text setting, he would only have to move the right-hand wheel back three places to encode his message. This type of Silly was known as JABJAB from the letters used in its first appearance, discovered by Babbage. But in JABJAB too our help came primarily from the use of keyboard patterns. If, for example, we found a three-part message in which the indicator settings were QAY, WSX, and EDC, it would be a good bet that the text settings were the same. It was extremely fortunate that both the Herivel tip and the keyboard Sillies had been discovered before the Germans changed their indicating procedure and defeated our method of breaking Enigma keys with the Jeffreys apparatus. Had we been foiled then, we would not have been breaking at the time of the last Eagle Day, and we would have lost the continuity that was to prove so essential later on in our use of cribs.

Those first few days after the change on May 10, 1940, were quite fantastic. Many people contributed bright ideas. Even at the time it was hard, and after all these years it is quite impossible, to determine who thought of what. We were like a pack of hounds trying to pick up the scent. Till now the observed habits of individual Enigma operators had been regarded as interesting oddities, rather than as a means of breaking Enigma keys. Suddenly they were all we had, and we had to find ways to take advantage of them. As it turned out, I believe, either there was no gap in our breaking, or any gap there may have been lasted merely a few days and we subsequently caught up with the skipped traffic. We were—though by a bare margin—still in the game.

During the early Hut 6 days Jeffreys was running the Machine Room and Sheet-Stacking Room; I was in charge of the Registration Room, Intercept Control Room, and Decoding Room, and also handled liaison with Hut 3, and all went extremely amicably. Shortly after the Germans' procedural change, however, there were definite signs of friction between us. Not only I, but many others who had worked closely with Jeffreys, became worried about what seemed to be his uncharacteristic irritability.

I hoped he was merely overtired by his heavy exertions. As Sidney Sussex College had allowed me to retain the use of my rooms throughout the war, I was able to suggest to Jeffreys that he take a short vacation there. He accepted, but only a few days later he was taken ill in my rooms and had to be rushed to the hospital. It turned out that he had both tuberculosis and diabetes, neither of which had been diagnosed before. This combination, on top of the strain of his work at Bletchley Park, was too much. Only a few months later he died in the hospital.

Jeffreys was very much liked at Bletchley Park. His death was a tragic loss to all of us. We felt deep sympathy for his fiancée, Pat Hempsted, who had been a member of his team from its beginnings in the Cottage. She was involved both in the initial punching of the sheets and in the testing of drops on which our early breaks depended. After John's death she continued to work in the Machine Room.

With Jeffreys gone, the burden of organization fell on me. The new method of breaking, based on Herivel tips and Sillies, called for twenty-four-hour operations in the Machine Room and the Decoding Room, as well as in the Traffic Registration Room and the Intercept Control Room. We would start looking for our clues on the midnight-to-eight-A.M. watch, as the traffic enciphered on the new day's key began to appear on the traffic register. The time of origin in the preamble of a message, together with the discriminant, would tell us whether the new day's key or the previous day's was being used.

The Machine Room watch consisted of two or three people. I

think that for a time the watch leaders must have been Alexander, Babbage, and myself. In fact I temporarily joined the wizards. The traffic register from Chatham became more important than ever, and we eagerly awaited the arrival of each sheet from the Bletchley Park teleprinter room. Our luck varied from day to day. Sometimes the key for the day would be broken by the midnight-to-eight-A.M. watch, sometimes by the eight-A.M.-to-four-P.M. watch, sometimes by the evening watch, and sometimes not at all.

In broad terms, the first task was to study the traffic registers, looking for clues to ring settings (Herivel tips) and text settings (Sillies). When the watch leader thought he had a plausible set of guesses, he would prepare a menu (set of instructions) for the DR (Decoding Room) operators, who would go through the series of routines he specified on their modified Type-X machines. The process would be repeated for all the 60 possible wheel orders. Each such routine would produce a jumble of letters related to a particular combination of wheel order and ring settings. A visual inspection would sometimes indicate whether the combination could be consistent with the set of guesses on which the menu had been based. If the combination could not be discarded by this visual examination, further tests were carried out. If our guesses were correct, these tests would reveal the steckers, and we would have the complete key for the day. If all the menus derived from a set of guesses failed, we simply had to try again with another set of guesses. If all three Machine Room watches failed to break the key for a day, as sometimes happened, the material would be set aside, and the night watch would concentrate on the next day's traffic.

For the more technically minded of my readers I would like now to explain more fully the processes involved in key-breaking over this period.

Suppose that, during the era of the Sillies, a particular day's Red traffic had given the Herivel tip of Figure 6.1 and the five Sillies of Figure 6.2. The Herivel tip suggests GRK, GSK, GRJ, GSJ, GRI, and GSI as the most probable ring settings. Suppose we decide to try GRK first, for all 60 wheel orders. For each wheel order we will prepare a menu. Let us consider wheel order 123.

The assumptions of ring settings GRK and wheel order 123 determine the turnover positions of the three wheels. Thus we can

KEYBOARD

```
Q   W   E   R   T   Z   U   I   O
  A   S   D   F   G   H   J   K
  P   Y   X   C   V   B   N   M   L
```

SILLIES

Three - Part Message

```
          W S X
Q A Y     M P R
```

```
          R F V
E D C     L I Y
```

```
          Z H N
T G B     V E A
```

Single - Part Messages

```
              A S D
Q W E     G J I
```

```
              O K L
Q A P     V Q N
```

CHAINS

```
X - R - L - N - A - G

Z - V - O
    I
    Y

P - S - J

F - I - D

H - E

K - Q
```

Figure 6.2 Sillies and Chains

deduce whether the encoding of WSX in the first Silly involves a turnover. Provided that Y is not a turnover position of the right-hand wheel, the encoding W to M will occur at wheel setting QAZ. Provided that neither Y nor Z is the turnover position, the encoding S to P will occur in wheel position QAA, and so on. Thus there are twelve turnover positions of the right-hand wheel that could cause a middle-wheel turnover during the encoding of one or more of the five Sillies; these positions are Y, Z, A, B, C, D, E, F, G, P, Q, and R. If a middle-wheel turnover does occur, it could cause a turnover of all three wheels. The point to bear in mind, however, is that the assumption of wheel order 123 and ring settings GRK determines the turnover positions of all three wheels, so we know what will happen. To simplify the explanation, let us assume that, with the assumed wheel order 123 and ring settings GRK, none of the Sillies will involve a middle-wheel turnover.

Figure 6.2 shows a number of chains that can be formed by pairs of letters that are the encodes of each other in the Sillies. Figure 6.3 illustrates the method of testing the output of a Silly menu derived from the six-letter chain. The instructions given by the Machine Room to a DR operator were very simple. She was to put wheels 1, 2, and 3 into her Type-X machine, having set the alphabet rings to G, R, and K. She was to put the turnover mechanism out of action, so that the wheels would not move. She was also to adjust her Type-X machine to operate as an Enigma scrambler without steck-erboard cross-connections. Then, with wheel positions QAB, she was to encode the letters of the alphabet, A to Z. The Type-X output, printed on tape, would be the jumble of letters MDH . . . K, as shown immediately below the alphabet A to Z in Figure 6.3. Every encoding, A to M, B to D, C to H, and so on, would have taken place with the wheels in the same position, QAB, in which, according to our assumptions, X goes to R through the whole Enigma, steckerboard included. The DR operator would stick the output tape of her Type-X across a sheet of paper, and would write the row of letters A to Z above the scrambled sequence, as in Figure 6.3. She would also write the letters X and R to the left of the two rows, as shown.

Before we go on to the next step in the menu, let us look at the meaning of this first step. Remember that we are testing a set of assumptions from which we have already deduced that, with wheel

SILLY   MENU

WHEEL	ORDER	1 2 3
RING	SETTINGS	G R K
WHEEL	POSITIONS	Q A B
		E D D
		G A S
		T G E
		Q W F
MAIN CHAIN		X - R - L - N - A - G

MENU OUTPUT

```
X    A B C D E F G H I J K L M N O P Q R S T U V W X Y Z
R    M D H B G Y E C O P Z V A U I J T X W G N L S R F K
L    Y K Z X W M T S I V H P Q R O N E B G A J F C U L D
N    R G N W X U A J V I E C K Y M Z H D U T S L P G F B
A    M O A E C Q N Y Z D W X L J R V S I P B H K U F G T
G    S R H K D B F W J C Y G P Z O U M T L Q A E V N X I
     ✓ ✓ ✓ ✓ ✓   ✓   ✓   ✓   ✓ ✓ ✓ ✓ ✓   C C ✓ ✓ ✓   C ✓
```

TESTING

```
O - V - Y
S - J
I - D,  P - S - J
H - E,  Z - V - Y
H - E
D - I
P - S
P - S
D - I
```

Figure 6.3 Inspection and First-Stage Testing
of the Output of a Silly Menu

setting QAB, X goes to R through steckerboard and scrambler. What the DR operator has produced shows that at this wheel setting the scrambler alone produces the substitution A to M, B to D, C to H, and so on. We can therefore make a series of logical deductions: if X/A (X is steckered to A) then R/M; if X/B then R/D; if X/C then R/H; and so on.

Now for the next step in following the instructions of the menu. The DR operator sets her Type-X wheels to EDD and encodes the jumble MDH . . . K that resulted from the first step, getting an output tape YKZ . . . D, which she sticks below the first, writing letter L to the left of this line. She encodes this second jumbled alphabet at QAS, a third at TGE, a fourth at QWF, and hands the results to the Machine Room, in the form shown in the six lines of menu output in Figure 6.3.

The first column of six letters shows that from the assumption X/A we can deduce R/M, L/Y, N/R, A/M, and G/S. But this involves a double contradiction, in that M cannot be steckered both to R and to A, nor can A be steckered both to X and to M. Consequently we can reject the assumption X/A, as is indicated by the check mark at the bottom of the first column. In this way, as is indicated by underlinings, the Machine Room operator can immediately rule out all but ten of the possible steckers of X.

The stecker X/F is not ruled out by this first inspection, but it implies O/N and Y/R. So the Machine Room man goes to his testing machine. From the chains of Figure 6.2 (p. 105) he knows that O goes to V in position QAQ, while V goes to Y in position EDF. From O/N he can now deduce the steckers of V and Y, and hopefully the stecker of Y will contradict Y/R. On the other hand the implied stecker of Y may turn out to be F—a "confirmation"— in which case the stecker assumption X/F cannot be ruled out so easily. A second stage of testing will be needed. Similarly X/H implies S/L and J/N, and hopefully this can be thrown out by using the fact that S goes to J in position QWG. The assumption X/J has a double possibility of being thrown out either from the implied steckers of I and D or from those of P and J. Similar possibilities of throwing out assumptions X/K, X/Q, X/R, X/S, X/W, and X/Z are indicated in Figure 6.3 under the heading TESTING. But in each case the test, which I will call a "first-stage" test, depends on the appearance in the same column of two letters that occur in one of the subsidiary chains of Figure 6.2. Thus in the column that shows deductions from the assumption X/F, the two letters are I and Y, which both occur in the first subsidiary chain. In this case, as I have explained, the stecker O/N, deduced from the assumption X/F, will imply a stecker of Y, which will probably contradict Y/R and so reject X/F. On the other hand O/N may imply Y/R, giving a confirmation rather than a rejection, in which case more complex wizardry will be needed. The same possibility of confirmation rather than rejection arises in each of the first-stage tests of Figure 6.3.

Note that the assumption X/X cannot be thrown out by this simple first-stage testing. It implies the steckers R/R, L/U, N/G, and A/F, which do not include a pair of letters that appear in one of the subsidiary chains of Figure 6.2. Note also that each of the three assumptions X/R, X/S, and X/X involves a "confirmation," indicated by the letter C at the bottom of the corresponding columns. The assumption X/R implies R/X. The assumption X/S implies both L/G and G/L. The assumption X/X implies both N/G and G/N.

As an example of the type of wizardry that was involved in a second stage of testing, let us consider what one might do to the assumption X/X, which refuses to be rejected by the simple first-stage test. The menu output shows that from X/X we can deduce R/R, L/U, N/G, A/F. From A/F, by using the fourth chain of Figure 6.2, we can also deduce the stecker of I and D. This could conceivably lead to a contradiction, ruling out the assumption X/X, but let us assume that it does not do so.

One might prepare a second Silly menu based on the second chain of Figure 6.2, which involves the four letters, Z, V, O, and Y. The output of this menu would show, in twenty-six columns, the sets of steckers of these four letters that can be deduced from assumed steckers of one of them, probably V for convenience of menu preparation. If every one of these sets contradicts one or more of the steckers that have been deduced from the assumption X/X, including those of I and D, this assumption can be thrown out. On the other hand, if some set of steckers of Z, V, O, and Y is found to be consistent with the deductions from X/X, it may include a pair of letters from one of the last four chains of Figure 6.3, in which case the testing can be continued, as in the first stage, with the possibility of rejection or confirmation. If the consistent set of steckers of Z, V, O, and Y contains only one letter of one of the last four chains, this will imply steckers for the other letter(s) of the chain, which could conceivably result in a contradiction. Failing this, one might produce menus for the remaining three-letter and two-letter chains of Figure 6.2, thereby making the fullest possible use of the letter pairings of the Sillies, just as the diagonal board of a bombe was planned to make the maximum use of letter pairings in a crib.

Occasionally one might come across an assumption that would be very hard to throw out, in which case the wizard would attempt to decode the first part of the three-part message with text setting WSX, using the set of consistent steckers that he had deduced. When he was working on correct assumptions, the tests would have involved many confirmations, and the decoding would soon enable him to discover the remaining steckers and so complete the key. Thus even when the German operators had given us a good Herivel tip and a set of Sillies, the actual breaking of the key for the day involved a lot of work, in the course of which one could not afford to make any errors. Although the number of possibilities would have been reduced very considerably, one would still have to test for 60 possible wheel orders and quite a number of ring settings.

I believe that Figure 6.3 gives an honest picture of the output of a Silly menu. I did not cheat to prove a point. The jumbled alphabets were obtained, without any intentional bias, from my teenage stepson's Scrabble set. In any case, playing the Sillies in Hut 6 was a fascinating game, a game with very high stakes, and we nearly always won.

The breaking of the Red key for the day did not by itself mean that the decodes of all Red messages intercepted on that day were at the disposal of the intelligence people in Hut 3 and available to Milner-Barry for his continuing analysis of individual habits of message formulation. A lot of work still had to be done in the Decoding Room. Our DR operator, having set up her modified Type-X to the newly broken key, would start decoding messages. Usually a message came out all right, but sometimes it didn't. Few of our DR operators had an intimate knowledge of German, but it didn't take them long to distinguish between German plain text and a jumble of letters. If a DR operator got a jumble of letters, something was wrong. What could she do about it?

Well, she might set the message aside, in order to deal with better-behaved messages, and come back to it later. By then several things might have happened. Perhaps the most likely cause of the difficulty was an error in interception of the indicator setting and indicator. So the DR operator, when she laid the faulty message aside, would probably request the Registration Room to find out, by consulting the traffic registers, if the same message had been intercepted twice. A second interception might give the correct version of the indicator setting and indicator, and the message would then decode properly. If there had been no second interception, the DR operator would consult her list of the most common errors in Morse code interception (such as the confusion between U and V) and try possible alternatives.

If it wasn't an error in interception, then perhaps the German Enigma operator had made a mistake; they sometimes did. The Hut 6 DR operators learned to guess aptly among the kinds of mistakes that might have been made. I cannot remember all the possible errors that our DR operators would investigate, but I clearly remember the satisfaction of knowing, either from radio chitchat or from other decodes, that we had succeeded with a message that even its German addressee had failed to decode.

There was another problem. Even if a message started to decode properly there might be a gap in the middle, due to fading signal strength or interference. The standard form on which the intercept operator had recorded the message would show the gap, and might even contain an estimate of how many five-letter groups had been missed. Obviously the first step would be to find out whether another intercept of the same message was available. Failing that, our DR operator would have to play around with possible lengths of the gap until she could decode the remainder of the message. In view of the pressure to decode all the traffic as soon as possible, the first decodable section of a message with a gap would be sent over to Hut 3 right away. If the Hut 3 watch found that it was an important message, they would come back with a request that as much as possible of the remainder of the message be decoded.

Sometimes a member of the Hut 3 watch would come over to the

DR with a decode in which some of the letters appeared to be wrong. Again the first step would be to find out if there was a second intercept of the same message. If not, a DR operator would experiment with the list of common intercept errors, trying to recover the true clear text.

As I write this narrative nearly forty years after the event, I realize that someone must have developed a very efficient method of keeping track of all the messages that arrived in bundles from the intercept stations so that they could be easily and quickly referenced. Although I originated many of the Hut 6 procedures, I have no recollection of starting this one. It was probably done by the staff of the Registration and Decoding Rooms, and it may well have been developed during the era of the Jeffreys apparatus. Anyway, when a key was broken, one copy of each message on that key, presumably the best-looking one, had to be ready for decoding, and other copies had to be readily available. This must have become quite a problem later on when Hut 6 was breaking several different keys each day.

My memory of breaking keys in the "Silly Era" is based on the short period during which I was actually working on the Machine Room watch. At that time our primary objectives each day were to break the Red key for that day, to intercept as much Red traffic as possible, and to send the decodes to Hut 3, giving priority to the messages that were likely to have the greatest intelligence value. But, time permitting, we also had some standby objectives, including dealing with unfinished business.

One of my happiest memories is of a night shift when I arrived to find that we were up to date except for one key, several days old, that had resisted all attacks. I settled down to try my luck, leaving the new day's traffic to other members of the watch. After going over previous work on the recalcitrant key, I discovered an unusual form of Herivel Tip that had been missed. The cluster of Figure 6.1 had gotten scattered to the corners of the Herivel square. To see how this could have happened, let us suppose that the true ring settings were ZAQ. Approximations to this, appearing as indicator settings on the traffic register, could have been YZP, ZAR, ABQ, and AZQ. These would have been entered in the four corners of the Herivel square.

Having spotted the dispersed cluster, I made up the usual menus for the DR and spent most of the watch with Pat Hempsted testing the results on the machine. She was one of the experienced members of the old Cottage team even before she worked with Jeffreys, and I don't think she had any confidence in my untutored efforts. (Having had little practical experience, I was painfully slow in my actual use of the testing machine, though I understood the theory of its operation.) In fact, as the night wore on, she got more and more fed up with the whole proceeding. Then, probably around seven A.M., I saw signs that I was at last working on the correct wheel order and ring setting. After a few more test operations Pat saw the signs too and exclaimed incredulously, "It's coming out." Tired but happy, we had almost completed the break by the end of the shift, when Hugh Alexander came roaring in, fresh as a daisy, to find out what had been going on.

There was another activity in the Hut 6 Intercept Control Room, and one that was to prove enormously worthwhile later on. Reg Parker, on his own initiative, was keeping detailed records of all sets of discriminants that we had identified; also of the wheel order, ring settings, and steckers of every key that we had broken. He hoped that some of these items might perhaps be repeated. Someone in Hut 6 thought of almost everything.

To conclude this chapter on the "Silly" days I would like to tell the strange tale of Uncle Walter, who visited us briefly.

One evening when I came in to head the night watch in the Machine Room I found considerable excitement. A decoded message on the day's Red key had indicated that a new *umkehrwalze* (turn-around wheel) was to be used in the Enigma machine. This new *umkehrwalze* had already been nicknamed "Uncle Walter," for obvious phonetic reasons. During the evening watch, headed by Babbage, a very long message had turned up. It was in at least six parts, and it wouldn't decode, even though it used the Red discriminants for the day. Could this long message have been enciphered by a machine equipped with Uncle Walter?

Babbage had studied the indicator settings and indicators of this multi-part message, and had found that the man who had done the enciphering was intensely lazy and a superb producer of Sillies. Babbage believed that he knew the text setting for each part of the message. If all this proved to be true, we would certainly be able to discover Uncle Walter's wiring in the morning. The assumption was that the text settings of all the parts of this long message had been enciphered on an Enigma machine fitted with Uncle Walter, but that the operator had not been instructed to change the wheel order, ring settings, and steckers from those of the key for the day, which we already knew. In other words, we knew how to set up an Enigma, and we knew that if we set up the wheels to the indicator setting and enciphered the indicator for each part of the message we should get the text setting that Babbage had guessed.

This was not a cryptological problem. All we needed was an electrician who could disconnect the cross-connections of the standard German *umkehrwalze* on one of our Enigmas or modified Type-X machines. Then, with the machine set to the known key, we could easily find out what cross-connection of *umkehrwalze* terminals would be needed to produce each of the letters Babbage had predicted. The only problem was that, at midnight, we could not call on an electrician.

We were up to date with the Red keys, so I was free to spend the night watch getting to know Uncle Walter without the help of an electrician. Fortunately I had David Rees with me. He had worked in the Cottage with Dilly Knox, and knew a lot more about the details of our Enigma studies than I did. He dug out the internal cross-connections of the movable wheels of the German Enigma, and from then on, though time-consuming, it was easy.

With the help of the Registration Room staff I constructed a paper version of the Enigma machine for the known wheel order of the day. Once this was done I could trace the paths an electric current would follow from the keyboard key to the *umkehrwalze* and from the *umkehrwalze* to the light bulb that had to illuminate Babbage's predicted letter. Thus I could determine the cross-connection of two *umkehrwalze* terminals that would produce the predicted result.

I went steadily through Babbage's predictions and when I got the same cross-connection for the second time (a confirmation), I was more than mildly excited. I had nearly finished the job at eight A.M.

when Hugh Alexander dashed into the Machine Room to find out what had happened. He had been present at the midnight conference, and one of my most pleasant memories is his remark: "I knew you would find a neat way of doing it!"

That, oddly enough, was the end of Uncle Walter. We never met him again.

PART
THREE

The Rest of the War

7

Hut 6 Faces New Problems

1940/41—1942—1943/44/45

There were four distinct phases of internal Hut 6 activity: the pre-paratory phase, the days of the Jeffreys apparatus, the era of the Sillies, and the period of the bombes. The end of phase one was marked by the completion of the Jeffreys sheets early in 1940, when Jeffreys, with his Sheet-Stacking staff and his Machine Room wizards, joined forces with my Intercept Control people, Registration Room staff, and Decoding Room personnel for the beginning of close collaboration with the Chatham intercept station and the then-embryonic intelligence organization that grew into a mighty Hut 3. The second phase ended abruptly with the change in German operating procedures on May 10, 1940, the date of the German invasion of France. This change completely defeated the Jeffreys sheets. The third, and almost incredible, phase of dependence on the Sillies ended somewhat less abruptly with the arrival of the first bombes, probably not earlier than September 1940.

I am sorry that, because I am writing from my own memory, assisted by the memories of a few close associates of Bletchley Park days, I cannot give an exact date for the operational availability of the first bombe. But it doesn't really matter much. The astonishing fact is that gross carelessness by German operators of the new cipher machines enabled us to continue breaking their main army/air coordination cipher, Red, for so many critical months in that summer of 1940 when Britain stood alone.

During the second and third phases Stuart Milner-Barry's patient studies of Red traffic decodes had shown that, given bombes, we would have had a good chance of breaking Red keys by means of cribs. So, in the autumn of 1940, as the advent of the bombes approached, Milner-Barry collected a small staff and founded a "Crib Room."

I want to reiterate here that the bombes did not break the Enigma keys. The cryptanalytic methodology that resulted in the breaks was developed and put into practice by the members of the Hut 6 watch, to whom the full credit should go. They had to face crypt-analytical problems of increasing complexity, particularly in later periods of the bombe phase, which they did with amazing success. But the bombe, although it was their principal tool, never did much more than perform the ancillary functions that were conceived by Turing and myself before the end of 1939. The bombes were useless without a crib. If a crib could be found by the Hut 6 watch, the task of the bombe was simply to reduce the assumptions of wheel order and scrambler positions that required "further analysis" to a manageable number.

I have talked of the last Eagle Day, September 15, 1940, as a major turning point, followed as it was two days later by a Hut 6 decode indicating that Hitler had abandoned his plans for the invasion of Great Britain. It was a turning point strategically, and it was also a turning point in our own organization.

Not long afterward our decodes began to tell us that German forces were being moved out of France, and by the end of October 1940 I began to get indications from Hut 3 that the area of operations of the German armies was going to expand very considerably—into the Balkans and through Italy into Africa. This was enough to suggest that not only Hut 6 itself, but all its supporting activities as well, would also require considerable expansion.

Indeed it was easy to foresee that the simultaneous conduct of operations on several widely separated fronts would cause the Germans to introduce additional Enigma keys to serve the various subdivisions of the overall command structure, and that the wide dispersion of theaters of operation would call for more radio nets and a much higher volume of Enigma traffic. Moreover it was clear that the distances involved would make interception a lot more difficult than it had been.

I remember making an estimate of how many German radio nets we would have to intercept, and how many keys we would have to attempt to break. I prepared a forecast of the numbers of Hut 6 staff, intercept operators, and bombes that we would need, and sent a handwritten memorandum to Travis on the subject. I think this was the memorandum that came back to me with BALLS scrawled across the front page in a brown ink that Travis always used. He was not going to believe anything without adequate proof. However, when I had improved my arguments, Travis was convinced, and moved with his characteristic speed and effectiveness. We got the additional supporting capabilities that we needed for the crucial developments of March, April, and May 1941. Although later developments were to show that my forecast of requirements was grossly inadequate, I still like to feel that the speed with which I developed that initial approach to Travis got things moving in the right direction sooner than would otherwise have happened, and so prepared the way for the major expansions of many Bletchley Park activities—not only those related to Hut 6—that were initiated early in 1942. This approach to Travis, incidentally, may have occurred before the first prototype bombe actually became operational, but it should be regarded as an event belonging to the fourth phase of Hut 6 activities.

In our team-building, we were still free to employ our piratical methods of recruiting until April and May of 1941 when I had three meetings in London with Dr. Snow, who, as I have explained, had been put in charge of the assignment of civilian scientific talent. However the "old boy" network for recruiting was not altogether defeated. For example, John Monroe happened to have a sister who knew Stuart Milner-Barry. Out of the blue, as it appeared to John, who was already in the army, his commanding officer received a letter asking if he could be released. Soon after this he had an interview at Bletchley Park, during which he met Tiltman and myself. About six months later he joined Milner-Barry's team.

My old school and university friend Harold Fletcher came to us two months later, also via the army, but his story was somewhat more complicated. I asked him to join me at Bletchley early in 1940, but at that time his occupation was "reserved." However, he wrote to me about a year later to say that his occupation would become "unreserved" on August 1, 1941, but that his firm would only release staff to join the armed forces. So, no doubt as a result of some string-pulling from Bletchley, Harold's local recruiting office was instructed by the War Office to recruit him into the Intelligence Corps. When he reported for the necessary swearing and documentation, the local recruiting officer and his staff were understandably disappointed that Harold could tell them nothing about what his duties were to be. The sergeant's parting shot was "I suppose you'll be in the desert in a few weeks' time, disguised as a Bedouin."

On August 6, with his firm's consent, he reported to an officer in London, and was told that he was just in time to catch the 3:06 P.M. train to Bletchley, where he would be met by someone. Sure enough, someone met him and took him to the adjutant of No. IV Intelligence School, who immediately made arrangements for a billet in nearby Linslade. From what he heard of the telephone conversation, Harold gathered that the billetor was unwilling to have a private soldier, and had to be persuaded that this particular specimen knew how to behave.

Harold's military career lasted some eight months. He was at once promoted to lance corporal, but, although Travis tried for the next six months to find a suitable military unit to which Harold could be attached as an officer, he had no luck. However, at that point Harold's firm changed its rules, allowing him to be "demobbed," placed on W reserve, and employed for wartime duties by the Foreign Office. Of course he had been working for Hut 6 from the day of his arrival at Bletchley and his duties soon became important. He only wore uniform when going on leave (in order to get a cheap fare). Otherwise he concealed the fact that he was in the army as far as possible. There were many Thursdays, though, on which a Hut 6 secretary would telephone the adjutant of No. IV Intelligence School to say, quite truthfully, "This is Lance-Corporal Fletcher's secretary speaking. He's very sorry he's too busy to come to pay parade this afternoon."

There were other examples of very able people who reached us through Dr. Snow or through the military, but I have singled out John Monroe and Harold Fletcher because they have both been kind enough to add their memories to mine in the revision of this book, which I started in May 1978. Until that time my account of internal Hut 6 activities was based entirely on my own personal memories. This help has been extremely valuable—especially because Travis began to assign me to other tasks in early 1943, and I would not have been able to give even an outline of the later phases of Hut 6 activities without assistance from John and Harold.

Harold remembers that, on his arrival at Bletchley Park, he and I sat on the lawn in the sunshine. He was utterly confused by what I was trying to tell him about Hut 6, could not see what on earth he was expected to contribute, and believed (mistakenly) that, in asking him to join us, I had credited him with a much better brain than he really had. However, with little if any help from me he very soon figured out for himself the ways in which he could help. He undertook control and administration of the highly intelligent female staff in the Registration Room and Decoding Room. Provision of space, buildings, alterations, furniture, pay, equipment, telephones, machinery, transport—the lot—was in his capable hands. He also managed liaison with the men who were maintaining the bombes, and with the British Tabulating Machine (BTM) company at Letchworth, who were manufacturing the bombes. His arrival in summer 1941 helped me develop the flexible organization of the various internal sections of Hut 6 that enabled us to keep on working as an efficient, coordinated, and happy team in spite of the explosive growth of our activities.

The "bombe phase" of the Hut 6 story can itself be subdivided into three successive chronological periods, though with somewhat blurred boundaries. The first ran roughly from September 1940 to the end of 1941 and involved a moderate increase in the number of Enigma keys with which Hut 6 had to deal. In North Africa, in March 1941, the Germans launched their first offensive under Rommel and the German army and air force each introduced a new key for its own use. We named them "Chaffinch" and "Light Blue." On our traffic charts for the former we used a reddish brown pencil that bore some resemblance to the color of a chaffinch's breast. I believe the pencil used for Light Blue was called "Azure" by its manufacturers. There was also a high-grade key called Pink.

Then, in April 1941, the Germans invaded Yugoslavia and Greece, and in May they took Crete. At this point our colors were exhausted. New keys appearing on the Russian front after the invasion of June 1941 had to be designated as birds, for example "Kestrel" and "Vulture."

The second period was roughly the year 1942. Early in that year the Germans, with their Italian allies, advanced toward Egypt until they were stopped in July at the First Battle of Alamein. Sebastopol in the Crimea had fallen to the Germans on July 3, so that in the summer of 1942 the gigantic German pincer movement toward Iran and the oil fields of the Persian Gulf had made considerable progress. However, the battle for Stalingrad began on September 13, 1942, and the British drove the Germans back at the second battle of Alamein on October 23. On November 8 the Allies landed in Morocco and Algeria, after which the Germans occupied southern France and Tunisia on November 11, 1942. Thus there were plenty of reasons for the Germans to need additional radio nets and Enigma keys.

The resulting jump in the number of keys called for a major expansion in the manufacturing program of the bombes and in the arrangements for housing and operating them. Clearly Hut 6 and Hut 3 were going to need more space, and plans were made for a new brick building to house both organizations. I believe it was in 1942 that a large radio intelligence organization that the army had built up moved to Bletchley and joined forces with Hut 6, under the name "The Central Party." I have mentioned the start of this activity in MI8, London, and will have more to say about it later. By the end of 1942 we even had a cafeteria, where I learned to enjoy dry sliced cabbage as a substitute for the unavailable lettuce.

The third period, which lasted until the end of the war, started early in 1943. At the beginning of 1943 the Germans began their retreat from the Caucasus, and on February 2 came the German surrender at Stalingrad. The German-Italian surrender in Tunisia came on May 10, and the Allied invasion of Sicily was on July 10. By that time there were enough teleprinters for virtually all the Enigma traffic intercepted in England. We were also receiving intercepts from overseas, encoded on Type-X and sent by radio. Having been encoded twice—once by the Germans and once by the British—they contained a fair number of garbles and were not very popular in the Hut 6 decoding room. Nevertheless, they produced a lot of good stuff.

By summer 1943, we had moved, with Hut 3, Hut 8, and our teleprinters, to the relative luxury of our new brick building. This third period was marked on the German side by a series of modifications of the Enigma machine itself and also critical changes of procedure, which added greatly to the cryptanalytical problems of the Hut 6 watch. Already, by the end of the first bombe period, their problems had been considerably complicated by the number of new keys they had a chance of breaking. Sillies had become rare, and the Germans had started to reverse the order of the wheels at midday. In the second bombe period the big jump in the number of keys had caused more trouble, but the worst cryptanalytical problems began early in 1943 and continued until the end of the war as the Germans introduced change after change in the machine itself. About two months before D-Day they gave up using discriminants, and they had already begun to change the frequencies of their radio nets periodically. Near the end, in February 1945, they took to changing all radio frequencies every day and to encoding callsigns by a simple method that we could not break for lack of sufficient data. So the Hut 6 watch had to face a whole series of cryptanalytical problems in the third period of the bombe phase.

Nevertheless, some eighteen or so keys a day were broken with reasonable regularity, and how the Hut 6 watch managed to do this, in spite of the increasing number of obstacles put in their way, would be a fascinating story. Unfortunately, I am not the man to tell it. From early 1943 Travis called on me more and more for assistance in non–Hut 6 matters, so that the many problems of methodology and technology that arose thereafter were handled entirely by other members of the Hut 6 staff. Near the end of 1943 Travis took me away from Hut 6 completely, to become his Assistant Director for Mechanization, a position that I held until the end of the war.

When we lost Jeffreys in May of 1940, I had become, in effect, head of Hut 6, though Travis did not make me official head for some time. In this task I had two tremendous advantages. First, Hut 6's work was of such obvious importance that everyone was willing to put in all he or she had and to put up with a lot of inconveniences and even, in some cases, real hardships. This advantage was typical of the national feeling of "all being in it together," which—

paradoxically perhaps—made Britain a wonderful place to live in during the war years. The second tremendous advantage was the high quality and good nature of the people of Hut 6.

What today would be called my "management team," the group with whom I discussed all management problems, was composed of five men: Colman, who headed the Intercept Control Room and was responsible for all our dealings with the intercept stations; Milner-Barry, who patiently prepared himself for the use of cribs, which became possible when the bombes came, and thereafter became the central figure in Hut 6; Alexander and Babbage, who were leaders in the Machine Room and in all matters related to the techniques of breaking Enigma keys; and Fletcher, who soon after his arrival had become a general Hut 6 administrator with specific responsibility for the Registration Room, the Decoding Room, and the expanding bombe capability.

During the first period of the bombe phase I insisted on frequent meetings, at which we six would discuss all aspects of Hut 6 operations. Usually we agreed unanimously on an issue. Sometimes this did not happen, and I as the leader had to make a decision. These friends made it a practice at such times to defer to my judgment and act on my decisions, even if they disagreed with them. I greatly appreciated this attitude, which made it possible for us to work always as a close-knit team with a clearly understood plan of action.

Neither was I only concerned with teamwork at the top. As Hut 6 grew, and the jobs got more and more separated, I realized the need for what today we would call feedback. The staff of the Registration Room, for example, who were laboriously taking items from traffic registers and entering them on the daily frequency/time-of-day charts and doing many other chores as well, must have had a vague idea that what they were doing was helping the war effort. But I wanted them to know whenever some specific thing they had done had contributed to some specific achievement.

With this in mind I asked each member of my management team to produce weekly reports of the activities for which they were responsible, reports that were to be pinned up on the bulletin boards of all the departments of Hut 6. These reports gave all Hut 6 staff members a feeling of what was going on. I urged the people who were having the fun of breaking Enigma keys or decoding messages signed by Adolf Hitler to miss no chance of reporting that some particular success had resulted from something done by the Registration Room or the Intercept Control Room. I also requested feedback from Hut 3 both on the highlights of what we had produced, and on the value of specific efforts by the Decoding Room to deal with garbled messages. I wanted the key-breaking people to be aware of the trials and tribulations of the departments on which they depended, so that they might be more understanding in whatever demands they might want to make. All this was aimed not only at boosting morale throughout Hut 6, but also at making sure that each part of the activity would know how its output was going to be used, so that it could itself devise methods that would increase the value of that output.

Indeed, I believe the whole of Hut 6 became that rare entity, a really effective team. The level of ability was high in all departments. Everyone knew how he or she fitted into the overall picture. Everybody had an opportunity to suggest improvements, and indeed many good ideas came from our highly sophisticated "rank-and-file." Everybody contributed to our successes.

Furthermore, the close personal relationship that grew up between Travis and myself proved to be an important ingredient in the success of Hut 6. Of course, Travis had many political problems of which I knew nothing. He had to fight hard for the things that were necessary to all of Bletchley Park's diverse activities; Hut 6 was only one of these, and sometimes had to yield to the others. Thus, even when he was convinced of a requirement he needed strong arguments to present to his superiors. And above all, he needed to be convinced himself.

As a wartime leader Travis had some of Winston Churchill's qualities. He was definitely of the bulldog breed, and he liked to have things done his way, but he also had a great feeling for what it took to create happy working conditions. We in Hut 6 saw more of him while he was still deputy director than we did after he took on full responsibility for all the expanding activities of Bletchley Park. He would get around to all our activities, making contact with staff at all levels, and he had the gift of the human touch. Once he personally organized a picnic for Hut 6 staff, which was a tremendous success. In spite of his heavy workload after he became director, he still showed his personal interest in our activities, including those at the bombe sites.

Winston Churchill himself came to visit us. Travis took him on a tour of the many Bletchley Park activities. The tour was to include a visit to my office, and I had been told to prepare a speech of a certain length, say ten minutes. When the party turned up, a bit behind schedule, Travis whispered, somewhat loudly, "Five minutes, Welchman." I started with my prepared opening gambit, which was "I would like to make three points," and proceeded to make the first two points more hurriedly than I had planned. Travis then said, "That's enough, Welchman," whereupon Winston, who was enjoying himself, gave me a grand schoolboy wink and said, "I think there was a third point, Welchman."

We were fortunate in having an inspiring national leader in Winston Churchill, whose oratory had a powerful effect. We were also very fortunate in having, in King George VI, a dedicated sovereign who was well able to command every citizen's loyalty to the country. I shall never forget the impact of his radio broadcasts to the commonwealth, in which his brave fight against a severe stutter won my heart. (I had a bad stuttering problem myself for many years, so I could sympathize with what he was going through.) Nor shall I ever forget my impression of the strength and warmth of his character when he awarded me the Order of the British Empire in recognition of my work in Hut 6.

Harold Fletcher has reminded me of some of the details of Hut 6 operations during the first period of the bombe phase. Soon after his arrival he found that, to get things done, it was necessary to be on the best possible terms with Captain Bradshaw, RN, who was in overall charge of administration for the whole of Bletchley Park. Although he knew what was going on in a general way, Bradshaw had little means and very little time to determine priorities. It seemed to Fletcher that Bradshaw worked on the principle of meeting any request he was unsure of with a stream of naval abuse. If the applicant crumbled, Bradshaw reckoned that the case was not a strong one. But if the applicant held his ground, Bradshaw would probably give his approval. Once Fletcher discovered this he had plain sailing.

Harold's first impression at Bletchley Park was that he had come to an organization where "first among equals" held almost universal sway. He had come from a factory with five managers, about sixty office staff, and five hundred factory staff; these were three very distinct classes and great respect was shown to the managers by the other two. In contrast there were no such classes at Bletchley Park, where respect was shown not because of rank but for ability.

Harold has also reminded me of the primitive but effective method developed for passing decodes from the Hut 6 Decoding Room to the Hut 3 watch in an adjacent building. To take them by hand was too slow and used up the time of valuable personnel, so it was done by means of a wooden tray, some string, a broom handle, and two hatches. The latter were cut opposite each other in the outer walls of Hut 6 and Hut 3, and the intervening space of six to eight feet was bridged by a flat piece of wood, boxed in with wooden sides and a roof to cope with the weather. The procedure was to place the decodes in the wooden tray and shout through the hatches to alert the Hut 3 watch, who would then send one of their staff to draw the tray across by the string attached to their side and remove the decodes. When the Hut 6 decoding room had another load of decodes ready, the wooden tray was retrieved by the string attached to our end and the transfer process was repeated. The purpose of the broom handle was to arouse the Hut 3 watch, if shouting failed to do so. It could make quite a loud noise when rammed against the Hut 3 hatch. The broom handle was also used to recover a tray when the string mechanism fouled up.

I can vouch for the truth of this account of our information-handling technology, but not for the following story, which Harold believes to be true. The toilets were in another hut, and it is said that a member of a night shift had not been warned that builders had started work earlier in the day but had not completed it. She switched on the light and sat down, only to discover that there was no outer wall and she was completely visible to the outside world. Since it was the middle of the night there was no one about, so the rules of decency were only notionally broken. But the same could not be said of the blackout regulations. Subsequent visitors to the toilet on that night shift had to make do with a torch.

In 1942, the second period of the bombe phase, the major prolif-eration of Enigma keys by the German army and air force burst on us. John Monroe suggests, and I think he may well be correct, that the Germans were getting worried that their Enigma traffic might be vulnerable to cryptanalytic attack if they passed too much of it on any one key. This may well have been a major reason for the introduction of so many different keys for handling different categories of traffic. But I also feel that to the Germans, internal security was another important consideration.

The proliferation of the Enigma keys had one very strangely helpful result. As I have said, most of the keys were issued for a month at a time and were changed every day. I assume that the production of the keys—no mean task—was entrusted to some back-room boy, whom we will call Herr X. One day Herr X hit upon a labor-saving expedient.

To produce one monthly key table, Herr X had to generate, for each day of the month, a set of four three-letter discriminants; a wheel order composed of three of the digits 1 to 5; ring settings for the three wheels, which required a three-letter group; and steckers, which specified pairs of letters of the alphabet to be connected by the double-ended cords. I can sympathize with Herr X because, in the course of preparing illustrations for this book, I have had to do a fair amount of random generation. For this purpose I have used letters from my sixteen-year-old stepson Tommy's Scrabble game. No doubt Herr X had devised some random or pseudo-random method of generating the monthly lists of discriminants, wheel orders, ring settings, and steckers. It must have been a time-consuming and boring job, but in the early days, when he would not have had to produce more than five or six key sheets each month, he was probably not too unhappy. As the number of keys increased, however, so did his workload. He probably asked for an assistant and was turned down. Anyway, at some point Herr X must have said "To hell with it!"

He had kept records of all the key sheets that he had created, and it must have occurred to him that he might save himself work if he used either the discriminants, or the wheel orders, or the ring settings, or the steckers for a previous month. This would reduce the amount of random or pseudo-random selection that he had to do. It must have occurred to him also that it would be all right if he used the discriminants from one earlier key sheet, the wheel orders from another, the ring settings from a third, and the cross-pluggings from a fourth. This would mean a great saving of work, and who would know?

Well, Reg Parker, of the Hut 6 Intercept Control Room, was on to this at once. As I mentioned before, he had set himself the task of recording all sets of discriminants and all broken keys. For some time he had been looking at the discriminants and the broken keys at the beginning of each month in the hope of finding a repeat. When, in 1942, Herr X finally said "To hell with it," Reg Parker caught him.

This sounds fantastic, but it did actually happen. We called the procedure "Parkerismus." At the beginning of each month the sets of discriminants of the various keys were compared with Parker's records to see if there were any repeats. Then, as each key was broken, the wheel order, ring settings, and steckers were also compared with the records to see if one or more of them were being repeated from earlier keys.

Thus, soon after the beginning of each month, we might know in advance some part or parts of the daily keys for some types of Enigma traffic for the rest of the month. It doesn't take much imagination to see that this was a tremendous help. Obviously, if we knew in advance one or more key components, our problem of breaking each day's key would be greatly simplified. Sometimes we knew them all—wheel order, ring settings, and steckers—from Parkerismus. Indeed, I seem to remember that at one time we knew in advance all the daily keys that Rommel would use in Africa for a whole month.

It was in 1942 also that crib hunting developed into a major operation, which involved many kinds of cribs. There were, for example, the lengthy, stereotyped addresses and signatures that I had spotted in my School days. These usually turned up in routine daily reports or routine orders, which the Germans were kind enough to send at regular times of day, with the time of origin in the preamble to help us identify the message as soon as it appeared on the teleprinted traffic register. These cribs presented difficulties, however. In a fast-moving war, both the command structure and the location of individual commanders could change. Nor was the format of address and signature ever quite completely stereotyped. At the end of a message, where the signature would appear, a few Xs might be thrown in to complete a five-letter group. In fact, the Enigma operators delighted in peppering Xs throughout the signatures and addresses. Thus to be able to use this kind of crib, it was necessary to be breaking a key pretty regularly, in order to follow people and habits.

Even so, it is hard to see why these stereotyped addresses and signatures were not coded, like our present-day five-digit codes for postal deliveries. Because the Enigma handles letters only, of course, letters would have had to be used rather than numbers, but one would think that a five-letter code would have been enough to identify every individual commander and unit. Even if we had learned to interpret such five-letter address or signature codes, they would have been no use to us at all, since we needed longer cribs than that. Furthermore, because letter-by-letter encoding on the Enigma machine was a fairly slow process, the Germans could have saved quite a lot of time by using coded identifications of originators and addressees.

Another type of crib was obtained from the repetitious content of routine daily reports, often passing between low-echelon commanders and their immediate superiors. We developed a very friendly feeling for a German officer who sat in the Qattara Depression in North Africa for quite a long time reporting every day with the utmost regularity that he had nothing to report. In cases like this we would have liked to ask the British commanders to be sure to leave our helper alone.

A third type of crib, and perhaps the most important of all, was a direct product of the proliferation of Enigma keys. A message encoded on one key, and originating on one of the many radio nets, might be retransmitted on several other nets without alteration. At some point, however, the message might reach a radio station from which it would have to be retransmitted to a commander who did not have the key. The message would then be reencoded on a second key that this commander was known to be using. Thus if we could break one of the two keys we would have a crib to the other. Because we had developed an intimate knowledge of the workings of the German radio communications system, it was not too difficult for us to detect these retransmissions.

We were astonishingly successful, even with traffic from the distant radio nets in the Balkans, in Africa, and on the Russian front. But the thinness of the ice on which we were skating was a perpetual worry. German enforcement of elementary cryptographic discipline could have put an end to our cribs. If the Germans had discovered that a sufficiently long crib could enable us to break an Enigma key, they could have monitored their own traffic and admonished the people who were unwittingly helping us. Apparently they never made this discovery, though we do know that, during the African campaign, their cryptographic experts were asked to take a fresh look at the impregnability of the Enigma. I heard that the result of this "fresh look" appeared in our decodes, and that it was an emphatic reassertion of impregnability.

The precarious nature of our success was not obvious even to some of our close associates in Hut 3, whose knowledge of our activities didn't extend beyond the decodes they received. Hut 6 seemed to them to be breaking everything, and some of the Hut 3 people thought we were capable of doing anything they might want us to do. Individual members of the Hut 3 watch would have their own special interests, and felt that they ought to be able to tell Hut 6 to give them what they wanted when they wanted it.

For example, some hard-worked member of the watch in Hut 3 might note that the decode of a particularly important type of report on one key didn't reach Hut 3 until late in the evening, although the report had been intercepted early in the morning. On investigation he might find that Hut 6 had been breaking another key in which he was not interested before even attempting to break his key. This seemed asinine behavior on Hut 6's part! Infuriated, he would complain loudly. The truth of the matter could well be that our chance of breaking his key for the day depended on a retransmission on that key of a routine message that originated on the other key. If so we would have to break the other before we could break his. Nor could we forewarn him, as the relationships among the keys changed rapidly.

Another complaint might be that we ought not to bother with a given key at all, because it had not produced any top-quality intelligence for weeks. In such a case our action would be even harder to justify. But if we should leave off breaking such a key for a while we risked being unaware when and if its traffic characteristics changed. In that event we would find it hard to pick up the thread again if and when Hut 3 wanted us to do so. Moreover, our whole experience in Hut 6 had shown that we could never tell what might lead to what. A key that was producing dull decodes might at any time prove to be the route into a much more exciting second key.

In 1942 Hut 6's game had to feature adaptability, for the opportunities were forever changing. We would get an occasional boost from Parkerismus, or an outburst of Sillies. Apart from these, however, our continued success depended on situations in the German command that would, first, lead to repetition in recognizable messages of predictable addresses, signatures, or content, and second, cause some German operator to reencode a message that had already been encoded on another key. Such situations, however, did not last forever. We had to take advantage of the most favorable ones while they lasted, and we had to be continually looking for new opportunities. It should be apparent that guiding our intercept facilities and assigning our bombes—of which we never had enough in 1942—were matters that required an almost inspired balancing of many considerations. We needed to think of the future as well as the present, and we needed a broad overview both of the cryptographic situation and of the present and future needs of Hut 3.

It happened that, just as I was seeing the need for a much closer interrelationship between Hut 6 and Hut 3, the organization of Hut 3 was changing. At the beginning of 1942 Commander Saunders was still in Hut 3, but, in view of the now obvious need for a greatly expanded bombe program, Travis asked Saunders to focus his efforts in that direction. Group Captain Jones came in to direct the obviously needed expansion of Hut 3, and appointed one officer, Wing Commander Oscar Oeser, as the spokesman for Hut 3 on matters of priority between our two organizations. This, in my view, was a very important step. Priority decisions might have to be made at any time of night or day, and procedures were agreed upon for round-the-clock collaboration between the people responsible for the principal activities in the two organizations.

Apart from enjoying working with him, I have one very personal memory of Oscar. Later in the war, when Katharine and I were awaiting the arrival of our second daughter, Rosamond, he came to visit us at our old manor house in the quiet village of Great Gransden. He distinguished himself in two ways. First, no doubt by the exercise of psychological wizardry, he instantly cured our three-year-old daughter, Susanna, of a particularly violent attack of hiccups. Second, he reduced our gardener to a state of helpless hysteria by his enthusiastic but unorthodox method of wielding a scythe.

As I have said, the third period of the bombe phase of Hut 6 started in early 1943. We had already been reinforced externally by the army radio intelligence group, the Central Party, about which I will have more to say later. We were also reinforced internally on August 30, 1943, by a strong team from the U.S. Army. Indeed I have a note that their train from London was due to leave Euston Station at 3:06 P.M., the same train that Harold Fletcher had caught on August 6, 1941.

Among my most pleasant memories of the whole war is the way those Americans came to Hut 6. By then we had moved to our new brick building, so I was able to receive them in respectable though by no means luxurious surroundings. There must have been eight to ten of them. They were ushered into my office to be briefed on our activities. I felt somewhat ill at ease as I started to tell them the Hut 6 story. But their attitude was simply that they wanted to be told what to do so that they could be helpful as soon as possible. There were no fanfares. No arguments. No difficulties. They simply melted into Hut 6 and were liked and welcomed by everyone. Very soon each of them had found a niche and was contributing. Their leader joined our management group and before long he became a major contributor to the key-breaking activities of the Hut 6 watch.

The arrival of this group of Americans came at a time when the new assignments that Travis was giving me were drawing me away from close contact with Hut 6. Consequently I saw very little of them. Nor did I hear any details of the way in which American equipment was able to augment our bombe facilities. The U.S. Navy developed a large installation of bombes similar to but faster than our own, and, although their primary commitment was the handling of the German Naval Enigma, their bombes were sometimes put at the disposal of Hut 6. The U.S. Army had developed a machine of their own design that could handle at least one problem that we were unable to handle: the problem of using Sillies derived from periods of a day during which different arrangements of the three wheels were in use.

The size of the Hut 6 watch and the complexity of its tasks continued to increase after the summer of 1943 as more bombes came into action, and as the Germans modified their Enigma machines and their procedures. One main job was to know what the bombes were doing and to have further bombe-fodder waiting as bombes became free when a key was broken or a bombe run was completed without success. Menus for the bombes had to be prepared, drops had to be tested, and, when the correct wheel order and wheel positions for a key had been determined, the ring settings had to be worked out by cryptanalytical techniques that sometimes proved troublesome.

A second job, known as e.p. (*en passant*), involved taking notes of cryptanalytical interest from the decoded traffic as it passed from our Decoding Room to Hut 3. This had to be done quickly, to avoid holding up the intelligence watch, but it was of vital importance to keep well-organized records for each key in order to detect crib possibilities. Indeed each key had one or more "parents" who would ensure that its records were kept in good order.

A third important job on each shift was to look for cases in which the same message was encoded on two or more different keys. For this purpose the Registration Room made out a slip for every message with brief particulars taken from its preamble (time of origin, length, callsigns, etc.). The key on which each message had been encoded was indicated by an X in the corner in the color associated with that key, or by the appropriate name when there was no color. The slips were consequently called Kisses. The reencodement man sorted the Kisses and, whenever a promising candidate for a reencoding was discovered he would take the necessary followup action. If one of the keys involved was already out, he had to obtain a copy of the decode either by having a duplicate done in our decoding room or by finding it in Hut 3.

In addition to the regular shifts, which operated round the clock, there was often a daytime team engaged on research. This became particularly necessary when the Germans introduced a new obstacle and a way around it had to be found. John Monroe tells me that in the last year of the war two serious research problems arose as a result of two mechanical adaptations of the Enigma. One made it possible to have nonreciprocal steckers (if A were steckered to R it would not necessarily be true that R was steckered to A). This demolished the principle of the diagonal board of a bombe. The other modification was the introduction of a new *umkehrwalze*, known as D. When the German army and air force started to use this *umkehrwalze*, the Hut 6 research people soon found that it was in fact variable by cross-plugging!

So it was that, right up to the end of the war, Hut 6, with an internal staff that peaked at around 250, was still having to contend with new cryptanalytical problems.

8

Bombes and Wrens

The two prototype bombes came into action as usable machines late in 1941—only about a year after the "idea" phase. This was a remarkable achievement, for it had taken a lot of skilled design, careful planning of manufacturing procedure, and a vast expenditure of general effort to turn mere ideas into complex operating machinery. From experience gained in the operation of the prototypes, the details were soon firmed up, and it was not long before bombes from the production line began to arrive. John Monroe remembers that when he arrived in June 1941 we already had four to six bombes, including the prototypes. Harold Fletcher believes that we had eight to twelve bombes by the time he arrived on August 6, 1941. So it seems that Doc Keen was already delivering production models at the rate of around three per month.

That the bombes performed so satisfactorily says a great deal for their basic design and manufacture. They had to operate twenty-four hours a day, seven days a week, month after month, and then year after year. Their only "time off" was the few hours during which they received their regular servicing by the RAF mechanics. Breakdowns were not nearly so frequent as might have been anticipated considering their unique nature and how quickly they had had to be developed.

In Chapter 3, I discussed the Enigma machine and how it was used. In Chapter 4 I discussed two important ideas that occurred to me in October and November 1939. However, to avoid delay in getting on to the exciting early days of Hut 6, I chose to put the detailed description of the bombes in the Appendix, which might now be read as an introduction to the actual use of the bombes after they began to be available in the second year of the war.

Soon after his arrival in August 1941, Harold Fletcher became involved in the administrative aspects of the bombe program, and his memory has been extremely helpful to me in reconstructing the sequence of events. In summer 1941, when Fletcher joined us, there were four to six bombes at Bletchley Park, housed in what was then known as Hut 11, and a similar number in converted stables at Adstock, the village where Travis lived throughout the war. Another "bombe hut" in the village of Wavendon was nearing completion, and, between them, Bletchley, Adstock, and Wavendon must eventually have accommodated some twenty-four to thirty bombes. Already authorized production at BTM was going steadily on, and Fletcher was asked to help the Admiralty requisition Gayhurst Manor and build a bombe hut there with a capability of utilizing some sixteen bombes. These early expansions of our bombe capabilities were not too difficult, but involved a problem of timing. The buildings had to be completely finished and ready for use before any bombes could be installed. No outsider could be allowed inside after bombes had been delivered. The machines themselves were operated by members of the Women's Royal Naval Service, who were called "Wrens," though the official spelling was WRNS.

When Gayhurst became operational, bringing the total to some forty to forty-six bombes, it was still felt that the limit would be about seventy bombes, which would require suitable accommodation for some seven hundred Wrens. In 1942, however, for reasons that I have explained, the picture changed completely. We would need far more than seventy bombes. Commander Saunders, then in charge of Hut 3 operations, was asked by Travis to devote his entire effort to the expansion of our bombe capabilities. In this task he was to be assisted by Harold Fletcher of Hut 6.

Because the bombes were being built at the BTM factory in Letchworth, not far from Bletchley, we were able to keep in close touch with the needs as they arose. Saunders worked with the Managing Director, a Mr. Bailey, while I continued to work closely with Doc Keen. The existing BTM factory was still able to provide a secure area for the assembly line and development laboratory, but it had become necessary to establish a new and quite large factory for the manufacture of parts, particularly those requiring machine tools. Keen directed the entire engineering effort from start to finish, did all the design and worked with his assistants on the final assembly and on troubleshooting and modifications after delivery. He visited Hut 6, as Ellingworth of Chatham had done, to get the flavor of our problem. He, together with a few of his principal assistants in the development laboratory and the man in charge of the new factory, were told the whole story of Hut 6. The workers on the assembly line and in the factory, however, never knew what the machines were intended to do. I hope this book will tell these people, and their children and grandchildren, that what they did was enormously worthwhile.

There were other workers involved in bombe manufacture besides those at BTM, for in support of the war effort part-time work had been organized in villages all over the country. Within a wide radius of Letchworth some of these village teams were making such parts for the bombes as did not have to be made by machine tools and other factory equipment. Some of the people who worked in those village halls may remember that they were making twenty-six-way cables, or other electrical subassemblies involving the number twenty-six, in which case they also may be glad to know that they were almost certainly making an essential contribution to Ultra.

There were problems of financing, because the first contracts with BTM were covered by Secret Service funds, whereas the expanded program was funded by the Admiralty, which caused a slight hiatus in the summer of 1942. Bailey explained to Fletcher at that time that one of the BTM workshops, making the basic frames for the bombes, had almost completed work on its current contract. If a further order was not received in time, he would have to put this workshop onto other war work, after which it would not be possible to transfer the workshop back to bombe work for a considerable time. Fortunately Bailey accepted Fletcher's personal assurance that a new order for at least as many bombes as they had already contracted for would shortly be forthcoming. It took another month or two for the new order to materialize, but no delay in the delivery of the bombes resulted.

Late in 1942 or early in 1943 BTM began to have difficulties in getting raw materials, which they could not resolve themselves. Malcolm Saunders was brought in, attired in his navy uniform, to apply Admiralty pressure on suppliers and Government departments. Though rather unapproachable, he did this sort of thing very well. He had an impressive manner and the much-needed supplies quickened up under his pressure. He also gave helpful pep talks to factory workers to encourage their efforts, as, for example, when he went with Fletcher to the Spirella corset factory at Baldock, which, instead of corsets, was making parachutes and miscellaneous bombe parts.

The biggest problem facing Malcolm Saunders and Harold Fletcher was where to put the projected quantities of bombes and the Wrens who would operate them. Fletcher recommended that a private school, Stowe, which was within easy reach of Bletchley, be requisitioned, but the suggestion was turned down at a very high level. He and Saunders had to settle for some brick office buildings at Stanmore, on the northern outskirts of London, which were nearing completion. This actually proved to be a very good solution to the problem. It was possible to provide nearby accommodation for the large staff of Wren operators. Furthermore it was possible to provide exclusive teletype and telephone lines to Bletchley Park.

For efficient operation of the anticipated number of bombes we needed large establishments, and, as a precaution against enemy air attack, we needed dispersed sites. So, having found the Stanmore scheme so satisfactory, Saunders and Fletcher readily settled for another site in Eastcote, in the western suburbs of London, where two buildings were nearing completion and there was space for a third. With effective encouragement from Saunders, in his navy uniform of course, the third block was erected in around six months. It housed some eight hundred to nine hundred Wrens. Bombes from Wavendon and Adstock were moved to Stanmore and Eastcote, but Gayhurst remained in operation throughout the war. A few bombes remained in Bletchley Park, but they were used for demonstration and training purposes only.

To understand the task of the Wren operators we must first consider the initial setup of a bombe in accordance with a menu prepared in Hut 6. In the Appendix, when I explain the idea of the diagonal board, I use the second diagram of Figure 4.4 and show, in Figure A.3, how the in-out and out-in terminals of nine double-ended scramblers would be connected by twenty-six-way cables to rows of the diagonal board in accordance with the diagram, which uses some of the letter pairings that occur in the first thirteen positions of the crib.

The same diagram is repeated as the main chain in the bombe menu of Figure 8.1, which is based on the same thirteen positions of the crib and on the assumption that there is no turnover in that stretch. But because our bombes had twelve scramblers we could use three more letter pairings: those of the two-link subsidiary chain R to L to S and also one of the single-link chains, say Q to O. This will reduce the number of drops by providing feedback from rows R, L, S, Q, and O. The Z to H link will not be set up on the bombe, but might be employed in testing drops.

The letters under the crib positions at the top of Figure 8.1 indicate initial positions of the top, middle, and bottom drums of the bombe's scramblers for the start of a run. Thus a Wren would set the first scrambler to AAA and connect its in-out and out-in terminals to rows C and T of the diagonal board. The second scrambler would be set to BAA and connected to rows Q and O, the third to CAA and connected to rows N and T. Because the letter pairing Z to H in position 4 is not to be used, the fourth scrambler will be set to EAA and connected to rows P and E, the fifth to FAA and connected to rows V and P, and so on, until the twelfth scrambler is set to MAA and connected to rows I and N.

When this initial setup has been completed for a selected wheel order and the test register of Figure A.3 has been connected to row E of the diagonal board, the bombe is ready for a run, during which its twelve scramblers will be driven in synchronism through all $26 \times 26 \times 26$ possible positions of the drums of each scrambler. Let us consider how Keen handled this mechanical motion and the associated electrical sensing. Remember that in each position of the battery a test had to be applied to determine whether some letter of the test register was not connected to any other letter. Thus, if current input was at letter A of the test register, Keen's sensing circuitry had to signal a drop when current failed to reach all the terminals of the test register. In fact he had to sense the occurrence of one of two possibilities. The first was a position of the bombe

THE CRIB

```
C Q N Z P V L I L P E U I K T E D C G L O V W V G T U F L N Z
T O T H E P R E S I D E N T O F T H E U N I T E D S T A T E S

I 2 3 4 5 6 7 8 9 IO II I2 I3 I4 I5 I6 I7 I8 I9 20 2I 22 23 24 25 26 27 28 29 30 3I

A B C D E F G H I J K L M
A A A A A A A A A A A A A
A A A A A A A A A A A A A
```

THE MAIN CHAIN

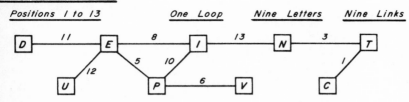

Positions I to I3   One Loop   Nine Letters   Nine Links

SUBSIDIARY CHAINS

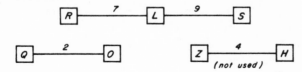

(Test Register Connected to row E of the Diagonal Board)

Figure 8.I   A   Bombe   Menu

scramblers in which current reached no terminal other than A, which would mean that, for this position, the bombe had failed to rule out the possibility that E is steckered to A. The second was a position in which current failed to reach some other terminal, say J, which would mean that the possibility of E's being steckered to J had not been ruled out.

For his sensing circuitry, Keen designed an electromagnetic relay that could operate in one millisecond. (It was similar to a Siemens relay that was about the fastest available at that time.) The top drums of all the scramblers were driven as fast as the sensing device would permit. The sensing for each position was timed to occur during periods when the drums' brushes would be making good contact with the commutator terminals.

As the top drums made a complete revolution, sensing would occur in all twenty-six positions. If no drop occurred in a revolution of the top drums, sensing was discontinued and a signal went to the drive mechanism to cause all the middle drums, and sometimes the bottom drums as well, to move to their next positions. Another sensing cycle was then initiated. When a drop was sensed, the top drums were not stopped but the motion of the middle and bottom drums was inhibited. Indicators would tell a Wren operator which letter of the test register was involved, and the position of the still-moving top drum of the first scrambler in which the drop had been sensed. She would also note the positions of the middle and bottom drums of this scrambler and the wheel order being run. Having noted all this information, which would be reported to Hut 6, the Wren operator would reactivate the drive mechanism for the middle and bottom drums. The remote possibility of two drops in one revolution of the top drums was taken care of.

The time occupied in dealing with drops would depend on the number of drops and on how quickly a Wren operator could get to the bombe. It is Harold Fletcher's recollection that an average bombe run took about twelve to fifteen minutes. When a run on a particular wheel order had been completed, another wheel order would be tried. It was possible to choose a sequence of wheel orders that would not call for more than one set of drums (top, middle, or bottom) to be changed between successive runs. Thus, allowing for the initial setup time, changing drums, and dealing with drops, it took one bombe rather more than twelve to fifteen hours to run one menu on all 60 possible wheel orders. When we had plenty of bombes we could put several bombes to work on the same menu, greatly reducing the time required to achieve a break.

The diagram of a bombe in Figure A.4 (page 308) shows an open door at the back. All the in-out and out-in terminals of the twelve scramblers were connected by an enormous cable to twelve pairs of twenty-six-way female jacks on the inside of the door, which also contained twenty-six jacks for the rows of the diagonal board, one jack for the test register, and the commoning boards. Thus the Wren operator would do all the cross-plugging on the door. The maintenance staff would have good access to the drive mechanism behind the front panel of the bombe.

When, very likely at the instigation of Travis, it was agreed that the operators of the bombes would be provided by the Womens Royal Naval Service, no one could have anticipated that the number of bombe Wrens would rise to around two thousand. In spite of this heavy demand, however, the high level of qualifications laid down at the outset was maintained to the end, and the Wrens were exceptionally good. So good that one felt that the pick of the recruits were being assigned to bombe duty in the WRNS organization known as HMS Pembroke V.

Although the bombe Wrens could not be given a taste of the sea, the WRNS authorities insisted that proper Naval nomenclature be used. This is why the organization to which the Wrens were assigned was given the name of a ship. Moreover, in their "ship" there were wardrooms, galleys, cabins, and berths. At one or two sites there was even a quarterdeck, which all Wrens had to salute. Harold found it refreshing to hear the humble minibus or shooting brake, which took Wrens to the station when going on leave, referred to as "The Liberty Boat."

Even so, he always felt a great deal of sympathy for them. Most of them had joined the Wrens, as opposed to any of the other services, in the expectation of seeing something of the sea, of warships, and of sailors. Instead they were stuck a long way from the sea, doing monotonous shift work that they couldn't talk about at home or anywhere else, with very little promotion, and not a male naval uniform in sight. It seemed to Harold that there was considerable danger of loss of morale, resulting in mistakes in operation and possible threats to security. So he devised a talk explaining in simple terms the problem the bombes were helping to solve, and its place in the chain of processes that, with luck, resulted in decodes.

This talk was an immediate success, and Harold was invited to deliver it, as a matter of urgency, some ten to twelve more times, so that all the bombe Wrens who had already arrived could hear it. Thereafter he repeated the talk for new Wren arrivals. The RAF mechanics also attended, and, later in the war, so did the U.S. Army personnel who operated a few of the bombes at Eastcote. Harold also gave or arranged for lectures on specific problems affecting bombe operations, such as the appearance of *umkehrwalze* D late in the war. He always tried to give, at the end of each talk, some comparatively innocuous items of intelligence in an attempt to show the work had a real connection with the war.

At the time Fletcher kept fairly quiet about the contents of these talks, in case he should be stopped on security grounds. He himself was quite certain that he was actually improving security, an opinion that would be confirmed by modern experience. Indeed the talks cannot have failed to make a real contribution to the welfare and efficiency of the Wrens, and they were certainly remembered by some. For several years after the war it was not unusual for him to meet socially a lady who would tell him that she had heard him lecture. The last occasion when this happened illustrates the deep and inviolate sense of security that Lewin mentions in *Ultra Goes to War*. During a tour of duty in Singapore in 1956 or 1957 a Lieutenant-Colonel arrived to join the intelligence staff of Far East Command and became aware of Harold's trade. His wife, on being introduced to Harold at a cocktail party, said, "I was with the Wrens during the war and went to hear your lectures." At which the Lieutenant-Colonel, with a triumphant grin on his face, turned to his wife and said, "So *that's* what you did in the war."

Inevitably the day came for an inspection of Hut 6 by the Director of the WRNS, Mrs. Laughton-Matthews, who held the appointment throughout the war. The inspecting party consisted of the Director; Mrs. Mackenzie, who commanded our Wrens with the rank of Chief Officer; Captain Bradshaw, RN, the senior naval officer at Bletchley Park; and Fletcher. After a short preliminary talk in Fletcher's office, the party proceeded to a Registration Room, where, of a total staff of about thirty, around ten were Wrens. The Director at once asked Fletcher, in rather supercilious tones, "Why are my Wrens working with civilians?"

Fletcher, caught off balance by this unexpected question, came out with the unadorned truth, which was that we were using Wrens because we couldn't get any more civilians. This shook Mrs. Laughton-Matthews to the core, and Captain Bradshaw retired behind a pillar for a giggle.

Mrs. Laughton-Matthews bore Fletcher no ill will, however. Indeed he met her later on a number of occasions, and she couldn't have been nicer or more helpful.

Fletcher was the man primarily responsible for establishing standard procedures for using the bombes, and for maintaining harmonious relationships among the various parties involved, particularly the Wrens who operated the bombes, Sergeant Jones and his men who maintained them, Doc Keen and his men who built them, and the watch in Hut 6 who gave them "menus" and used their output.

Sergeant Jones was one of the original maintenance engineers. Travis had decided to give him overall responsibility for maintenance of all the bombes and, working out of Bletchley Park, Jones established effective maintenance procedures. His experience of BTM techniques was extremely valuable, particularly in the care of around 15 million delicate wire brushes on the drums that had to make reliable contact with the terminals on the templates. (There were 104 brushes per drum, 720 drums per bombe, and ultimately around 200 bombes.) Later in the war, when other people tried to operate them, we realized how lucky we had been to have had Sergeant Jones. He was a tireless worker, very ingenious, and willing to take on any technical problems that Hut 6 might throw at him. By the end of the war he had been promoted to Squadron Leader.

All the bombes had names. The first prototype was called Agnes, but after the first few bombes had arrived, the responsibility for naming them was given to the Wrens, who tended to use warships and ports. Thus one might hear a Wren duty officer call out "Put

Warspite, Victorious, and Tiger on Chaffinch job 81." This was better for morale than saying "Put machines 110, 111, and 112 on job 9–81."

Later in the war the German navy modified its Enigma by splitting the *umkehrwalze* into a fixed left-hand part and a rotatable right-hand part, creating a machine with four rotating wheels instead of three. When Keen was brought into the picture, he immediately produced a sound approach to the problem, and was soon manufacturing four-wheelers instead of three-wheelers. And his solution was simplicity itself.

When he had started building his bombes he did not know how fast he could drive his drums and still obtain reliable contacts between their brushes and the commutator terminals, so he based his drum speeds on the testing speeds that he expected to achieve with electromagnetic relays. Now, however, he knew from experience that he could safely drive his drums much faster, and it was an easy matter to use already well established electronic techniques to perform the very simple testing function at speeds much higher than those achievable by his relays. So Keen simply added a set of twelve super-slow drums below the top, middle, and bottom drums of his existing bombes. This involved making higher frames and providing a simple addition to the bottom of his drive mechanisms. The drums were already in large-scale production and no change in the electrical circuitry was called for, other than the simple matter of introducing electronic sensing of electric current reaching the terminals of the test register. Hey presto! With very little additional effort Doc Keen was building four-wheel bombes that could do twenty-six times as many tests as the three-wheel bombes in only twice the time.

9

From Interception
to Intelligence

The big expansion of our intercept facilities began in 1941, when the RAF opened a big station at Chicksands, a little to the east of Bletchley, under Wing Commander Shepherd. In the meantime we depended almost entirely on the highly experienced intercept operators at the army station at Chatham. This station was a good site for interception, except that, being on top of a hill, it probably did not have enough level space for the large rhombic and Beveridge aerials that would be needed to intercept traffic from considerable distances. But another consideration limited its suitability. Chatham was too exposed to enemy air attack. Accordingly, the Chatham intercept organization had to be moved.

Our crack intercept operators' new home was Beaumanor, a country estate in Leicestershire some 50 miles to the north of Bletchley. On a flat part of Beaumanor's grounds the necessary large aerials were erected, and several huts were built. One hut housed Commander Ellingworth and his controllers, and had tele-printer circuits to Bletchley Park. The other huts were for the intercept operators. The interception huts all had pneumatic tubes leading to the control hut; these were used for sending across hand-written forms containing logs and intercepted messages. The pneumatic tubes were laid underground, and in the winters, which were quite rugged, they would collect condensed moisture; thus the arrival in the control room of a container from one of the other huts would often be announced by a spurt of water.

As for the motorcycle dispatch riders, they had a somewhat shorter ride to Bletchley Park than they had had from Chatham, but it was still a long one in bad weather and in the blackout.*

I visited Ellingworth several times at Beaumanor, and found that the dedication of the operators and of the staff was just as impressive as it had been at Chatham. I don't know how many new operators had been recruited, but I believe the station had grown considerably. Nor was interception at Chatham entirely defunct, for Ellingworth kept a small group of intercept operators there so as to have diversified reception. This could make the difference in the case of the weaker signals, some of which might be more audible at Chatham than at Beaumanor, or vice versa.

The RAF intercept station at Chicksands, a large station from the outset, opened in 1941 with male operators. In August 1942 it was augmented by operators from the WAAF (Women's Auxiliary Air Force). Late in 1942, an auxiliary station was established at Shaftesbury, initially staffed by WAAF operators, to provide diversified reception. Thus by early 1943 we had four widely separated principal intercept sites: Beaumanor in Leicestershire, Chatham in Kent, Chicksands in Bedfordshire, and Shaftesbury in Dorset.

Wing Commander Shepherd, at Chicksands, was a tremendous help to Hut 6. He was eager to cooperate with our Intercept Control Room, and he realized that his operators and staff had much to learn about the interception of German radio nets carrying Enigma traffic, particularly those that were almost inaudible. The RAF was now running a training school for intercept operators, which must have helped a good deal. The Chicksands operators were well indoctrinated and well led from the outset; my early visits there gave me the same impression of dedication that I had observed at Chatham and Beaumanor. In a remarkably short time Chicksands was making a valuable contribution. The quality of its interception went on improving, and the station became more and more expert at

---

* We gradually acquired more teletype equipment, and when we moved to our new brick building in 1943 we had enough to carry virtually all the intercepted Enigma messages. By that time we were also receiving intercepts from overseas, sent by radio after being encoded on Type-X. The double encoding produced a good many garbles, so these intercepts were not too popular in the Hut 6 Decoding Room, but they produced a lot of good stuff for Hut 3.

picking up weak signals from Africa, the Balkans, and the Russian front.

During the war the dedicated operators and staff of these intercept stations were doing a job that was absolutely vital to the production of Hut 6 Ultra intelligence. Recently, thirty years after the end of the war, Winterbotham's *The Ultra Secret* made it known that what they did resulted in intelligence of immense value, but, not having been in touch with the intercept stations, he does not pay adequate recognition to their contribution to Hut 6 Ultra. The tribute that I am able to pay in this book is long overdue.

When, in 1971, I retired as a regular employee of MITRE, another of the many happy chances of my life led me to choose the historic and beautiful city of Newburyport, about an hour's drive northeast from Boston, as my retirement home. It was a fortunate move for my story, as well as for myself, because in Newburyport my wife already knew Diana Lucy, who, as Diana Stuart, had been a WAAF operator at Chicksands. She has given me an account of how she came to be there and what it was like to be an intercept operator.

Quite early in the war young unmarried women who were not in "reserved" occupations such as teaching or nursing were subject to a system of "directed labor," which might mean having little or no choice as to one's assignment. One could end up working in a munitions factory or on a farm, occupations that might be congenial to some, but not to others. However, one could volunteer for the assignment of one's choice before one was actually called up.

Diana was training as a speech therapist, which was not considered a "reserved" occupation, so at age nineteen, in October 1941, she volunteered for the Women's Auxiliary Air Force (WAAF), known today as the Women's Royal Air Force. She became Leading Aircraft Woman 2082928 and was sent for six weeks to a camp outside Gloucester for basic training and aptitude evaluation. It was decided that she was to be a radio operator, and she was sent to Manchester for an intensive six-month course in the dreary Post Office building, where her instructors were GPO* telegraphists.

After further training in Blackpool, Diana and many other

* General Post Office.

WAAF radio operators were posted to RAF fighter stations on the south coast of England. Then, in the summer of 1942, after an intensive course on the maintenance of radio equipment, she found herself at Chicksands Priory, having been told only that she was to do "specialized radio work."

At the Chicksands intercept station conditions were primitive. The WAAFs slept in Nissen huts and shared bathing facilities with the men. They worked eight-hour shifts, and reported for duty in a cobblestoned courtyard of the old Priory, where a roll call was taken. Then the thirty-odd members of a shift would proceed to a "watch room" high up in an old wing of the Priory, with cold stone floors, Gothic windows, and a vaulted ceiling. The only access used by the WAAFs to this eerie watch room was a narrow circular stone staircase, with a stone column in the middle and steps that showed centuries of wear.

The radio sets were lined up on shelves above working benches running along the walls. Bats had been accustomed for some time to make use of the vaulted ceiling of this watch room. On one occasion the bats were disturbed and swooped screeching all over the place. Pandemonium ensued. Interception ceased, because the WAAFs were under the benches, until the bats were somehow caught or driven out. As soon as possible much better working conditions were provided in new concrete block structures with fluorescent lighting.

Late in 1942 Diana and a party of around twenty WAAF interceptors were sent to the Chicksands satellite station at Shaftesbury in Dorset to operate an evening watch, roughly from six P.M. to two A.M., when reception of distant radio transmitters was particularly good. Diana much enjoyed this assignment in a particularly lovely corner of England. The WAAFs were billeted with families in the town, who had no idea what was going on. The intercept facility was referred to simply as the "radio station," and there were plenty of those around the countryside. Diana herself was somewhat reluctant to return from the cozy atmosphere of a billet to the regimentation of Chicksands in the summer of 1943. The Shaftesbury activity continued to expand after that date.

Diana has the distinct impression that the pressure on intercept operators increased considerably toward the end of the war, starting with the winter of 1943/44. There seemed to be more stations on each German radio net, and more traffic too. It was just about all she could do to record on log and message pad all that was going on. When one remembers that the German retreats in Russia started early in 1943, and that their troubles in Italy started only a few months later, this seems understandable. They would have to deal with deep infiltrations and clandestine operations. More and more they would need to keep track of what was going on everywhere.

To indicate how specialized was the task of our intercept operators, I must say a little more about how the Germans controlled the radio nets that carried the Enigma traffic. I understand this far better now than I did during the war. Only recently have I learned that the frequency stability of radio sets in those days was very poor, particularly under field conditions.

Diana tells me that the drifting of German radio frequencies often made it extremely hard for our intercept operators to keep in touch with the stations of a net. There was no problem when the signals were coming in strongly, but she was often listening to distant nets on the Russian front. Usually the control station of a net was relatively easy to pick up; the problem was to identify the very weak signals from the outstations, which would fade out with the slightest drift in transmitting frequency. Our intercept operators would be continuously tuning, trying to pick up outstation transmissions, and it was only too easy to pick up a signal from a different net on a nearby frequency. By following a net for a long enough period, an intercept operator could learn to recognize the individual German outstation operators by their "fists"—the way they keyed their Morse code transmissions—and this proved the most reliable method of keeping in touch with all the stations of a net and avoiding confusion with other nets. When contact had been established with a particular net, prediction of callsigns could be a great help to the intercept operator, but often he or she would be looking for new nets, created to meet the requirements of a new tactical situation.

If the task of our intercept operators was not an easy one, neither was that of the controller of a German radio net. The Germans had great difficulty in keeping their nets operating efficiently. The procedures they developed to cope with this problem were very thorough, further demonstrating their regard for the importance of reliable communications in fast-moving military operations. But the problem continued to plague them throughout the war. The same frequency drift and fading that made it difficult for our intercept operators to pick up signals on a specified German radio net hampered the German operators in hearing each other. Let us think about what this implies.

We are talking about a very simple and flexible type of radio net. Its radio frequencies are in the high frequency (shortwave) range to permit communication over considerable distances. A number of radio stations use the same frequency both for transmission and for reception. All the stations monitor this frequency all the time, one of them acting as net control. Stations may join or leave the net as necessary, and the control function can be transferred from one station to another. If there were no problems of drifting and fading, the function of the control station would simply be to control traffic. Any message transmitted by any one of the stations would be heard by all the stations. The controller would simply have to ensure that no two stations transmitted at the same time.

But the Germans' problem was not so simple. Diana, and many hundreds of skilled British interceptors, would follow the chitchat by which the German net controller struggled to keep his net in working order. This involved a lot of very short messages using the callsigns of the individual stations and a so-called Q-Code. This needs a little explanation.

The creation of Q-Codes, still widely used today, dates back to the sinking of the *Titanic* on April 15, 1912. Radio distress signals from the ship were picked up in New York, but although there were ships of several nationalities near enough to have assisted, they would not have been able to understand the distress signals even if they had picked them up, because of language difficulties. This incident showed that to handle emergencies at sea it was necessary to introduce an international code that, in combination with figures (e.g., for latitude and longitude) and names (e.g., of ships), would permit effective communication anywhere in the world, regardless of language differences. The three-letter international code that was soon introduced was called the "Q-Code" because each three-letter group began with a Q. Typical meanings of code groups are:

QRA   What is the name of your station?

QRG   What is my exact frequency?

QRM   Is my transmission being interfered with?

QRO   Shall I increase transmitter power?

QRQ   Shall I send faster?

QTH   What is your location?

QTX   Will you keep your station open for further
       communication with me?

QUA   Have you news of —— ?

In the international code of today there are some forty such three-letter groups, together with a few special signals, such as the well known SOS.

To control their military radio nets in World War II, the Germans needed a specialized form of Q-Code. After all these years Diana does not remember all the code groups, but she believes that the list was similar to that used today by the Amateur Radio Relay League.

Without going into further detail, we can now understand the general nature both of the German task of net control, and of our task of following the "whispers" of the German nets. For our intercept operators would record all the chitchat on logs, and the analysis of these logs, known as "log reading," was the basic tool of the "Central Party," whose radio intelligence activities I am about to discuss.*

The individual stations of a German radio net identified themselves by callsigns usually consisting of two letters and one figure; these changed at midnight, as did all the Enigma keys and their identifying discriminants. When the new net controller came on at midnight, his first task was a roll call. Using their callsigns and the appropriate Q-Codes, he asked each outstation to transmit an acknowledgment if it heard him. If he failed to get an acknowledgment from one of the outstations, he would ask another one to try to make contact with the one that had not answered. This initial procedure gave our interceptors a chance to record on their log for the day all the callsigns of the nets they were covering. We in Hut 6, however, would be aware only of the callsigns that were involved in message traffic, because only these would appear on our traffic register.

---

* The early log-reading effort in MI8 was mentioned at the end of Chapter 5.

Having established contact with all his stations, the German controller proceeded to arrange for the handling of traffic. If he had an Enigma message for a particular station, he would make sure that the station was ready to receive before transmitting the message preamble and text. If he had an Enigma message for all the stations of the net, he would announce it with an all-station (CQ) call. He would also ask each station in turn if it had a message to transmit, and give permission for the transmission. For a message addressed by one station to two or more others, the controller would check that the addressees were receiving from the sender before permitting the transmission.

From midnight to midnight, successive watches of German net controllers would struggle to keep the communications lines operative, so that when a message needed to be sent it would reach its destination(s). Sometimes the recipient of a message would be unable to receive the whole text, and would ask for a repeat; or one of them might be unable to decode the message at all, and would ask for a repetition of the indicator setting and indicator. Sometimes we found ourselves doing better than the German recipient. Provided that one or more of our intercept operators was steadily following a particular net, the log would show all the chitchat involved both in keeping the net operative and in arranging for the transmission of messages. All callsigns would appear, and the existence of the net would be revealed even if no messages were passed.

The existence of the net! Looking back I am sorry that I did not recognize the significance of the fact that log reading could reveal the existence of a German radio net even without message traffic. I have been told that, in the official accounts of Bletchley Park activities, I have been regarded as the originator of traffic analysis, commonly shortened to "TA." To put the record straight, however, I had no hand in developing the possibilities of chitchat analysis, as distinct from the analysis of Enigma message traffic. Rather naturally, because I was developing my kind of TA as an aid to breaking Enigma keys, I was concerned with the messages that we hoped to decode. Very early on it seemed certain that we could achieve our goal with the information contained on our traffic register— information related to the transmission of an Enigma message. I was hardly aware of the Q-Code signals used by the Germans to keep their nets operating. I never read a log myself. It never occurred to me that the Germans might inadvertently reveal their intentions simply by exercising a radio net, without passing any message traffic on it.

However, the leaders of the expanding log-reading effort were well aware of this possibility. Their objective was pure radio intelligence, derived from detailed analysis of enemy radio transmissions. They studied the chitchat in the logs, they used direction-finding facilities to locate the transmitters, and they collected callsigns used on successive days by the same station so that, when the yearly repetitions appeared, log reading could begin to identify military units served by radio stations.* No doubt they used the intercept operators' identifications of the German radio operators by "fist" when they could. They studied the preambles of the encoded messages, and particularly the retransmissions of the same message on different nets, in order to piece together the whole structure of the German radio communications system, which had to reflect the command structure and the order of battle (what units were where under whose command). By getting to know the regular pattern of message traffic in relatively quiescent periods, they could hope to detect something unusual and to guess what it might mean. Occasionally the logs would contain short messages in the clear, giving names of individuals or units.

All this effort had started in a small way in London in the early days of the war, while I was beginning to study message traffic in the School. When the Chatham intercept operators moved to their huts in the grounds of the Beaumanor mansion, the log readers moved into the mansion itself, and grew to a large organization. During this period they must have gained a good deal from close proximity to the intercept operators, but as the RAF station at Chicksands expanded, and carried an increasing portion of the load, Beaumanor became a less advantageous location. I believe it was in 1942 that the log readers moved to Bletchley Park, where they became known as the Central Party.

By now the Central Party was a large organization of British army men and ATS (Auxiliary Territorial Service) women. They worked in a separate hut, but they became an integral part of the

---

* This identification became much easier when the German callsign books were captured, but by that time the log-reading party had gone a long way toward the reconstruction of the books.

Hut 6 organization. At last, now that they were with us, I was able to tell them that we were breaking a great deal of Enigma traffic, how we were doing it, and how their log reading could help. Their leader, Philip Lewis, joined my management group, and the Central Party was included in the circulation of weekly reports. They were reinforced by a group of U.S. Army men.

The arrival of the Central Party at Bletchley Park was a boon to me for a personal reason. My wife, Katharine, having young children, was not subject to conscription, but, like many young married women, she had volunteered for service in the ATS, leaving the children in the care of her mother. She went first to the ATS Depot at Aldermaston and was then assigned, as Private No. W/75856, to 1st AAMT Company ATS at 8 Rutland Gate, London, which meant that she could easily get home on leave. However, after a period as a driver, she was posted to the log-reading group at Beaumanor and moved with them to Bletchley Park. Now she could live at home, and she was permitted to know what I was doing. One of the tasks in which she became involved was the continual updating of a huge wall chart showing all the German radio nets on the Russian front.

The Central Party's intimate knowledge of the German radio nets was of immediate value to the Hut 6 Intercept Control Room, and they were soon able to cooperate a good deal with the Hut 6 crib hunters, with the Registration Room, and even with the Decoding Room. I think we were all amazed by how far they had been able to get without ever seeing a single decode. They maintained a detailed picture of the structure of the German communications system, and this was updated as the logs from the intercept stations were analyzed. They were already familiar with the routine messages that interested our crib people, they had followed successive retransmissions on different radio nets, and they could help Hut 6 to detect cases in which a message originally encoded on one key had been reencoded on another key before being retransmitted. They would notice situations in which the recipient of a message who was having difficulty with the decoding would ask for a repeat of the indicator setting and indicator and might receive a correction that would help our Decoding Room.

The Central Party was sometimes able to assist Hut 6 in breaking Enigma keys and in exploiting the breaks. Sometimes its contribution was a matter of helping the Hut 3 people develop the full implications of Enigma decodes; sometimes the Party people were able to produce independent intelligence. Always they were trying to keep up their expertise, so that they could act as a backup to the key breaking. If Hut 6 had had a temporary setback, as could easily have happened, the Central Party could have continued to produce intelligence, and could have been a great help in attempts to start breaking again. Moreover, if Hut 6 had become unable to break Enigma keys altogether, the Central Party would have become the principal source of radio intelligence derived from nets carrying Enigma traffic. Fortunately that never happened, but if it had, the Central Party's close association with Hut 6, and still more with Hut 3, would have greatly enhanced their ability to produce valuable radio intelligence without decodes.

I will have more to say in Part Four about the potential value and actual achievements of radio intelligence. At this point I am concentrating on activities directly related to the breaking of Enigma traffic by Hut 6. I have spoken of the expansion in bombes, interception, and log reading. We now come to intelligence derived from the decodes.

The expansion of the Hut 3 intelligence activity was vital to exploitation of Hut 6 Ultra in an increasingly complex war. Peter Calvocoressi, who was first deputy head and later head of the Air Section of Hut 3, has given some indication of the magnitude of the task in an article of November 24, 1974, in the London *Sunday Times Weekly*. As Hut 6 succeeded in breaking more and more Enigma keys—for example, at some point we began to break the SS traffic as well as the operational traffic from the many fronts—it was obviously necessary to expand the organization that was to squeeze the last drop of reliable intelligence from the decodes.

Calvocoressi points out that this was no simple matter. The expanded Hut 3 revolved around its twenty-four-hour watch, which occupied a room about 30 or 40 feet square containing a large horseshoe table. The Head of the Watch sat in the middle of the horseshoe, with some ten members of the watch facing him around the outside—all working on the stream of decodes from Hut 6.*

---

* After the move to our new brick building the decodes were transported from the Hut 6 Decoding Room to the Hut 3 watch by a conveyor belt that never stopped. Another conveyor belt brought the raw intercepted messages from the teleprinters to the Hut 6 Registration Room.

Some of these people had been schoolteachers; others came from universities, museums, and business. One thing they all had in common was that they knew German. Most of the members of the watch belonged to one of two main Hut 3 sections—Army and Air. During Calvocoressi's time as deputy head and head, the Air Section grew to a strength of around fifty.

At any time of day or night two army and two RAF "advisers" were working in the corner of the watch room. Their job was to take the translated decodes, annotate and comment on them, and send messages to commanders in the field who could use them. The secure communications system used for this purpose had been originated and continually expanded by Winterbotham, who discusses it in *The Ultra Secret*. He organized Special Liaison Units (SLUs), which were responsible for operating the secure communications links and for seeing that rigorous security procedures were followed to protect the source of the intelligence. If the expansion of the SLU organization had not been able to keep pace with the increasing complexity of the war, Hut 6 Ultra could never have been used so effectively on many fronts.

Everything deciphered at Bletchley Park (known in the intelligence world as Station X), including the Hut 6 decodes, went to the various intelligence departments in London, but only the cream went to commanders in the field. The advisers in the watch room decided what went to whom and paraphrased the original message as a security precaution. As the reader of *The Ultra Secret* will know, many of the most important messages went to Winterbotham, to be passed on to Winston Churchill.*

Calvocoressi points out that, next to the decodes from Hut 6, the most important tool in Hut 3 was the indexing system. His Air Index, of which he is justly proud, was in a large room just off the watch room. On each shift of the watch a team of indexers would take each decoded message and underline key words to be put on cards—names of people, places, units, weapons, code words, scientific terms, and such special subjects as oil. It was a huge job, and the Air Index grew to many thousands of cards, so precious that they were photographed and the duplicates stored away in another

---

* Far more information about intelligence derived from Hut 6 decodes will be found in Ronald Lewin's *Ultra Goes to War*, and in R. V. Jones' *The Wizard War*.

location in case Bletchley should be bombed. Over and over again, reference to the index would be essential to proper interpretation of a decoded message.

In addition to the watch, the regular indexing operation, and the advisers, Hut 3 had three or four special units that were on the lookout for technical and background information related to such matters as new scientific developments, radar novelties, and V-weapons. Indeed, Calvocoressi's article emphasizes the important fact that proper interpretation of a newly received message usually depended in some way on associating the message content with information acquired at an earlier time—days, weeks, months, or even years before. Calvocoressi speaks of an occasion in September 1943 when, rummaging routinely through a pile of the previous day's decodes, he noticed an order that indicated that something unusual was being sent to the Mediterranean theater. The German cover name rang a bell in his mind; checking the index he was able to piece together what was happening, and concluded that a radio-controlled bomb, which had been under experimentation in the Baltic, was now moving to an operational base. Britain was not immediately helped by this knowledge; the weapon was first directed against the Italians, who were in the process of changing sides, and it was used to sink an Italian battleship a day or so later. But the event is a good example of the way in which intelligence, built up bit by bit over a considerable length of time, can reveal a picture to the analyst that could not have been generated without a good filing system.

Patient gleanings are of course part of the larger-scale, continuing work by which commanders must prepare themselves for their encounter with the enemy, using whatever information they can lay their hands on, from whatever source, that describes the enemy's intentions, the capabilities that he may bring into play or the characteristics of the terrain. With respect to the terrain, an example from World War I that links up remarkably with the distant past will show how even a most unlikely source—in this case the Bible—can produce guidance that can win an engagement. About 1050 B.C. Israel was on the verge of falling under the yoke of the Philistines when Saul collected a small standing army and began guerrilla warfare. By good tactics and surprise attacks he hunted the Philistine occupation troops out of the tribal territory. One night during World War I, almost three thousand years later, a brigade major in Allenby's army in Palestine searched his Bible by the light of a candle. His brigade had been ordered to take a village that stood on a rocky prominence on the other side of a deep valley. The name of the village, Michmash, seemed to stir a faint memory. Eventually the brigade major found the name in the First Book of Samuel, Chapter Thirteen, and read:

> And Saul, and Jonathan his son, and the people that were present with them, abode in Gibeah of Benjamin but the Philistines encamped in Michmash.

The action was described. Jonathan and his armor-bearer crossed the valley at night. They came to a path where there was a sharp rock called Bozez on one side and another sharp rock called Seneh on the other side. They followed the path, climbed up a cliff, and overpowered a Philistine outpost "within as it were an half acre of land, which a yoke of oxen might plough." The main body of the enemy were awakened by the fight, thought they were surrounded by Saul's troops, panicked, and began fighting each other in the dark. Then Saul attacked with his whole force and won a victory.

The brigade major woke the commander. Patrols were sent out. They found the narrow passage, and it led past two jagged rocks—Bozez and Seneh. Up on top, beside Michmash, they could see by moonlight a small flat field. The brigadier adopted the tactics of Jonathan and Saul. He sent one company through the narrow passage under cover of darkness. The few Turks they encountered were overpowered without a sound, the cliffs were scaled, and before daybreak the company had occupied the half acre of land. The Turks woke up and fled in disorder, thinking they were being surrounded by Allenby's army. History, through the brigade major's cleverness and the fortunate survival of a bit of military intelligence data in biblical form, had been made to repeat itself.

10

A Comedy of Errors

That we managed to stay in the game until the end of the war was made possible only by a comedy of errors committed by the Germans, who failed in many ways to do what could and should have been done to protect the security of their command communications. Their failures may perhaps be excused on the ground that they were the first to experiment with large-scale use of a machine cipher under battlefield conditions. To reduce the chance that our own people may make comparable errors in the future, it seems important to be fully aware of what went wrong with the supposedly impregnable German system based on the Enigma. Let us therefore survey the ways in which we were helped by the planners, users, and operators of the Enigma machine that was issued to the German army and air force. For this we must return to the period from the beginning of the war to the end of 1941.

The German errors were of several kinds. They stemmed from not exploring the theory of the Enigma cipher machine in sufficient depth; from weaknesses in machine operating procedures, message-handling procedures, and radio net procedures; and above all from failure to monitor all procedures. In their planning they failed to make proper use of history, and they failed to recognize new characteristics that had no historical precedent. Looking back, it is amazing that so much could hang on such slender threads.

Perhaps the most spectacular single error was the Germans' failure to think of the principles of our bombes, which made an Enigma key vulnerable to a sufficiently long crib. But this would not, by itself, have been fatal. Our bombes, if we could ever have justified their development, would have been useless without cribs, and we would never have found our cribs if the Germans had not made a number of errors in procedure. At any time during the war, enforcement of a few minor security measures could have defeated us completely.

The double encipherment of each text setting, standard practice until May 10, 1940, was a gross error. It enabled us to attack the million-odd combinations of wheel order and ring settings without bothering about the vast number of steckerboard cross-connections (more than 200 trillion of them) in which the German experts apparently had placed their trust. To exploit this weakness, all we needed was manually operated apparatus that could be developed at Bletchley Park. Once we had our Jeffreys apparatus, an Enigma key became vulnerable whenever the volume of traffic on that key produced enough female indicators. About a hundred messages would be sufficient.

This gross error was compounded by a relatively minor mistake in procedure. In any application of the Jeffreys apparatus, we had to be quite certain that all the female indicators we were using had been enciphered on the same Enigma key. We could afford no mistake in determining which sets of four discriminants indicated the same key. And, as I have explained, we were greatly assisted in this aspect of our problem by the German procedural error of using different discriminants in the preambles of the successive parts of a multi-part message, and thereby indicating to us that these particular discriminants must belong to the same set of four.

I do not know whether the Germans abandoned the double encipherment procedure because they had discovered its vulnerability. However, this early error was extremely important to us, for without it the Hut 6 balloon might never have gotten off the ground. We would have been in bad shape in four ways. First—and I cannot stress this too strongly—if, in the early days of the war, we had not been developing apparatus that would undoubtedly enable us to break Enigma keys, we would not have been able to obtain permission to build up Hut 6 quickly as an exploiting organization. We would probably not have been able to recruit the key people who made such important contributions later on. Herivel, in particular, might not have joined us, and it is by no means certain that anyone but he would have discovered the "Herivel Tip," without which we could not have used Sillies to break Enigma keys by manual methods.

Second, if before the period of the Sillies we had not been able to use the females to break the Red and Blue keys for a few months, we would not have been able to make a thorough study of the habits the Germans followed in encoding message settings. Even if we had suspected the existence of the Sillies, which sometimes enabled us to guess message settings, we might have had far less confidence in them if we had never seen the actual decoded message settings.

Third, without decodes to study, we would have been unable to establish the cribs on which the bombes depended. And fourth, without the early successes with Red and Blue keys we would not have obtained timely support for the considerable expansion of interception and bombe capabilities that proved so essential as the number of German radio nets and Enigma keys increased.

The Sillies and the Herivel tip were two gross errors in operating procedure that should have been spotted if the Germans had been monitoring their own traffic adequately. The situation that arose when the Germans stopped using double encipherment of message settings in May 1940 was quite extraordinary. Just when we appeared to have been dealt a knockout blow by a change in operating procedures, we were saved by these two types of error, perpetrated by a small number of German operators. Neither type of error would have been any help without the other, but in combination they brought our problem within the range of manual methods based on our modified Type-X cipher machines.

Thanks entirely to this combination of errors we were able to continue breaking the important Red keys with almost complete regularity. This produced valuable intelligence at the time. It also gave us the continuity that we needed to detect the cribs that we would use when the bombes came. I would assume that the intelligence derived from Hut 6 decodes during the eras of the Jeffreys apparatus, the Sillies, and the early bombes was of less operational value than that produced later in the war, as by then we and our allies had gained strength and were able to make more effective use of Hut 6 Ultra intelligence. But if the German errors had not allowed us to become well established as a valuable intelligence source by the end of 1941, we would not have been supported by the greatly increased interception, bombe, and intelligence-processing capabilities that became so necessary in the remaining years of the war, and it might have proved impossible to find ways around the new obstacles that the Germans put in our path from 1942 on. The members of the Hut 6 staff can certainly claim credit for vigilance in habit-watching and for ingenuity in exploitation. However, our success, achieved with all the flavor and excitement of a game of chance, most certainly was owed to the gifts the German operators were unknowingly giving us.

After the advent of the early bombes and the subsequent proliferation of keys in 1942, we depended above all on continuity. To find a crib we had to discover who was talking to whom, and perhaps what they were saying in a particular intercepted message. This required up-to-date knowledge of the radio traffic pattern, together with decodes of messages transmitted on recent days. In that war of rapid movement, the traffic pattern and the message content were not likely to remain unchanged for long. There were relatively quiescent periods, but we had to maintain continuity during the many periods of rapid change. It was not always easy, but we were kept alive by more German errors. I have spoken of the Germans' failure to think of the principles of the bombes, of their foolishness in double-enciphering message settings, of their use of different key discriminants in multi-part messages, and of the Sillies and the Herivel tips, for which we were indebted to the laziness of a few operators. But to succeed with cribs we needed further inadvertent assistance, and we got it. The Germans committed errors in message generation procedure, message relay discipline, and callsign protection.

Our best chance of finding cribs lay in examining the routine reports and routine orders. These might be expected to contain stereotyped addresses and signatures; they might even include usable content as well. The Germans helped us by establishing times-of-origin for such standard reports, and presenting these times in the preambles of the transmitted messages, which appeared on our teleprinted traffic registers. Thus the Hut 6 crib experts, by studying the registers and watching the charts in the Registration Room, could usually spot without difficulty the messages in which they were interested.

Since the individual Germans who generated the messages tended to be very punctilious in giving the full titles of the addressee and originator, they managed to give us cribs long enough for use in bombe programs. If message generation procedures had called for the use of coded addresses and signatures, we would have been sunk. Furthermore, we would not have been able to take advantage of routine message content if strict instructions against repetition had been issued and enforced.

With regard to message relays, it is thoroughly bad cryptographic procedure to transmit the same message in two different ciphers without radical changes. Yet the Germans committed this error too. It was often necessary for a message enciphered on one Enigma key to be retransmitted after reencipherment on another Enigma key. This was frequently done without any rearrangement of the text, with the result that, once we had broken one of the keys, we had a usable crib to the other key too.

There were two more errors. One was Parkerismus, and of all the errors that gave us our success, this must be the most flagrant. It is difficult to credit that the person or organization responsible for generating Enigma keys should have repeated entire monthly sequences of discriminants, ring settings, wheel orders, or steckers. It may seem almost equally improbable that we should have spotted this error as soon as it was committed. But both of these things actually happened.

The Germans' biggest error of all was failure to monitor all their procedures. A team of German devil's advocates, analyzing their own Enigma traffic, could have discovered seven of the twelve errors I have identified: use of different key discriminants in multipart messages, Sillies, Herivel tips, giveaways in routine messages, errors in message generation procedure and in message relay discipline, and Parkerismus—just as we discovered them. Of course such monitoring would have been a major operation, but it would have stopped us cold. Why didn't they establish it as a precaution? It may well have been considered, but if so it was considered unnecessary. My guess is that the German theorists were dazzled by the enormous number of stecker connections, and if they thought about the kinds of carelessness in operating procedures that we discovered, they must have considered them tolerable.*

It is clear that, although the designers of the Enigma with which Hut 6 had to deal may be accused of not having done a perfect job, the real culprits were the people who laid down the operating procedures, the people who were communicating with each other, and the cipher clerks who operated the machines. The machine as it was would have been impregnable if it had been used properly.

There is another side of the coin, however. While analyzing all these types of German errors and reconstructing the methods we used to exploit them, I have been struck by the fact that modifications in the design of the Enigma could have defeated us completely in spite of the procedural mistakes. We would have been in grave trouble if each wheel had had two or three turnover positions instead of one—a simple modification if it had been introduced in the planning stage. It would also have been possible, though more difficult, to have designed an Enigma-like machine with the self-encipherment feature, which would have knocked out much of our methodology, including the females. But the change that fascinates me most is a devastating one that could have been made without too much difficulty during the war.

Look again at Figure 3.6, a diagram of the electrical connections of the Enigma. This diagram shows the pairs of upper and lower sockets of the steckerboard, which were used for the variable cross-plugging. Each Enigma was supplied with double-ended connectors by means of which the upper and lower sockets corresponding to any one letter, say X, could be connected to the lower and upper sockets corresponding to any other letter, say Y, thus producing two cross-connections, X to Y and Y to X.† Suppose that, at any point during the war, the Germans had simply issued sets of single-ended connectors to replace the sets of double-ended ones. This would have meant that the upper socket corresponding to each

---

* On the other hand the Sillies and Herivel tips had virtually disappeared by the end of the war, and Parkerismus flourished only in 1942, so perhaps the Germans did monitor some of their procedures. But the real damage had been done by the end of 1941.

† As I have explained, I am not sure how many connectors were provided, but it doesn't matter. There were certainly less than thirteen, so that some pairs of upper and lower sockets were not plugged, leaving the corresponding letters steckered to themselves.

letter, say X, would be connected to the lower socket of a specified letter, say Y. The lower socket corresponding to X would also be connected to the upper socket of some specified letter, but this letter need not be Y.

All the Enigma operators would no doubt have complained bitterly, because every night they would have had to handle twice as many connectors. Herr X would have been furious, because for each key he would have had to write out twice as many letter pairings, but the output of Hut 6 Ultra would have been reduced to at best a delayed dribble, as opposed to our up-to-date flood.

The Jeffreys sheets would still have produced their drops, and the Silly menus would still have produced their output of jumbled letters, but what about the second stages of these key-breaking processes, the testing by the Machine Room people? We could no longer have deduced that if one letter, X, was steckered to another, Y, then the second letter, Y, must be steckered to the first. In both eras, Jeffreys sheets and Sillies, our ability to accomplish the actual codebreaking would have been almost, if not completely, washed out. In the bombe era, if we had gotten as far as that, the diagonal board would have been out of business, because it depended on being able to deduce B/A from A/B.

We were lucky.

11

My Tasks as A.D. (Mech)

1943 to 1945

I remarked earlier that when Travis took me away from Hut 6 and made me his Assistant Director for Mechanization, commonly abbreviated to A.D. (Mech), I became far less aware of what was happening or was likely to happen on the battlefields, and of what it might mean for Hut 6. I will, however, mention a few aspects of my A.D. (Mech) work that are in some way related either to the Hut 6 experience or to what I will say about the future. Other aspects, although of great interest to me at the time, do not belong in this book.

My first assignment was to work closely with the Canadian Colonel B. deF. Bayly, always known as Pat. Pat had been a Professor of Communications Engineering at Toronto University before the war, and was now handling a good deal of sensitive radio and cable traffic between Washington and London. He had invented a new cipher machine to handle teletype traffic, and was working to develop it further. Travis wanted me to work with Pat on the security aspects of this machine, and indeed on the whole problem of the security of government communications. He also wanted Pat, who was already in touch with the U.S. Army and Navy counterparts of Bletchley Park, to help me carry on the American–British technological liaison on Enigma and other problems, initiated by Turing and himself. Pat's headquarters were in the Rockefeller Plaza complex in New York, but he spent a good deal of time in Washington.

My appointment as A.D. (Mech) was timed to coincide with his first visit to Bletchley Park, and Travis told us to educate each other. Pat was to teach me what I needed to know about the technology of communications, and I was to introduce him to what he needed to know about Bletchley Park's problems if he was to function as an on-site liaison with our American counterparts on matters of mechanization.

Fortunately we liked each other from the start. Indeed it would have been hard not to like Pat. He was an exuberant person with infectious enthusiasm.

When Travis had introduced us, Pat's first request was to be taken to the teleprinter room. When we got there, he tapped away at one of the machines for a while and explained that he was asking his office in New York to call his wife at their nearby apartment and ask her to be at the office in half an hour. Sure enough, when we returned, she was on the line, and, since they were both proficient teletype operators, I witnessed a husband-and-wife conversation via transatlantic cable. It was my first introduction to the actual operation of teletype equipment, an area in which Pat and I would do a good deal of work later on.

Together we explored many of the technological activities that were going on at Bletchley Park, which included far more than the Hut 6 operation, to which, however, we paid special attention. After showing him all the activities in Hut 6, I asked him to give me his candid comments on the organization. His reply was that everyone he talked to seemed to know exactly what he or she was supposed to be doing, and seemed to be happy about it. This, in his view, meant that the organization must be sound.

Indeed, in building up the internal communications of Hut 6, I seem to have hit on something that is now being recognized as important in studies of business management. Not long ago General Motors, which had acquired a reputation for training particularly successful managers, wanted to find out how this had happened, so they called in Peter Drucker, one of the leading professionals in the rapidly developing field of organizational communications, to look into the matter. After many years of study, Drucker's key finding was that, no matter whom he asked, at any level from top to bottom, each employee could state his objectives clearly. This finding echoes Pat Bayly's remark to me, and I have often wondered recently whether Peter Drucker's finding could be turned around to test whether or not an organization is well prepared to act effectively in some contingency that is expected or could well arise. Such a test might be particularly valuable in the field of preparedness for military operations. If every single member of a military force, from private to commander, were asked to state exactly what his or her objectives would be in several clearly defined situations, any weaknesses in training and indoctrination would be likely to show up.

Apart from Hut 6, Pat and I concentrated on two areas of activity in which Bletchley Park depended heavily on supplies of American equipment, and on ways of achieving compatibility between British and American practice: cryptographic applications of punched-card technology, and the handling of government communications. One of our chief concerns was the interface between British long-distance radio communications using Morse code and the radio teletype preferred by the Americans. Both systems used punched paper tape for automatic transmission and reception. Pat was in some way responsible for the operation of a high-speed Morse code radio link between Canada and England that had a very attractive feature. The speed of transmission could be adjusted to the atmospheric conditions, so that at any time information could be passed at the highest rate that the conditions would allow. Pat was also deeply involved in government teletype communications via transatlantic cables.

To help the reader get back in imagination to the communications technology of those faraway days, let me describe two procedures. On a visit to the British Admiralty communications center in London, I saw messages to ships at sea being transmitted in Morse code by means of punched tape. For the larger ships, with automatic receiving equipment, the tape was run through at full speed. Then, for the smaller ships, the same tape would be run through at a speed slow enough for aural reception of the Morse code characters. This flexibility could not be matched by teletype.

The second procedure was one adopted at Bletchley Park to deal with the tremendous volume of teletype traffic that we had to receive. There was no chance at that time of acquiring enough automatic receiving equipment to handle the problem. So we had to use readily available oscillographs that recorded signal strength on a paper tape. This tape was handled by typists who were trained to recognize the thirty-two characters of the Baudot code used in tele-printer transmissions. I believe we had a large room with twenty to thirty typists handling teletype traffic in this way. Pat Bayly, and some of our American visitors too, were amazed by the efficiency of this makeshift method.

After our preliminary work at Bletchley Park I joined Bayly in America for a time. On February 17, 1944, I caught the ten A.M. train from St. Pancras, London, to Glasgow, and proceeded to Gourock, where the *Queen Mary* was at anchor in the Firth of Clyde, looking wonderful in the evening light. On the tender that was taking passengers from the Gourock dock to the *Queen Mary*, a small American boy was maintaining hotly that this *Queen Mary* was not nearly as big as the ferryboats in New York. But the boy's reaction was not as absurd as it may sound. The *Queen Mary*, though mag-nificent, was dwarfed by a background of mountains, including 2,433-foot Beinn Mhor, whereas the boy had probably seen the Staten Island Ferry coming in to the southern tip of Manhattan in a mist, which is a truly impressive sight.

When I reached America, Pat and I would spend Monday to Friday working in Washington and the weekends working in New York. Travis was no stranger there. Indeed, Bayly told me that at some earlier date Travis had visited the laboratory in the Rockefeller Plaza complex in which the new on-line cipher machine was being designed and built. As he was trying to think of an appropriate name for the machine, Travis happened to look out of the window. Below him, on a flat roof adjoining Radio City Music Hall, he saw some of the famous Rockettes sunbathing. He immediately named the machine The Rockex.

I was made to feel very much at home by the cryptanalysts and the technical staff of the U.S. Army and Navy establishments. Meeting and working with these people was a most exhilarating experience; the good feeling that developed then was one of the principal reasons for my decision to emigrate to America in 1948.

An anecdote that I heard several years later is appropriate in this context. It is said that Charles Babbage, who invented the principle of the general-purpose digital computer in the last century but could not implement the idea with the mechanical technology then avail-able, was once asked to define the difference between an Englishman and an American. "Well," said Babbage, "suppose you invent a gadget for peeling potatoes and show it to an Englishman. He will immediately declare that it couldn't possibly work. If you peel a potato in front of his eyes, he will promptly complain that the gadget is no good because it will not slice a pineapple. On the other hand," said Babbage, "if you disclose your idea to an American, he will immediately apply his energy to determining how the idea could be exploited." The story may be apocryphal, but it really does justice to my reaction to the technological discussions that I had with Americans, on this first visit and on a second one at the end of the war.

The Americans, I found, are particularly good at putting people at their ease by preliminary talk about this and that before serious matters come up for discussion. When I first arrived in Washington, before I was allowed to make contact with the cryptanalysts, I had to be introduced to some of the top brass, whose approval was needed. No doubt they would have made things easy for me by a period of general conversation, but in my case no such ice-breaking was necessary. I had only just arrived from England, where our wartime diet was simple, and I was suffering from my first exposure to American food. As soon as we reached the building, I had to ask "Where is it?" Pat talked to the dignitaries who were to receive me, and when I finally arrived everyone was grinning and there was no ice to be broken.

I was welcomed in Washington by several groups, and very much enjoyed working with them. Though I would like to mention several of them by name, I am not certain that their wartime participation in cryptanalysis is public knowledge even today. However, I am free to mention how much I appreciated my association with Frank B. Rowlett of the U.S. Army and Howard T. Engstrom of the U.S. Navy. Rowlett is mentioned in Kahn's *The Codebreakers* as one of W. F. Friedman's original team. Engstrom is mentioned in a paper on the "Colossus" by B. Randell of the University of Newcastle-upon-Tyne Computing Laboratory. My association with Engstrom continued after the war, when I joined him in Engineering Research Associates, pioneers in digital computers.

In our liaison work in Washington, Pat Bayly and I found ourselves in a curious position. The technical staffs of the U.S. Army and U.S. Navy organizations were only too willing to discuss all their activities and ideas with us. Yet they could not exchange ideas with each other directly. They would have liked to do so, but interservice friction made this virtually impossible. So Bayly and I found ourselves acting as go-betweens. It may seem foolish that we were just about the only means of contact between the leading cryptanalytic experts on Enigma of the U.S. Army and Navy, and indeed it was foolish. But it was a very real problem then, and similar problems exist today, not only in America.

When I left Hut 6 to become Bletchley Park's Assistant Director for Mechanization, I did not realize that I was moving into a corner of the strange world of Sir William Stephenson, the *Man Called Intrepid*. After reading that book, it is clear that Colonel Pat Bayly, with whom I worked so closely, was one of the highly qualified Canadians whom Stephenson recruited and put into army uniform.

In summer 1940, buses in the Bletchley Park grounds were held in readiness to transport some of us to Liverpool if the threatened German invasion of Britain should materialize. Evidently the threat was taken very seriously by Winston Churchill's government, which was determined, if need be, to carry on the war from the other side of the Atlantic. Churchill sent Stephenson to America to establish a second British "Secret Service" organization that would be able to carry on if Britain should be occupied. Stephenson established the headquarters of his British Security Coordination (BSC) in Rockefeller Plaza, New York City, and developed related activities in Canada and Bermuda.

I did not become aware of Stephenson's existence until I went to America on the *Queen Mary* in February 1944, and found myself sitting at the Captain's table with several well-known people, including a minister in the British cabinet, the head of the British National Physical Laboratory, and film producer Alexander Korda. During the voyage it became apparent that the cabinet minister resented the presence at the Captain's table of this Gordon Welchman, who didn't seem to be doing anything important. However, when we reached New York, and the passengers were awaiting instructions, we heard a broadcast announcement: "Will Mr. Alexander Korda and Mr. Gordon Welchman please disembark?" I happened to be standing near the cabinet minister and saw the look of amazement on his face!

At the time I was told that this VIP treatment was due to the fact that Stephenson, who was in charge of British Passport Control in

New York, was in control of disembarkation procedures, and that Alexander Korda was a personal friend of his. All I had discovered about Korda was that he was a man of wide interests, who got annoyed when the subject of conversation at the Captain's table kept on being brought back to film production, usually by the cabinet minister. I remember his protest to the effect that "The trouble with film business is that everyone regards it as *their* business." Not until I read *A Man Called Intrepid* did I have any inkling why Korda was crossing the Atlantic. He was one of the many brilliant people from a wide variety of professions whose talents and contacts were used by Stephenson in the many forms of special means that contributed so much to the Allied victory.

After my trip to America I became deeply involved in and intrigued by several activities that are not particularly relevant to my Hut 6 story. I was in touch with Turing's experimental work on an entirely new method of achieving security for voice transmissions, much needed at that time because voice "scramblers" attached to telephone circuits were too easily broken. I took over from Hugh Alexander the liaison between Bletchley Park and the people who were concerned with the design and use of the British Type-X cipher machine and other cryptographic systems. I also worked with Bayly, Turing, and Alexander on the design of a new rotor-type cipher machine that would handle the thirty-two characters of the Baudot code rather than the twenty-six letters of the alphabet and would be capable of both on-line and off-line operation. I established a committee that discussed desirable improvements in our various technological capabilities. Its members were Alexander; Turing, now working on his speech scrambler; Freeborn, in charge of our large punched-card installation; Morgan of the Army section; and Newman of that remarkable machine, the "Colossus."

I very much enjoyed my association with the technological aspects of the other Bletchley Park projects, though I do not feel qualified to write about them from memory. I should point out, however, that "Colossus" was a very different machine from our bombes. In Hut 6 we were concerned with messages encoded on the off-line Enigma, which handled the letters of the alphabet only. But the Germans also developed on-line cipher machines that handled the Baudot code used in teleprinter transmissions. For example, a Siemens machine, the *Geheimschreiber* or "secret writer," was used by the Germans on Swedish landlines and was broken by Arne Beurling in what David Kahn describes as "quite possibly the finest feat of cryptanalysis performed by the Swedes." A similar problem had been encountered at Bletchley Park, but in our case we were dealing with radio teletype, intercepted by Kenworthy's Foreign Office station at Knockholt. This was the problem for which Colossus was designed. I made contact with the very competent people who were handling this problem, but I was concerned primarily with what, if anything, they needed. I believe I made a very minor contribution to the way in which errors in the traffic reaching Bletchley Park could be minimized by procedures at the intercept station. But I was too occupied with other work to find out much about what had happened before I became A.D. (Mech). There were many developments of which I knew nothing until I saw Randell's paper on the Colossus, mentioned above. In particular I was not aware of the major contribution that had been made by Max Newman.

As an undergraduate at Cambridge University in 1925–28, I had been inspired by Newman's lectures on topology. Several years after the war I was intrigued by his contributions to the theory of the general-purpose digital computer. Somewhere in between I enjoyed visiting the Newmans at their charming home at Comberton, a small village between Cambridge and Great Gransden. Toward the end of the war I worked a little with Max, but I was not aware of his early work at Bletchley. According to Randell, Newman volunteered his services, joined a research section under Major G. W. (Gerry) Morgan in September 1942, and was assigned to the team known as the "Testery." This was a sub-section under Major (later Colonel) Tester that was struggling by manual means with the radio teletype problem.

I was never in close touch with Tester's work, and have forgotten the details of the problem, but Randell claims that it was Newman who had an idea for tackling the problem by mechanical means. He went to Travis, as I had done in 1939, and obtained permission to set up a new section that came to be known as the "Newmanry." He collected a team of mathematicians, and got Wynn-Williams of the Telecommunications Research Establishment to build the first machine, an electromechanical device known as Robinson. The name was from Britain's Heath Robinson, who was comparable to America's Rube Goldberg.

Randell tells us that, some time after the start of the Robinson project, T. H. Flowers—who was a high-ranking telephone engineer in the British Post Office research organization—was brought into the picture, probably at the suggestion of Turing who had worked with him on an earlier project and had acted as an advisor to the Testery. Flowers threw all his electronic expertise into solving Newman's problem with the machine that became known as Colossus. Randell claims that Flowers' achievements were a major and highly original step toward postwar electronic computers in England.*

Flowers seems to have realized at once that synchronization of punched-tape operations need not depend on the mechanical process of using sprocket holes. He used photoelectric sensing, and at that early date he had enough confidence in the reliability of switching networks based on electronic valves (tubes, in America), rather than electromagnetic relays, to risk using such techniques on a grand scale. From his prewar experience, Flowers knew that most valve failures occurred when, or shortly after, power was switched on, and he designed his equipment with this in mind. He proposed a machine using 1,500 valves, nearly twice the number used in the pioneering ACE computer built in England after the war. Randell also brings out the value of the support provided by Flowers' boss, Radley, the director of the Dollis Hill research laboratories of the British Post Office. Max Newman supported Flowers, but the initial financial support, refused by Bletchley Park, came from Radley.

Flowers and his group built the first Colossus in eleven months. Its photoelectric punched-tape reader operated at five thousand characters per second, a remarkable speed for those days. Flowers was a pioneer in the redesign of the electronic decision-making circuits that had been invented before the war. The first "string and sealing wax" (Flowers' own description) version of the Colossus was

---

* I do not agree with this claim. Flowers did a magnificent job for a specific problem. But developments in America had a much greater effect on the postwar electronic computers, in England as well as in America.

a tremendous success. Again Flowers and Radley anticipated a future demand and made preliminary arrangements for production. Around March 1944 Dollis Hill received an urgent request from Bletchley Park for more Colossi. They produced them, thanks to their preliminary arrangements, and the effective speed of sensing and processing the five-bit characters on punched paper tape was now twenty-five thousand characters per second. Moreover, as Randell points out, Flowers had introduced one of the fundamental principles of the postwar digital computer—use of a clock pulse to synchronize all the operations of his complex machine.

It seems to me that, in spite of the continuing attempts to preserve secrecy, Randell has been able to piece together a pretty reliable story of the relationship between some of the wartime developments and postwar computer technology. Because I happen to know about activities that were going on in America, as well as in England, I would differ with him on matters concerning the origin of ideas that have since proved to be important.

My last assignment as Assistant Director for Mechanization was to help Travis with his plans for the future of Government Communications Headquarters. A small planning group had been formed, but I remember very little about our deliberations, except that I very much enjoyed working with Hugh Foss. He had returned from Washington, where he had worked with U.S. Navy cryptographers on Japanese ciphers. Before the war he was one of the most brilliant of the professional cryptographers of the Government Code and Cypher School; and during the war he made a considerable contribution. I had met him in Washington on my first trip, and was told that he was highly esteemed by the Americans. I remember him as tall and thin, full of interests, and very friendly. He was certainly one of the GCHQ people to whom I felt strongly drawn, though our separate areas of work did not allow us to develop a close friendship. (Incidentally I feel that same way about Josh Cooper, who helped me so much in the early days.)

To the best of my recollection Foss alone among all the members of the planning group was seriously interested in a set of ideas that I was beginning to put forward, ideas that had largely grown out of my experience in Hut 6. As I have shown, this organization was an unusually happy one and was unusually effective. Our harmony stemmed internally from the fact that everyone was doing a clearly defined job for which he or she was well qualified. Externally we had established excellent relations with the technological organizations on which we depended for our success: the intercept stations, the engineering group that developed our bombes, and of course the intelligence people in Hut 3 who processed our output and gave us priorities.

I thought all this over for a time. As I asked myself why Hut 6 had been successful in these two important areas, and what could be done to ensure similar success in a peacetime Government Communications Headquarters, I thought I saw valuable hints for future organizations in our experience. I finally drew up my personal recommendations; these probably took the form of a memorandum to Travis. Some years ago I heard that this memorandum was still in existence and that it was still considered to be of interest. But I was told my recommendations had not been followed.

I think my main points warrant repeating here, though, for they have a bearing on the Hut 6 story. In regard to the internal organization of the future GCHQ, I believe my dominant theme was that people with particularly valuable capabilities should be able to reach the top levels both of salary and of prestige without having to perform tasks for which they might not be particularly well qualified. For example, it should be possible for the most brilliant cryptologist in the place to be drawing a higher salary than the Director without having to undertake any administrative duties whatever. His value would lie in his own research activities, and in the inspiration that he would provide for budding cryptologists. At the same time, as Hut 6 had shown, there would be a need for middlemen like myself who would not be either brilliant cryptanalysts or experienced administrators, but who would see how to combine and exploit other people's successes. Such men too should be able to reach the top levels of salary and prestige without being looked down on because they were neither brilliant technicians nor experienced administrators. And so on for the other kinds of people who would be needed. Each individual should be assigned a type of work that would make the best use of his or her talents. Furthermore, promotion and prestige in an organization such as GCHQ, I was convinced, should depend more on an individual's value to the organization than on the number of his subordinates.

In regard to relations with external technological activities, I felt very strongly, and still do, that the cryptological staff of GCHQ should not set themselves up as experts in other fields. Instead they should attempt to establish enough mutual understanding with such experts so that the cryptological, technological, and intelligence aspects of a problem can be jointly discussed by the people who know most about them. In technological matters they should encourage their counterparts to suggest ways in which further developments in technology might help. Above all, they should avoid trying to tell technologists how they must contribute to the solution of a given cryptological problem, and they should not attempt to dictate to the intelligence community.

It seemed to me that this idea of sharing initiative with the experts in other technologies was one of the basic reasons for the success of Hut 6. We owed a great deal to the contributions of Commander Ellingworth and his interceptors, and to Doc Keen and his engineers. These contributions would have been hamstrung if I, or anyone else at Bletchley Park, had told Ellingworth and Keen exactly how they were to do their jobs. Yet this is precisely the way in which some of the cryptanalytical staff at Bletchley Park would have liked to handle their relationships with other technologists. I discovered this when, as Assistant Director for Mechanization, I first came in contact with technological activities in support of cryptanalytical work on ciphers other than the Enigma. These supporting activities included both interception of radio traffic and development, manufacture, and operation of new equipment. There was also a very large installation of standard IBM and BTM tabulating equipment under a professional in the field, Freeborn of BTM.

Freeborn's operation was giving strong support to many of Bletchley Park's cryptanalytical activities. As I began to learn a little about it, however, I became convinced that the capabilities of his installation were not being used to full advantage because some of the cryptanalytical departments had a tendency to try to tell Freeborn how to use his machines in support of each problem. What I learned from Freeborn about the problems of programming a very large installation of tabulating equipment (probably one of the largest the world had known up to that time) made it plain that the cryptanalytic sections would have had better service if they had simply discussed their needs with Freeborn instead of dictating to him. This would have given him a chance to program the overall use of his equipment and staff in a way that would have been advantageous not only for each individual problem solution, but for the overall service he was providing to the Bletchley Park departments. Of course not all the cryptanalytic sections at Bletchley Park made the mistake of dictating to Freeborn. But those sections that did, and had the priority to get away with it, reduced the service that Freeborn could give to other sections, and probably made it harder for themselves as well. A visit to a very similar installation of tabulating equipment in America bore out my conclusions by presenting a very different picture. As far as I could tell, the American cryptanalysts, who made extremely good use of their installation, did not make the mistake of dictating their own ideas on how the equipment and manpower should be used.

Looking back I still feel that I was largely right in my attitude toward the use of technological developments in a specialized field such as cryptology. My views were confirmed in the mid-1950s, when I was able to compare the attitude of British government agencies toward digital computer development with that adopted by U.S. government agencies. I worked on the technological side of the fence in both countries, first in America from 1948 to 1953, and then in England from 1954 to 1956. In my experience the American agencies in those days were pleased to get ideas from computer technologists, and were ready to find funds to pay for proposed new developments that seemed to offer better ways to perform their special tasks. In England, on the other hand, the dictatorial attitude tended to prevail. One British agency told me that it would wait until commercial firms had developed computers at their own expense, at which time the agency would decide how it wanted to use the machines. In my view this difference in attitude was one of the factors that gave the American computer industry a tremendous advantage over what was a very promising young industry in England.

The connection between all this and the way in which Charles Babbage described the difference between an Englishman and an American is painfully apt. In the early 1950s I was essentially a computer applications engineer trying to suggest ways in which, with adequate funding, the new machines could be developed so that they would fulfill some useful purpose—in Babbage's example, peel a potato. In America the response of a government agency was often "Let's go." In England the answer tended to be "Don't tell me what you can do. When you have developed your gadget, I will tell you what I want it to do."

Certainly in summer 1945 at Bletchley Park in England, it had become obvious that my ideas on planning for a postwar GCHQ organization—based fundamentally on my Hut 6 experience, which stressed the benefits of cooperation and shared initiative—were not going to be accepted. By then I was a changed person. I had been thoroughly shaken out of my old academic way of life by my challenging experiences at Bletchley Park and in the United States, and it seemed impossible to return to what I had been doing before the war. Thanks to a glowing testimonial from Hugh Alexander, I was offered his old post as Director of Research in the John Lewis Partnership.

This Hugh Alexander, the British chess champion of the day, has been mentioned several times in this book. As to the John Lewis Partnership, it was at the time the largest group of department stores in England, with a staff of about ten thousand. The Chairman of the Partnership, the brilliant Spedan Lewis, always hoped that bright people from other walks of life might be valuable in his business. At the end of the war Spedan wanted Hugh to return. Hugh said, however, that he would be willing to return on one condition only: that he would be Assistant Director, with me as Director of Research. Who could ask for a more perfect testimonial? I took the position, severing my ties of some six years' standing with the British intelligence community, and entered a very different world. I had come far: from an academic life through wartime secret activity to retail business.

So ended my part in the Hut 6 story. Or did it? After all these years I find myself returning to my World War II experience in Hut 6—not to retell old war stories, but to discover how up-to-date it seems. What I learned then keeps providing fresh insights into today's problems of secure battlefield communications, on which I have been working at the MITRE Corporation. In many other ways also, the Hut 6 experience of 1939 to 1945 seems to have its meanings for the present generation. The Hut 6 story, in fact, deserves to be reviewed and related to what has happened since, and to what may happen in the future. I will continue my personal story in Part Four, in which I will make a big jump from the World War II experience to the military's communications problems of today as I see them.

12

The
Bletchley Park
Environment

In my discussions of successive phases of Hut 6 activity I have, I hope, given many glimpses of what it was like to work in England and in particular at Bletchley Park during the war years. Yet this book would be incomplete if it did not contain a few additional comments on our overall environment and on the marked contrast between the peaceful life at Bletchley and what was going on elsewhere.

Like everyone else, we had to contend with routine problems such as food rationing, gasoline rationing, the blackout, and acute shortages of important supplies. Because of the nature of our work one of the most irritating shortages was that of ordinary writing paper. We used the reverse sides of no longer needed documents. Knowing this, an American, whose office I visited in Washington, teased me by deliberately tearing up an unused sheet of scribble paper. It hurt.

The national food rationing in Britain was well organized. What food was available was evenly distributed, and price subsidies made it possible for everyone to buy what was needed. Indeed it was said that those with the lowest incomes were better fed during the war than ever before.

For some reason the traditional British fish and chips, when it was available, could be bought without coupons. I found this a great boon. Because my work schedule as head of Hut 6 was apt to be extended beyond the time for which official transport was provided for shift workers, I was allowed enough gasoline coupons for journeys to and from home—and this allowed me to drop in at the village fish and chip store quite often. Even so, because of the paper shortage, I still had to provide my own piece of newspaper for wrapping before I could take my meal home and eat it.

The scarcity of liquor was a problem, too. One could usually buy a drink of some kind in a pub, but it was hard to obtain a private supply of hard liquor. I was fortunate in that I knew the sales representative of a firm that had sold wine and liquor to Sidney Sussex College for many years before the war. He was able to send me a case of twelve bottles from time to time. Once, however, a wooden case arrived, was ceremoniously opened by Katharine and myself, and was found to be full of coal! Reporting this, I found the liquor was insured against theft, and that another case would be sent. Later we decided that we might as well use the coal in our stove, so we took it out of the case. At the bottom we discovered a bottle of rum. Evidently the thieves were only interested in the gin and whisky that had constituted the remainder of the consignment. I reported this also, but was told that the insurance claim had already gone through, and that I had gotten a free bottle of rum.

Billeting was a problem from the start, but this got worse in summer 1940 when the Phony War came to an end and section after section had to operate around the clock. The problem became even more acute with the major expansion of activities that started in 1942. The distances at which people had to be billeted increased steadily, and in the end a good many were living in Bedford, some 20 miles away. An extensive bus service had to be instituted.

The three eight-hour shifts were hard on billetor and billetee alike. Each would have to be quiet while the other needed to sleep. It was impossible to settle down to a regular routine, because the billetees would change from one shift to another. One billetor might have two billetees on different shifts. Moreover, there being a big railway junction close by, many billetors were railway workers, who also had to work on the night shift.

Nevertheless the people who came to Bletchley Park found themselves at least in pleasant rural surroundings. This, combined with the pleasant atmosphere of the whole place, contributed to our overall well-being. Moreover our minds were on our work, and we were happy to be doing something that was really helping the war effort. For the great majority of "B.P.-ites," that converted estate with its jumble of huts was a very happy place in which to live and work. As I have said, many of us look back to Bletchley Park Days as the best period of our lives, and it has been a real trial that until recently we have been unable to discuss our activities there.

As the numbers of personnel expanded, so did our social activities. We had a fine collection of people drawn from a great variety of peacetime activities, including the stage, the arts, the sciences, and the professions. In spite of the problems of shift operations and transportation to and from scattered billets, people managed to get together for many social activities, large and small.

Because my wife, Katharine, was a very good amateur singer and pianist, I was more in touch with the musical activities than with others, and we certainly had plenty of very good musicians, professional as well as amateur. Concerts were held in the cafeteria, and they were excellent. I think the musical community at Bletchley Park put on Purcell's opera *Dido and Aeneas,* and I am sure that the theatrical community put on several plays. The two groups joined forces in at least two highly successful revues. I also remember a madrigal-singing party on the bank of a canal on a perfect summer evening. When Katharine and I moved to an old house on the Watling Street in Stony Stratford, we would often fill our paneled drawing room with musicians who would perform as the spirit moved them. On these informal occasions I would carry in enormous jugs of draught beer from a pub across the road. Incidentally, our Stony Stratford house, with its Queen Anne front and a much older rear portion, was halfway between two famous pubs, the "Cock" and the "Bull." It is said that the term "cock and bull story" originated here, as someone in one pub would recount what he had heard from someone in the other pub, who had no doubt got his information from someone in the first pub, who had . . .

In the Bletchley Park grounds we had some extensively used hard tennis courts. There were a few very good players—one had been at Junior Wimbledon—and many lunch hours were enlivened by exhibition games. Shortly after VE day, matches were arranged between British and American teams at cricket and baseball. Appropriately enough the United States won the cricket and the United Kingdom won the baseball.

Most of the sections held dances at regular intervals. The Hut 6 Dance Committee was particularly efficient and the dances they arranged, about three or four times a year, were very successful. A particularly memorable dance, arranged for early June 1944, caused a nice problem in security. Leave had been canceled and everyone knew that D-Day would be at the end of May or the beginning of June, but in Hut 6 only Milner-Barry and Fletcher knew that the planned date was June 5. The dance had been planned for the evening before the D-Day operations were due to start, and Fletcher asked Milner-Barry if it was all right to proceed; no one wanted to do anything to prevent the utmost effort being available for the period of the invasion of France. After consideration Milner-Barry said yes, and how right he turned out to be. He was afraid, of course, that if he said no he would be giving a strong indication that D-Day was planned for June 5. In the event, the invasion had to be postponed twenty-four hours anyway, because of the weather, and so took place on June 6, giving ample time for the dissipation of any hangovers acquired at the dance.

From this account of some of our social activities, it will be evident that we had play as well as work. Even during working hours, the fact that most of us were involved in friendly teamwork meant that we were in an atmosphere conducive to good comradeship and the development of lasting friendships. There were many Bletchley marriages. Yet many people at Bletchley were, to say the least, disturbed by the contrast between our happy existence and what was going on elsewhere. In impotent rage we watched the flames of Coventry. We saw huge bursts of flame over London during the big air raids. Those of us who knew through the Enigma decodes what the Germans were saying about their military successes had some faint idea of what hell our troops went through, particularly in the early days when they were so completely outmatched by German preparatory planning. No wonder many of the brightest young men in Hut 6 pleaded to be allowed to get into the fighting, and were disappointed to be turned down because, knowing our secrets, they could not be permitted to come within the enemy's reach!

It was a time of strange contrasts. When our third child, Rosa-mond, was on the way Katharine left the ATS and went to live in Rippington Manor, a medieval priory in the village of Great Gransden that we had bought just before the war started. We had to share our territory with a good many Italian prisoners, who were quartered in Nissen huts in the grounds and probably worked on farms. Nevertheless the old manor, with its walled garden sloping down to what must once have been the monks' carp pond, was and still is one of the most peaceful places I have ever known.

Fortunately it was near the railway line from Bletchley to Cam-bridge. The Bletchley Park staff were encouraged to take a day off once a week, to keep fresh. Even in the war there were four or five trains each way on this line on weekdays and two on Sundays.* I could take an evening train from Bletchley and return the next evening or the following morning. I left a bicycle at the nearest station, Gamblingay, and as I came down the hill into Great Gransden I would often hear the old carillon in the church tower playing one of its tunes. The whole atmosphere seemed so peaceful and so remote from what we were thinking about at Bletchley. For others, however, the contrast between the peace of the village and their war work was far greater. Just a few miles away was an airfield from which bomber crews would fly at night into the hell of anti-aircraft fire over Germany.

I never had to endure one of those nights in London during the period of heavy bombing, when the underground stations were used as sleeping quarters. But toward the end of the war, after the V-bombs had been introduced, I had to go to London several times. I was full of admiration for the way people just carried on. Once, having spent the morning in the communications room at the Ad-miralty, I went into a pub in Whitehall for a sandwich lunch. The drone of a V-1 flying bomb was heard through the open door to the street, but nobody seemed to take any notice, and I followed suit. On another occasion I was at a meeting in Mayfair when a V-1 was heard; the only reaction was that "perhaps we had better move a little further away from the window."

The striking contrast between our life in Bletchley Park and that of Londoners was brought home to me after the war when I joined

* There are none today.

the John Lewis Partnership and talked with Michael Watkins, the man who had run the business throughout the war. By keeping the Partnership operating in spite of bomb damage, Watkins performed a valuable wartime service. Moreover he was, I believe, the principal originator and organizer of the "utility goods" scheme under which the manufacturers of a variety of merchandise, including clothes, furniture, and china, agreed to produce only a limited number of designs. The selected designs were good, and the scheme enabled people to meet their essential needs at the lowest possible prices while releasing a considerable part of the manufacturing labor force for other work.

Discussing our respective experiences, Michael Watkins and I found many differences. I lived in quiet surroundings that were never subjected to anything more than trivial accidental bombing. (I do not remember hearing of anyone's being hurt.) When I had to travel any distance on business, I was provided with a car and a female chauffeur. Because of the importance of my work I was excused from Home Guard duty. Watkins, though a man of some prominence doing an important, exacting job, was shown no such consideration. He lived at Cookham on the Thames, in normal times a railway journey of about an hour from London. At the end of each day's work at his office in Cavendish Square near Oxford Circus, he had to struggle across London to Paddington Station in the hope that a train would take him home. The journey was often nightmarish, delayed either by bomb damage or by actual bombing attacks. Yet when he got home to Cookham he would do his full share of Home Guard duty.

Certainly our work at Bletchley Park was important. Still, our lives were very easy in comparison with those of civilians like Watkins who were doing important jobs under fire. Furthermore, no matter how hard some of us may have worked, we made no sacrifices that could remotely be compared to those made by the men who were doing the actual fighting on the land, on the sea, and in the air.

In my own case exemption from military service involved a curious sequence of events. At the beginning of the war, when I became a temporary civil servant in a branch of the British Foreign Office, I was thirty-three years old. In due course my age group was called up, and I received a notice telling me to report to a unit of the Royal Artillery somewhere in the north of England. I took the notice to the Foreign Office administrative people. They assured me that they would handle the matter, and that I was to do nothing.

A little later I received a polite letter from the Colonel of my artillery unit, saying that there was no doubt a good reason for my nonappearance, but would I please report at once. I took this letter also to the administrative office. Again I was told that the Foreign Office would handle the matter.

The next development was a phone call to my mother-in-law, from her brother, Ned, who as chance would have it was Chief Constable of Buckinghamshire, the county in which I was living. He had a warrant for my arrest.

This raised an intriguing point. Bletchley Park was enclosed by a high fence and was under military guard. Its cafeteria was open night and day, and sleeping accommodation was available. Suppose I had kept on living and working there and never emerged? I suspect the police might have had some difficulty in arresting me. As it turned out, however, I did not need to resort to any such dramatic delaying action. The Foreign Office and Army Administrators finally resolved the matter.

One problem remained. Army regulations included no means of simply letting go of a man who had been called up but had not enlisted. The regular discharge procedure applied only to those who had gone through the enlistment process. It developed that, in order to sever my relationship with the Gunners, I would first have to enlist. I had to report at a Royal Artillery establishment, and it was arranged that I should go to the nearest one, which was a few miles south of Bletchley Park. I was given a gasoline allowance and drove my own car. The "establishment" turned out to be a small office presided over by a sergeant.

The sergeant had received detailed instructions, and after filling in a few forms, he shook me by the hand, congratulated me on being a Gunner, and said that he would arrange for me to be discharged some other day. When I explained that my office did not want me to take time off for a second trip, he said that he could not discharge me at once because a medical examination was needed and the doctor would be at lunch.

I had to get back to Bletchley as soon as possible, so I discovered where the doctor lived, dashed round and just caught him before he went to lunch. A few minutes later I had whatever medical certificates were necessary for my discharge, only to find that the sergeant had gone to lunch. I found him in the nearest pub and persuaded him to come back to his office. After filling out a few more forms, he told me that I was now a civilian again. My length of military service was almost exactly twenty minutes. Then, having arranged my discharge, the sergeant gave me a few appropriate papers, one of which I treasured for many years. It urged me to join the Home Guard, where my experience in the Army would be extremely valuable.

So much for the lighter side of my wartime experience. In the last part of my book I will be talking very seriously about the dangers that we face today. In my view we are in a real mess. Something needs to be done urgently if what we value most is to survive.

PART
FOUR

Today

13

Danger Signals

INTRODUCTION

More than thirty-five years have passed since victory in Europe in summer 1945. For me personally it has been a long and roundabout journey from my last task at Bletchley to my recent activities. At the end of the war, Bletchley Park was a flourishing and highly successful activity. It had been given all the funding needed for its many wartime objectives. And the planning problem with which Travis asked me to help in 1945 was to keep the organization alive and effective in peacetime, when objectives would be of less obvious importance and funding would be hard to come by.

At that time we and our British allies* had a long, bitter, and difficult war behind us, its lessons fresh in our memories. We had learned what did and did not work in conditions of combat. Some important aspects of the war had to be kept secret, but on the whole we were in reasonably good form to think about ways to keep our wartime capabilities alive and effective in peacetime. In the thirty-five years since, however, we have forgotten much—and we have gained little (if any) new experience to improve our understanding of what war could demand of us. (The actions in Korea and Viet-

---

* Along the way from 1945 to 1981 I became an American citizen. So, instead of talking about "we" (the British) and the Americans, I will now talk about "we" (the Americans) and the British.

nam tended to teach us how war ought not to be fought—and have left us divided and uncertain about our goals.) We are far less able than in 1945 to think positively about the capabilities for war that we should be developing. Unpreparedness now is likely to be more disastrous for us than it has ever been in the past.

This issue did not directly concern me until I joined the MITRE Corporation in 1962. My first postwar job was in the world of department stores—a far cry from Bletchley activities. In 1948 I emigrated to America and became involved in computers and information technology. When I joined MITRE, however, I embarked on a series of military studies that, over eighteen years, deepened my understanding of the defense problems that face us, and gave me increasingly grave concern about our unreadiness to cope with them.

My knowledge of war was derived from my Bletchley Park experiences. Later, I studied shortcomings in the communications of the North American Air Defense Command (NORAD), which at that time were quite incapable of surviving an attack by nuclear missiles. Next I worked on capabilities for fighting limited wars outside Europe with conventional (nonnuclear) weapons; this phase led to the concept of a battlefield communications system that would meet the requirements of combat forces and their commanders. I switched in 1971 to a series of studies of the threat to NATO posed by the conventional forces of the Warsaw Pact. Finally, in 1978, I came back to communications, working on security measures for a revolutionary system of tactical communications that was being developed with support from the U.S. Army, Navy, and Air Force.

These assignments made me an informed, and I am afraid a rather disillusioned, student of several vital aspects of our military posture. It has convinced me that our national defense is in shockingly bad shape. We are not well prepared as a nation to fight any kind of war. We are utterly unready to deal with the nonmilitary threats with which we may be faced, though these may be just as significant as the military dangers, if not more so. We have failed to learn from history, we have failed to recognize the implications of change, and we have been doing a very poor job of anticipating the future. The handwriting on the wall is clear. It spells DANGER.

In this part of my book I will draw on my experiences at Bletchley Park and at MITRE to talk about what is wrong today and what I believe needs to be done. My experience does not cover every defense problem, but it is broad enough to demonstrate that we are in a very serious predicament. In one area, that of communications security, I am in a unique position. Because I was in on the beginnings of Hut 6, I know more than anyone else about why the security of the German Enigma traffic broke down. Then, in 1978, 1979, and 1980, I learned a good deal about the as-yet-unsolved problems of providing both security and flexibility for the future battlefield communications capabilities that we so badly need. Thus I can see this crucial problem, as it were, from both sides.

I am convinced that our tactical communications constitute a glaring gap in our national defenses. In our craze for technological achievement in weapons systems we have put the cart before the horse.

With this in mind I shall have good deal to say about bridges between the past and the future, about changes in military doctrine that may be on the way, about the type of battlefield communications we need, and finally about matters of secrecy, security, and survival. I will start with a review of the danger signals I have seen during the last nineteen years.

NORAD

My first NORAD assignment at MITRE in 1962 revealed several dangers. A system designed for one particular threat had not been modified when that threat subsequently changed. Far too little attention had been given to the survivability of the communications on which system performance was entirely dependent. Also, system planning had been compartmentalized, and there was a marked lack of overall coordination based on total grasp of the problems involved. The necessary collaboration among all fields of expertise that could contribute to a solution had not been achieved. At first we could not make contact with NORAD's operational commanders, to learn the true nature of their problem. And even at the end of our study, the rigidity of military procedures still prevented direct contact with the NORAD high command. On balance, however, this first exposure of our failures in military planning did not disturb me nearly as much as my later studies. When we were through with the NORAD study, it did at least appear that remedial measures were under consideration.*

Our first large-scale computerized defense system was known as SAGE, for Semi-Automatic Ground Environment. It was aimed at the defense of the United States and Canada against the threat of Soviet bombers carrying nuclear weapons. The NORAD system was based on regional commands, each of which had a number of SAGE control centers whose radar and computer equipment were to follow the tracks of enemy bombers and be able to direct attacks on them by our intercept aircraft. Early warning of impending attacks by enemy bomber formations was to be provided by a variety of forward radar installations. A teletype network, known as SURTAC (for Surveillance and Tactical), allowed formatted digital messages to be passed among the forward facilities, the control centers, the regional command posts, and the headquarters of NORAD's Commander in Chief, CINCNORAD, at Colorado Springs.

By 1962 the threat of attack by nuclear-armed ballistic missiles had become a reality, and a Ballistic Missile Early Warning System (BMEWS) had been put into operation. It was thought that an attack by Soviet bombers would be preceded by a missile attack, the first salvo of which could well knock out CINCNORAD's headquarters.† When I came into the picture, plans were going ahead for a "hardened" underground facility for CINCNORAD. The Canadians had already constructed an underground headquarters for the North Eastern Region, for which they were responsible. A system was sought that would allow the hardened Canadian facility to act as an Alternate Command Post (ALCOP) if CINCNORAD's headquarters became inoperative. MITRE was asked to establish Project SNOCAP (Survivable NORAD Capability) to look into

---

* I hope the reader will pardon the acronyms and jargon that follow. These are the terms our military establishment uses to discuss its systems and its organization. Once one gets acclimatized to them, they are not all that bad. Any attempt to translate into ordinary language might well be even more confusing.

† Indeed all the SAGE facilities in the United States were "soft," or vulnerable to nuclear missile attack.

the matter. At first I was in charge of the communications aspects of the study; later I became project leader.

It was worrying to find that little attention had been paid to the survivability of the communications on which everything depended. If one of the BMEWS sites had detected a missile attack, it would have been extremely important to get the warning to the national command and to the strategic air command immediately. Yet these commands could only get such warning from CINCNORAD (which might be knocked out by the first strike), and each BMEWS site had only one primary communications channel to CINCNORAD, a channel that frequently failed.*

The SURTAC teletype circuit network, leased from public utilities, ran through areas that could be regarded as prime targets for a missile attack. In fact the communications network on which the SAGE system depended could well have been put out of action by missiles before the Soviet bombers arrived. Working closely with a Canadian communications engineer, we prepared a plan that would reroute teletype circuits to avoid prime target areas and provide alternate routing between any two terminals. It was disturbing that no such steps had been taken before our study.

NORAD's telephone circuits were also leased from public utilities, but we soon found that the NORAD people had done far less to ensure survivability under nuclear attack than had the AT&T planners of the public telephone system, who were doing a very good job. Each of the many agencies and organizations involved in the operations at NORAD headquarters had been demanding its own separate dedicated telephone lines, which made it prohibitively expensive to provide redundancy. It was gradually being accepted that far greater survivability, and equally good service, could be obtained by a common-user voice communications

---

* This was a high-capacity channel designed to carry raw data for processing by a computer at Colorado Springs, even though each BMEWS site had its own computer, capable of processing the raw data. When the primary channel failed, the warning to CINCNORAD, derived in that case of necessity from the BMEWS site computer, would be sent by voice. If voice communications failed, the warning could be sent by teletype. In fact the need could have been met at far less cost by teletype circuits with switches to carry the warnings directly to all the places where they were urgently needed, including the Canadian ALCOP we were studying. Moreover, because teletype circuits are relatively inexpensive, it would have been possible to provide redundant circuits and switches that could come into operation if and when the normal routing of messages failed.

system employing enough circuits and switches to provide many alternative paths between any two terminals. This was the birth of the present AUTOVON (Automatic Voice Network) system in the CONUS (continental United States). Still, however, system design had not taken account of the threat of sabotage. At some switching centers and relay stations military circuits were on the same racks as commercial circuits. The military circuits were colored red, to facilitate restoral, but this also was extremely helpful to any potential saboteur, who would at once see which wires to cut!

By the late 1970s CONUS AUTOVON, linked to the AT&T system, had nearly seventy switching centers and was thought to possess considerable survivability. But technicians who worked for several years on the installation of the similar European AUTOVON system for NATO stated categorically that this communications network could not survive a massive attack by conventional Warsaw Pact forces—which would undoubtedly make use of sabotage. Thus, some fifteen years after the SNOCAP period, a system designed to serve U.S. forces in Europe and to connect them with the CONUS was not survivable. Furthermore it provided little traffic capacity. So little, in fact, that a study concluded that if a random 90 percent of the West German commercial toll network were knocked out, it would still work better than a fully operational AUTOVON in the same area.

As I have noted, in the first phase of SNOCAP, we could not make contact with NORAD's operational commanders. Instead we had to accept the description of the ALCOP problem given us by a few staff officers who did their best to guess what their chief would think. In their anxiety not to do anything of which he might disapprove, they gave us rigid guidelines that proved to be absurd. Largely because some of the stated requirements were unrealistic, we designed a thoroughly bad system. Fortunately General Muehleisen, a NORAD regional commander who had been acting as Alternate CINCNORAD for some time and had thought deeply about his task, got wind of our proposed system. He made a personal trip to Colorado Springs and convinced CINCNORAD that the restrictive requirements must be removed and the system redesigned.

At that point I became project leader. I was allowed to take my whole group for a week to General Muehleisen's regional command center, where we made contact with all sections of his staff. The general put on an exercise for our benefit. I myself was able to spend a lot of time with his deputy, learning about the functions of an operational commander. For this was a real live situation: Every day there would be tracks of unidentified aircraft to investigate; many of them would be tracks of Soviet planes. Continual vigilance was needed.

We spent a week at the hardened regional command center in Canada, where the commander and his staff were willing to discuss what would be involved in taking on ALCOP duties as well as those of a regional command post. Armed with a far better grasp of the problem, we were then able to come up with a workable system. When this was presented to CINCNORAD, we were told that "never had so many generals agreed to anything so quickly."

This of course was gratifying. However, our proposed system was not implemented—for a variety of reasons, some good, some bad. The political implications of putting the only survivable NORAD command center in Canada were obviously a serious concern, and may well have been the basic cause of the rejection of our proposals.

I personally had learned a great deal, however. It had been an unusual opportunity to discuss problems with operational commanders and their immediate staff. But the handling of our presentation to CINCNORAD revealed a serious malaise of our peacetime military establishment. CINCNORAD was not prepared to listen to a presentation by a civilian. Our proposals had to be presented to him by someone wearing the uniform of an officer in the U.S. Air Force. In our case fortunately this did not matter, because the Air Force officer supervising Project SNOCAP had worked closely with us, had contributed a great deal, and was well able to present our ideas. But in principle it was bad. It was an example of a serious fault of peacetime military establishments, which tend to be "role oriented" rather than "task oriented." They are more interested in having things done in accordance with established procedures than they are in the successful accomplishment of a task.

LIMITED WAR ENVIRONMENTS

Early in 1964 I was transferred to a department that was studying air operations on a conventional battlefield outside Europe. I was to study offensive missions against ground targets. My department head was seriously concerned that everyone seemed to be thinking about what happened at command posts. There was too much talk of using computers. I was asked to concentrate on what was involved in the actual attack. I soon ran into more danger signals. The higher levels of our military establishment were paying far too little attention to the individual characteristics of the different types of limited war in which we might become engaged. Imaginative thinking was suggesting changes, but the establishment was not responding.

In the early 1960s, for example, during John F. Kennedy's presidency and for some time after his assassination in November 1963, realistic consideration was being given, at the national policy-making level, to three broad issues. First was the need to identify the different kinds of war in which U.S. forces might have to fight. Next, the need for military policies, procedures, a procurement appropriate to all the different situations had somehow to be met. Lastly, special emphasis had to be placed on what the Communists call "wars of liberation," which they had selected as their primary method of attack on the free world. But this period of realistic consideration, although it produced some very good thinking, did not lead to appropriate action. Established military doctrine was unaffected, as were the aims of military procurement.

When, in early 1964, I was starting to think about air attacks on ground targets, I was also asked to prepare an analysis of future limited war environments, which I completed in summer 1964. I found plenty of help in earlier studies, and plenty to worry about. In 1957, for instance, the *Military Review* had published two articles on "readiness for the little war" by a group of eight U.S. Army officers, all of whom were members of the faculty of the U.S. Army Command and General Staff College. They concluded that:

> The United States does not have a highly mobile military force in being that gives us the capability of immediately retaliating against small-scale Communist aggressions on a graduated retaliatory basis. Small aggressions do not warrant big bombs.

They recognized that the mobile force would require a political as well as a military capability; it would include and utilize the capabilities of all services; and it would be capable of participating in, as well as augmenting, indigenous capabilities in the conduct of unconventional warfare.

Another example of the increasing concern about the rigidity of military thinking was an article in the *Military Review* of May 1960 entitled "Dual Strategy for Limited War," which stated:

> Americans should study the Communist campaign which was waged in the Philippines because it may be a harbinger of a type of warfare to come, a classic example of one type of limited war. In addition it should be studied because Magsaysay won his war and thus became the only democratic leader in Asia, and one of the few in the world, who for all intents and purposes completely defeated an overt Communist armed rebellion in his country.

Today, who remembers Magsaysay and his "dual strategy," which was essentially a blending of military actions with political reform and aid for the people? Yet in 1964 this chapter of history seemed to me to be of great importance. Greater attention to it might have made a big difference in Vietnam.

Another source I found helpful was Seymour Deitchman's *Limited War and American Defense Policy*. Deitchman points out that terrain and climate will govern both the mobility of the ground forces and the size of each ground force that can operate as a coherent unit. From his geographical studies Deitchman deduces that, outside the highly developed areas of the world, wars will be fought by armies organized in relatively small units. In underdeveloped areas, unconventional warfare is likely to be an important, if not a dominating, element in any war. Indeed in the early 1960s there was much talk of counterinsurgency, or COIN.

Using ideas from such sources as these I did my analysis in what seemed a very obvious and straightforward manner. With help from the Foreign Technology group in the Electronic Systems Division of the U.S. Air Force Systems Command, I listed the most probable trouble spots around the world. For each of them I reviewed:

Political-military considerations
Types of warfare and terrain
Enemy capabilities
Air mission requirements
Principal capability developments needed

The analysis was accepted and used immediately in an Air Force advanced planning document called, I believe, "The Five-Year Plan, 1964." It was also used in a "master plan" for an advanced tactical air control capability, prepared in MITRE and published in April 1966. It was used again in the report of a Vietnam study group with which I became involved, probably in late 1966. In fact my analysis, completed in a few months by a newcomer to tactical advanced planning, seems to have been treated for some years as an authoritative statement on limited war environments! I find this far more worrying than flattering. Why had no such document been prepared before 1964? Why was it not revised for the master plan and the Vietnam study?

One can only conclude that there was no serious Air Force interest in the characteristics of possible future wars. This is a real danger signal. How can we hope to be well prepared if we are not willing to study what we should be prepared for? Moreover, my analysis, though derived entirely from open literature, was classified. Other students of limited war would thus have difficulty getting access to it. They might not even hear about it.

PRESIDENT KENNEDY'S CALL

In September 1964 I attended a course at the Air Ground Operations School at Eglin Air Force Base in Florida. The AGOS course was concerned with the system that had been designed to control direct air support to ground forces in battle. That system seemed to me unnecessarily clumsy and complicated. I had the feeling that the officers in charge of the course felt so too, and that something better was needed.

For me the most interesting part of the AGOS course was a visit to the Special Air Warfare Center (SAWC), where the 1st Air Commando Wing had been activated on June 1, 1963. This was part of President Kennedy's response to his meeting with Khrushchev in May 1961, in which the latter predicted the triumph of Communism in the new and less developed countries as a result of wars of liberation supported by the Kremlin. In a special message to Congress on May 25, 1961, the President said that our special forces and unconventional warfare units would be increased and reoriented. Throughout the services new emphasis was to be placed on special skills needed to provide efforts short of open conflict but necessary to counter Communist-sponsored guerrillas or insurgents. In the same special message Kennedy stated that assassins had taken the lives of four thousand civil officers in the last twelve months in South Vietnam. The war of liberation in that country was already in full swing.

Working closely with U.S. Army Special Forces teams, the air commandos of 1964 were trying to help the South Vietnamese fight their own war. I was able to talk with commandos who had been working with the South Vietnamese in those early days. The Commander at SAWC (General Pritchard, I believe) was frustrated because he could not persuade the authorities to put money into production of new simple aircraft. Even the OV-10, originally designed for counterinsurgency, was, in his opinion, far too complicated for use by not-very-well-trained Vietnamese pilots.

Another worrying aspect of that day at SAWC was the antagonism of an Army officer on the AGOS course to the air commandos. He considered that they were doing a job that should be done by the Army Special Forces. At the same time he did not seem to be happy about having Special Forces in the Army. He was a tank man, and may have thought that fighting without tanks is for the birds. Anyway, this sign of friction between branches of the service was disturbing. Perhaps the effect of President Kennedy's May 1961 call to Congress for a revised doctrine was already beginning to fade; later on it disappeared completely.

In March 1965 I visited R. F. Futrell, Air Force Historian at the Aerospace Studies Institute, Air University, Maxwell AFB. He had written *The United States Air Force in Korea*, an extremely valuable book. I found that there had been a strong response to President Kennedy's call for new doctrine to meet changing threats. In 1962 the Concepts Division had started a study program to examine the role of airpower in guerrilla warfare. Lessons were to be drawn from the many small wars that had been fought since World War II. I talked to a colonel who had just completed the seventh study in the series, "Guerrilla Warfare and Airpower in Algeria." This was particularly interesting because it described a highly effective organization of joint air/ground operations, supported by an extremely effective method of achieving rapid information exchange with small units scattered all over the country.

I also talked to an officer who was completing a year's research on the problem I was studying at the time—air attacks on ground targets in various types of warfare. We had both concluded that Air Force doctrine on the matter was far too rigid. Futrell helped me by criticizing my draft report on the subject and allowing me to browse through official reports from Vietnam. He also lent me a copy of a valuable but hard-to-get analysis of U.S. Tactical Air Force operations in Europe. Many of its recommendations have been ignored, though they were made by the commanders who had actually carried out the air operations in support of ground forces.

The activities of the air commandos in Vietnam were being taken very seriously at the Air University. A special course was being given for Air Force personnel assigned to duty there. The course was described to me and I thought it was absolutely first-rate. At the time of my visit the Aerospace Studies Institute was, I believe, regarded as a source of new doctrinal ideas. It seemed well able to exercise this function. However, as I understand it, the establishment in Washington disapproved of this arrangement and transferred all responsibility for doctrinal studies to Air Force headquarters in Washington. The promising attempt to modify doctrine in the light of innovative thinking and imaginative pictures of different types of future wars was killed.

In the early days of Vietnam few people were aware of what was going on, so the story is obscure and difficult to trace. But it needs to be dug out, because it illustrates a danger that we face today. People have a tendency to filter out what they do not want to hear. Before World War II, an appeasement-minded government in England filtered out the information on Hitler's Germany that they were receiving from their Secret Service. The British, French, and Americans took no notice of the German theory of tank warfare that was published in open literature by a German, Max Werner, in 1938. During the Korean War General MacArthur chose to ignore Chinese public statements of their intention to intervene, and received a rude shock, costly in American lives, when Chinese General Lin Piao sprang his trap. In the early days of North Vietnam's subversive activities in South Vietnam, we did not listen to clear evidence of what was going on.

In 1961 General Vo Nguyen Giap, the North Vietnamese commander, published his book *The People's War—The People's Army*. He explained his concept, largely taken from Mao Tse-tung, of the three phases of a war of liberation: guerrilla warfare, mobile warfare, and the final offensive.

The preliminary phase would start at the village level with the arrival of specially trained commissars from North Vietnam. In each village the commissars would convince the population that their troubles were due to their own government. They would wait until the assent of the majority of the village inhabitants had been won. Then the commissars would ask the people of the village to indicate the traitors and government agents among them. Assassination committees would be entrusted with carrying out executions. Guerrillas would be recruited. The village would become a paramilitary base, capable of bringing effective aid to regular units in the later phases of the war.* General Giap even explained a weakness of this kind of war: that, if the mobile stage does not continually expand, it will dwindle back to guerrilla warfare, which will ultimately peter out.

President Kennedy was doing his best to exploit the weakness that Giap himself had pointed out in his concept of the "people's war." The President wanted to help the South Vietnamese prevent expansion of mobile warfare, so that operations would indeed dwindle back to guerrilla warfare and peter out. But how many people know about this early phase of U.S. involvement in Vietnam? It never hit the news because, after President Kennedy's death, "tradition" became dominant. The regular troops of North Vietnam came into the picture, as did those of the U.S. Army. The whole nature of the war changed, and unfortunately it is this second phase that most of us remember.

The history of the area was distorted in the public mind, and not insignificantly by the leadership in Hanoi, which was deliberately trying to attack the minds of the American people—with considerable success. A strong feeling grew up, particularly among young Americans, that our involvement itself, rather than its manner, was

---

* The details of the preliminary phase were published in the *New York Times*, August 16, 1964, by Max Clos, a correspondent for *Le Figaro*, under the title "The Strategist Behind the Vietcong."

wrong, and that North Vietnam had right on its side. In recent years the same young people who were influenced by this propaganda have been coming round to the opinion that the North Vietnamese are a ruthless nation, whose expansionist ambitions and general callousness should not be condoned.

The true story of the earlier history of South Vietnam (which was once the independent country of Champa), North Vietnam, Laos, and Cambodia, though fascinating, is hardly a subject for discussion here. But it is worth making the point that North Vietnam's deliberate influence on the minds of the American people is a type of clandestine warfare against which we should be continually on guard.

MASTER PLAN OF 1966 AND VIETNAM STUDY

I mentioned that my 1964 analysis of limited war was used in a "master plan" for an advanced air control capability completed at MITRE in April 1966. My own contribution was a proposal to improve our ability to attack ground targets by providing additional capabilities for an Airborne Forward Air Controller (AFAC). I want to say a little about this, because it brought me in touch with a vivid example of faults in our methods of military procurement for changing or newly perceived needs. Innovative thinking, though accepted in the initial phase, was frustrated in the end by lack of continuity in the planning process.

In October 1965 a MITRE group produced a working paper describing a new concept known then as the Airborne Electronic Grid and Information System (AEGIS). Using available technology, the system would enable some 120 aircraft operating in a battle zone to determine their positions in a common grid, to report their positions to a ground-based command center, and to receive commands from that center. The position reports were to take the form of short coded digital messages. They would be repeated in a broadcast on a single frequency so that each subscribing aircraft would receive all of them. Electronic equipment in the aircraft would present the pilot with a screen display showing his own position and the relative positions of other aircraft.

I had been studying the highly successful use of AFACs in Korea. Each AFAC, working in close touch with ground units, would spot enemy targets and control air attacks on them. It occurred to me that, with the new capability of laser ranging, an AFAC pilot could determine the position of a target and report it, together with his own position, by means of AEGIS. The target location would thus appear on the screen display of an attacking pilot, helping him to find it. Working with a MITRE engineer, Lou Williams, I developed a proposal for an Airborne Tactical Air Support Team (ATAST) that used a small two-seater aircraft.

Remember that during the early part of the Korean War and again in South Vietnam, a small low-flying aircraft could fly over enemy territory without getting shot down. Not so today. In Vietnam, in the early days, an AFAC could fly slowly at low altitude over the same bit of territory day after day and so be able to spot subtle changes that would indicate the presence of a small enemy unit. But, because the AFAC would be seen flying nearby, the enemy unit might guess that it had been spotted. Later in the war the AFAC, in order to survive, had to fly at much higher altitudes at much higher speeds. I am told by a pilot that, after flying over the same territory for about a month, an AFAC could still spot small targets on the ground. Moreover, because he would be observing a much wider area and would appear only as a speck in the sky, an enemy ground unit would be far less likely to know that it had been observed.

Not long after the completion of the master plan I became involved in a Vietnam study group, formed to look for ways of improving capabilities in South Vietnam. At that time we were still trying to support the South Vietnamese in something like Magsaysay's "dual strategy," combining military and political action. I proposed, in some detail, a countrywide organization of two-man airborne teams, somewhat similar to the ATAST, that would act as observers and controllers, keeping in close touch with the civilian administration as well as with military forces. Possibly as a result of this, Lou Williams and I were asked to spend a day at the Aeronautical Systems Division (ASD) of the Air Force Systems Command, where a group had been convened to study means of improving capabilities for nighttime operations in South Vietnam. It was part of a project called SHEDLIGHT. We found that the members of the group were all promoting weapons systems and other capabilities already under development. None of them seemed to have thought about the special problems of the small-scale dispersed operations that characterized the situation in South Vietnam at that time. Williams and I argued that in this peculiar environment our capabilities had to be coordinated by something like the well-known AFAC, but with added capabilities for nighttime operations.

After many hours of argument (the discussion lasted well into the night), the Air Force officer in charge of the study saw our point and agreed with us. He went to a blackboard and showed, from his practical knowledge, how our ideas could be improved. We had been proposing that an AFAC, having spotted a target, would control an attack by giving directions over voice radio. The experienced officer suggested that the AFAC, having spotted a target, should fly on as if nothing had happened. Then, as the attacking aircraft approached, he would return to the scene and head for the target he had spotted. The navigation problem of the attacking aircraft would be reduced to getting on the AFAC's tail and following him—a beautifully simple and practical scheme.

The outcome of that discussion was that the need for an AFAC with nighttime capabilities (dubbed a NIFAC) was included in the study group's recommendations. The OV-10 was selected for the mission: Its manufacturers understood the objectives and were enthusiastic about them. The clear view from the rear door of the OV-10 offered additional advantages for unconventional warfare that I need not go into here.

Now comes the sad part. The development of NIFAC capabilities was approved, but direction of the development was entrusted to a completely new group of people, none of whom had had any contact with the earlier study group. I attended one of their meetings, probably the first, with representatives from the manufacturers of the OV-10. I have seldom been so discouraged. The group seemed completely incapable of understanding the purpose of the project. They had closed minds. All they could think about was putting weapons systems on the OV-10. I heard afterward that they had added so much weight that the aircraft could barely get off the ground to perform its NIFAC mission.

CHANGE OF FOCUS TO EUROPE

After its escalation, the Vietnam War dragged on into the early 1970s. Before it was over, our military thinking was reacting to a major change in NATO policy, which is still, to a surprising degree, unknown to the general public, a fact that I regard as a danger signal. In January 1968 the NATO policy of "flexible response" replaced the "trip wire" nuclear strategy. Under the earlier strategy any incursion of Warsaw Pact forces into West Germany would have triggered an immediate full-scale nuclear response. Under the new policy of flexible response, a conventional attack by Warsaw Pact forces would be met by a conventional response until things got out of hand, at which time NATO would use tactical nuclear weapons in a "flexible" manner. This new policy insisted on the concept of "forward defense," which meant essentially that every inch of West German territory must be defended.

The focus of our military thinking switched to this new problem of high-intensity conventional war in Europe—to the total exclusion of limited war elsewhere. The thinking of the 1960s was forgotten—a pity, since some of it was very good and is still applicable to non-European threats that we may have to face in the future.

As a result of this change of focus I was asked, early in 1972, to study the Soviet capabilities for military operations in and around Europe. I found that, as early as 1953, R. L. Garthoff's *Soviet Military Doctrine* had made it evident that U.S. and Soviet views on fundamental military problems were widely different. Eighteen years later, in 1971, the Royal United Services Institute published a defense study, *Soviet Military Power*, by Professor John Erickson of the University of Edinburgh. It was a study in depth, based on a large number of Warsaw Pact sources. The reshaping of the Soviet military command between 1965 and 1970 was analyzed and many inferences were drawn from Soviet military training and from the large-scale exercises that had been carried out in the 1960s. Of considerable importance was the "Shield-72" exercise of mid-September 1972, discussed by Erickson in the December 1972 issue of the *RUSI Journal*. (Remarkably quick reaction.) In this exercise several new trends appeared. It was becoming increasingly evident that Warsaw Pact forces were being structured to conduct a "lightning war" with little capability for protracted conflict. Clearly NATO needed a "lightning response" capability well tuned to what was known about traditional Soviet methods of fighting and about the latest thinking of their military planners. NATO's "lightning response" needed a defense against enemy ground forces pouring across the borders, but also needed to be prepared to deal with enemy activity in rear areas all over the country.

The situation is clarified by Figure 13.1, which shows the narrowness of West Germany. It must be reckoned that, if they choose to do so, Warsaw Pact forces could probably occupy Austria without much difficulty. If this were to happen, no corner of West Germany would be more than 200 miles from them. Indeed, in the extreme north almost the entire extent of the West German coastlines on the North Sea and on the Baltic, together with the border with Denmark, already lies within 100 miles of Warsaw Pact territory.* Soviet thinking envisaged that the planned penetration in a major offensive might reach up to 250 miles. Successive echelons of the attacking force would be organized in depth, so that a new hammer blow could be struck as soon as each echelon lost its momentum. Night-fighting capabilities were already being improved to permit round-the-clock operations. Massive air attacks were to concentrate first on enemy reserves, while many small-scale airborne infiltrations and a number of large-scale airlifts would disrupt the enemy rear. To many military thinkers in the early 1970s it seemed that the response being planned by NATO was utterly inadequate to meet the new situation presented by the Warsaw Pact threat. Yet the doctrine of U.S. Army Field Manual FM 100-5, designed mainly to deal with operations in central Europe, was similar to that stated in French doctrinal manuals of 1940 in that of the two elements, fire and movement, fire was considered to be predominant. The Germans did not think this way—nor do the Soviets.

Clearly our military establishment as a whole is still not attempting to acquire a deep understanding of the military concepts of our major enemy. We are still neglecting the vital need to anticipate how the enemy will fight, and this is, to my mind, one of the gravest of all our many danger signals.

From 1972 to 1978 my studies centered more and more on anticipating what the Soviets, with their Warsaw Pact allies, might try

---

* These geographic distances explain why U.S. forces stationed in Europe, feeling the proximity of a strong enemy, tend to have views very different from those of the military experts who sit at desks around the United States.

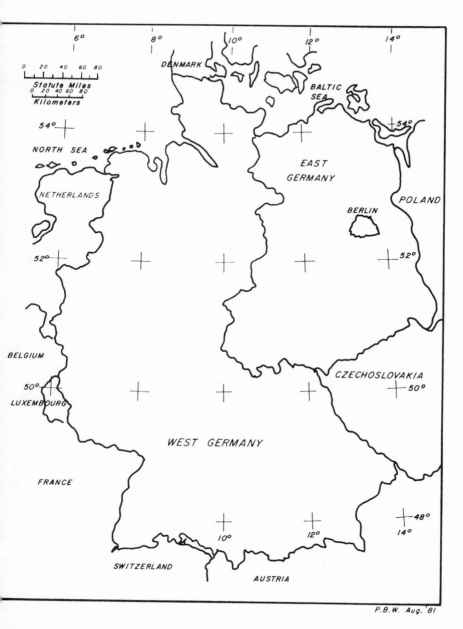

Figure 13.1 The Narrowness of WEST GERMANY

to do in the first few hours of a conventional attack against West Germany. In open literature I found a good deal of information on recent trends in Soviet thinking and in their development of offensive capabilities. Today the Soviets are capable of launching a new version of the German blitzkrieg, still based on conventional weapons, but far more devastating than the World War II version. If we were to be caught unprepared, as were the French and British in 1940, our chance of muddling through would be dim, if not nonexistent. Yet today many of our politicians still call only for more defense spending, as if that were the answer. What matters is not the amount spent, but the thinking and planning that directs the spending. The development of increasingly sophisticated weapons systems is easily understood and glamorous. It appeals to our military command, to our armaments industry, to our politicians, and to the general public. But it is by no means the whole answer. In deciding how to spend defense funds, our military has put too much emphasis on spectacular technological achievements, and too little on less glamorous but equally important requirements such as communications—too much on providing computerized capabilities for commanders, and too little on the needs of the combat units that will do the actual fighting. Success on a future battlefield will depend in large measure on how effectively the actions of the many diverse combat elements can be directed and coordinated, particularly in response to a new threat or a new opportunity. This in turn will depend on availability of means of communication that can adapt quickly to new situations and can handle information at the speed called for by ever-advancing technology. As I will show, we have no such tactical communications today—and of what use is any ultra-advanced weapon, or superbly armed combat unit, without a means of communication to bring it into play at the right time and with the right objective? If this planning and development area does not get its proper share of defense money, the vast sums we have spent on weapons and other glamorous items may as well have been poured down the drain.

STRATEGIC COMMUNICATIONS AND GLOBAL THREATS

In 1978 the focus of my studies switched to the achievement of suitable tactical communications for possible future battlefields.

The emphasis, however, was still on situations that might arise in Europe. I will be talking about this later—it brought me back to memories of the Hut 6 experience. First, however, to conclude this discussion of danger signals, I will draw attention to two other sadly neglected areas: strategic communications and global threats.

Our strategic communications capabilities, which include those needed to bring nuclear weapons into play, appear to need urgent attention and adequate defense spending. Even the decision to use low-yield tactical nuclear weapons in Europe, in accordance with NATO's doctrine of flexible response, would involve the governments of the NATO alliance, and that would require communications of a strategic nature. Awareness of, and response to, critical situations in other parts of the world would depend on adequate communications. Yet today one keeps reading public statements about the unreliability of important strategic communications systems. For example, according to the *Wall Street Journal* of March 10, 1980, government auditors have concluded that the World Wide Military Command and Control System (WWMCCS), the computerized communication system designed to warn the President of an enemy attack or international crisis, is prone to breakdown. The auditors said the network is unacceptably slow, unreliable, and has failed in at least two recent critical situations. (And this without any enemy intervention.) It has also been reported in the press that, on more than one occasion, we have been dangerously near to launching nuclear weapons, an act that would have started a nuclear war, through communications foulups. What more do we need to convince us that our survival may well depend on having the right strategic communications capabilities?

In regard to global threats, I have shown that although in the 1960s a lot of thought was given to conflicts that might arise outside Europe, not much was done to prepare for such conflicts, and then in the 1970s the focus moved on to Europe. But events in Angola, Abyssinia, Afghanistan, and Iran, as well as alarming situations nearer home in the Caribbean and Central America, are forcing us to realize that we need new environmental analysis and conceptual thinking about possible threats outside Europe, some of them by no means directly related to the Soviet Union.

We should not, for example, neglect the possibility that, if some Latin American neighbor becomes sufficiently irritated with the

United States, its government—or a powerful rebel force making a bid for power—might ask for Soviet military assistance. There is little doubt that, with their tremendous development of merchant marine and airlift capabilities, the Soviets could very quickly transport a substantial military force to an area from which they could then threaten the United States.

Thus global threats are not only very real but also continually changing, and they call for frequent reappraisal. If we fail to anticipate the special communications problems that may be involved in countermeasures, we are likely to find ourselves in trouble. In this context I am reminded of a lecture on crisis management given at MITRE in March 1973 by Dr. Thomas G. Belden, then Chief Historian, Office of U.S. Air Force History. He analyzed the glaring weaknesses in communication that had showed up in the stories of Pearl Harbor and the *Pueblo* incident. In each case he exposed failures to anticipate and to set up the proper communications procedures ahead of time. He also stressed the vital need in a crisis for rapid establishment of secure conferencing, both vertical and horizontal, among the elements involved—very true of a crisis that might call for a decision on whether or not to use tactical nuclear weapons in Europe. He argued that even the most advanced means of establishing secure voice conferencing were far too slow, which is still true. He urged a return to "conversational teletype," which would have been perfectly satisfactory for the types of crisis conferencing he had studied. This still makes good sense, but teletype communications are old-fashioned—definitely not glamorous.

Belden also introduced the idea of developing standard message formats to ensure that, in various types of crisis situations, no essential items of information would be omitted. This is an old idea that has been applied to many management problems, but it calls for imaginative thinking and it does not involve glamorous technology.

Belden was absolutely right, I believe, in suggesting simple measures that would greatly improve our response to future crises, large and small. The danger signal is that such ideas have not been implemented. We are no better able to handle a crisis now than we were at the times of Pearl Harbor and the *Pueblo* incident.

As we have seen, the Germans in World War II were on the whole well served by their communications system. But as I have pointed out, the part of the system with which I was concerned operated reliably only because the controllers of the nets worked continuously to keep them in good order. A communications system whose satisfactory operating condition is not frequently verified by actual tests is liable to fail when it is needed. Indeed, failure to make sure that an important line of communication remained continuously open was one of the main troubles in the *Pueblo* incident. Taking steps to see that our vital means of communication are kept in working order may be less glamorous than improving the performance of a weapons system, but surely the expenditure needed for this purpose should have high priority in the allocation of defense funds.

14

Military
Considerations

THE PEAK AND THE RUT

The nature of our present situation was brought out in a lecture on "Advanced Technology in Modern War" given at the Royal United Services Institute, Whitehall, London, on November 26, 1975, by Mr. John A. Morse, formerly Deputy Assistant Secretary of Defense, Pentagon; International Security Affairs, Europe and NATO. He argued that our main problem at that time was a thinking rut, thirty years deep. Both political and military leaders were stuck in it. Morse said that this rut simply must break up before long, and predicted a revolution in military operational concepts, doctrines, and tactics. If we do break out of the rut, he went on to say, the military technology already available, or likely to be available within five years, offers great promise. This advanced technology can provide better ways to deal with problems we face now, and with those we will face in the future, and it will do so at costs we can afford if we use our assets more effectively and efficiently.

Since 1975 a conceptual debate has been building up, resulting in increasing pressure for change, but the predicted revolution has not yet materialized. In what follows I will be discussing ways in which my personal experience, and what I have learned in the course of my work, may be applicable to today's problems. My experience in

Hut 6 was concerned with communications of the German army and air force. In recent years, too, my study of military communications has been focused on the needs of ground and air forces. I have searched for military case histories, drawn from actual combat, that can help us to prepare for the realities of future battles. I have also been in close touch with one particular development of military communications technology that does indeed offer great promise.

This example of available technology will be discussed in the next chapter. Its potential value will be illustrated by showing how it could have been used to great advantage by the U.S. Air Force in Vietnam. In the present chapter I will present a few historical episodes that can help our military planners to achieve a realistic approach to problems of the future. In particular I will draw attention to events that took place in the African desert during the short period from May 26, 1942, to July 10, 1942. In nearly twenty years of study I have never found an episode in military history that contains so many lessons for the future in the areas in which I have been working. Nor have I found a story of actual war that so clearly mirrors what I believe to be wrong with our current army thinking, at least in the areas discussed in this book.

Let us first go back to the time, in World War II, when the Allies were preparing to invade France. American air offense against targets deep in enemy territory was to be handled by the U.S. Eighth Air Force, based in England. The U.S. Ninth Air Force under General Hoyt Vandenberg was preparing to support the ground forces by attacking targets at the front and in the immediate enemy rear. The planners, in spite of protests from Washington, refused to be governed by earlier doctrinal thinking. They were designing an organization for joint ground/air operations on a scale without historical precedent. Experience in the African desert had shown that cooperating air and ground headquarters must work very closely together. Consequently Ninth Air Force headquarters was so designed that a compact, highly mobile "advance headquarters" could move with the Army Group and handle air operations, while the large "main headquarters" handled administrative matters. Under the Ninth Air Force there were three Tactical Air Commands (TACs) cooperating with the First, Third, and Ninth Armies. Again each TAC headquarters was divided into advance and main sections, so that the former could move with the associated Army headquarters. Thus XIX Tactical Air Command under General Otto P. Weyland supported Third Army under General Patton. In its first month of operation Weyland's advance headquarters moved five times to keep up with Patton's headquarters. For periods of particularly rapid movement a "super-advance" headquarters was used, consisting of Weyland, an operations officer, an intelligence officer, and communications personnel. Similar arrangements applied to the other TACs, and there was also close cooperation with the British Second Tactical Air Force, which was the air partner of the 21st Army Group.

Army–Air cooperation was carried down to corps and division levels by Tactical Air Control Parties, and sometimes right down to the front line by Air Liaison Officers. An ALO could ride with the lead elements of an armored column and be given authority to divert fighter missions headed toward targets of opportunity in the enemy rear to targets in the immediate vicinity of the column. The ability of the overall organization to adapt to an unexpected situation was tested on many occasions. Commanders and their staffs were encouraged to introduce new functions and more efficient operating procedures, and to eliminate functions and sections that had outlived their usefulness. The Allies had come a long way from the rigid, outmoded doctrines with which they had entered the war. They had outdone the Germans with their own ideas of blitzkrieg. Driven by necessity, they had reached a peak in military thinking and accomplishment.

After many months of careful study by officers who were directly involved, a "Condensed Analysis of the Ninth Air Force in the European Theater of Operations," with many conclusions and recommendations, was published in March 1946, while memories were still fresh. The basic conclusion, as General Vandenberg declared in a foreword, was that flexibility and mobility in thought, policy, and action are essential to success in war. He warned that, if a tactical air war were to be fought in some other part of the world, it would be highly dangerous to assume that the policies and procedures developed in the European theater would be appropriate. Each new environment would call for new thinking.

As far as I can discover, this excellent "condensed analysis," which recorded the experience of our tactical air forces at the peak of their performance, was almost totally ignored by the peacetime military establishment. If its recommendations had been followed, we would have fared better in Korea and Vietnam. Instead a thinking rut developed in the area of tactical air operations. I imagine that much the same is true in other areas, resulting in the overall situation that Morse perceived.

Morse also pointed out that, in prolonged periods of peace, the development of a thinking rut in a military establishment is perfectly normal. This being so, it is not going to be easy to develop the kind of military thinking that we will need in war. But, until we wake up, the development of new capabilities will continue to be far too slow. There is the grave danger that we may be overrun in our sleep, as were the French and British in 1940, and, in view of the far greater pace at which things move today, our chance of muddling through to a turn of the tide will be far less than theirs.

BATTLE OF FRANCE

Because the realities of war involve so much that is absent from peacetime experience, and because we need to form realistic pictures of what the initial phase of a Soviet blitzkrieg may be like, it seems clear that we will do well to examine the causes of the phenomenal success of the German blitzkrieg in France against an allied force that outnumbered them and had weapons superiority in some areas. Indeed when, around 1970, the focus of our military attention switched to conventional war in Europe, it became important to study World War II. Far from being out of date, that war seems extremely up to date when compared with our peacetime thinking. It was the most recent major European conflict. Its events and patterns can be expected to have at least some similarity to those of future non-nuclear combat in that part of the world. Hence its firsthand source materials, which are largely unknown to most Americans, should not continue to be neglected. We live in a world very different from that in which the Second World War was fought, yet parts of the story, including the matters I have described related to Hut 6, contain lessons that are still valid. They may be the best lessons we have. It would be foolish to ignore them. Two books in particular that tell us a great deal are *Panzer Battles* by F. W. von Mellenthin, and *Panzer Leader* by Heinz Guderian.

Guderian, who was one of the principal architects of the German blitzkrieg, led a German panzer drive through the Ardennes. Starting early on May 10, 1940, he reached the river Meuse on the evening of May 12. A major panzer breakthrough beyond the Meuse was achieved on May 16. The coast of the English Channel was reached on May 20, and by May 21 the Allies had lost all hope of recovery. The distance covered in ten days was a little over 200 miles, an achievement well worth our attention.

Guderian's detailed story of his drive to the Channel coast is fascinating. Even today it is extremely relevant to our thinking about the possibility of a Soviet blitzkrieg in Germany. It emphasizes the critical importance of quick response to the "initial test"—to a new situation that is suddenly thrust on us. It shows that the Germans could have been stopped in that campaign if the Allies had responded quickly enough with appropriate countermeasures. At the onset, the critical crossing of the Meuse near Sedan was forced by infantry units without waiting for the arrival of artillery. Air attacks substituted for artillery fire, and succeeded in neutralizing the French artillery. This decisive use of air power to support the river crossing had been planned to the last detail by Guderian and Lieutenant General Bruno Loerzer, commanding Air Corps II. The army–air discussions on the matter had taken a month, but on the previous day the plan had been countermanded by General von Kleist, Guderian's superior commander, in agreement with General Sperrle, Loerzer's superior commander. Much to the surprise of Guderian, who was watching the long-planned crossing by the 1st Rifle Regiment of his 1st Panzer Division under Lieutenant Colonel Balck (later to become a distinguished panzer general on the Russian front), the air attacks went according to plan, and were extremely effective. General Loerzer had decided that the new orders from higher command had come too late to be implemented!

This was the first of several occasions on which Guderian's chances of success were nearly ruined by the German higher command, which did not have an intimate knowledge either of the planning of their operational commanders or of the opportunities that were arising on the battlefront. Guderian, however, was on the spot and managed to drive his troops on, taking full advantage of the slowness of his enemy's response.

A major factor was the dismal failure of the French to keep pace with the German development of military radio communications.

This is discussed in "France 1940: Anatomy of Defeat" by Lieutenant Colonel Frank E. Owens, U.S. Army.* After the war General Gamelin (the Allied Commander in Chief) testified that it normally took forty-eight hours for an order issued at his headquarters to be executed at the front. A British liaison officer with the French in Belgium reported that there were no radio communications whatever among the 1st Group of Armies. The French were forced to rely entirely on dispatch riders. Indeed they had no means of communication speedy enough to coordinate their operations against the well-coordinated and fast-moving German armored attack. This held true from the highest headquarters to armored units, where flag signals were the only means available to dispose and maneuver tanks—just as in the U.S. Army before the winter of 1940–41.

Von Mellenthin, author of *Panzer Battles*, was a staff officer who saw a great deal of the fighting throughout the war. We will do well to look carefully into his analysis of the principal reasons for the success of the German forces in France, Belgium, and the Netherlands in 1940. He says:

> Our panzer corps and divisions not only had the advantage of excellent training and communications, but the commanders at every level fully appreciated that panzer troops must be commanded from the front. Thus they were able to take immediate advantage of the rapid changes and opportunities which armored warfare brings. Perhaps I should stress that although we attached the greatest importance to armor, we realized that tanks cannot operate without the close support of motorized infantry and artillery. Our panzer division was a balanced force of all arms—that was a lesson which the British did not learn until well into 1942.

Notice that von Mellenthin, in his analysis of the Battle of France, makes no mention at all of the excellence of Germany's weapons systems! (Indeed in 1940 the British Matilda tanks were superior to the German tanks.) He ignores weapons to concentrate on others aspects: the importance of a balanced force of all arms, command from the front (not a part of recent U.S. doctrine, though

* Owens was Deputy Director, ADP Support Division, U.S. Army War College. The article appeared in *Army Magazine*, December 1972, and in *Signal*, December 1973.

practiced in U.S. forces in France after the Normandy invasion), and, first and foremost, excellent training and communications.

The British learning process, to which von Mellenthin refers, occurred while their Eighth Army was fighting Rommel's Afrika Corps in the African desert. It occurred before Montgomery's first defeat of Rommel in the battle of Alam el Halfa at the end of August 1942. I will summarize the story here because it brings out so many of the dangers that must be faced again today. Special attention should be paid to the short period from Rommel's attack on the Gazala line on May 26, 1942, to Auchinleck's success in stopping him in the July fighting, which became known as the first battle of El Alamein. (The second battle of El Alamein was Montgomery's victory of October 1942.)

An account of the desert campaigns, which clearly reveals the learning process, is to be found in Correlli Barnett's *The Desert Generals*. The story, however, should also be studied from a different point of view; it brings out the fact that the coordination of overt military actions is not enough. Clandestine activities, too, need to be included in our concept of combined operations. After the turn of the tide in Africa, the Allied victories were greatly facilitated by well-coordinated clandestine activities such as deception, sabotage, and counterespionage. Moreover it is extremely important to recognize that cryptology, intelligence, and secrecy are all weapons of war that need to be coordinated with all the other activities, both military and clandestine. Thus, it is worthwhile to review briefly the seesaw campaigns in the African desert from Rommel's arrival to his defeat by Auchinleck in July 1942.

THE EARLY PHASES OF THE DESERT CAMPAIGNS

To bring out what was wrong with British thinking and what was done in the middle of a campaign to remedy the situation, it is convenient to divide the story into three parts. First, what led up to the beginning of the Gazala battles. Second, the British defeats of Gazala and Mersa Matrûh. Third, the defeat of Rommel at First Alamein. The territory covered by the desert campaigns is illustrated in Figure 14.1. Very roughly we may think of Tunis to Tripoli to Benghazi to Tobruk to Alexandria as being four compar-

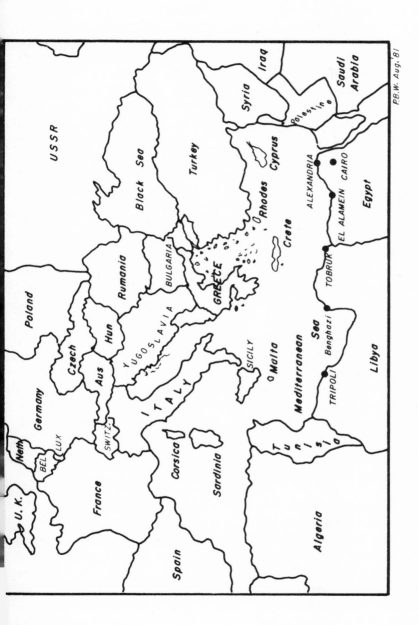

Figure 14.1 Scene of NORTH AFRICAN CAMPAIGNS of 1942

able distances along a narrow coastal strip flanked by inhospitable desert.

In 1940 the British under Sir Richard O'Connor had won overwhelming victories over the Italians, culminating in the capture of Benghazi in February 1941. Then Rommel came to Africa. In his first offensive, Rommel took Benghazi and besieged Tobruk, a bastion that for the moment held out against all his efforts. At that time Hut 6 was breaking Enigma traffic pretty regularly, and our decodes told the story of the arrival of German forces in Tripoli. They revealed that by May 1941 General Wavell, the British theater commander at the time, was faced with two armored divisions much sooner than he had expected. Winterbotham remarks that it was the accurate knowledge that Wavell and O'Connor received from Ultra of the buildup and strength of the Afrika Korps that enabled the fighting withdrawal of the British and Imperial forces to be carried through without complete disaster. But if the British had a valuable asset in intelligence, the Germans had a big, if not decisive, advantage in communications. British tank radios in Africa had components that could not survive the environment. So long as the British were fighting the Italians it was tank against tank—one on one—and the British were victorious. When the German Afrika Korps came in, the British found themselves up against a force that was well coordinated by good tank radios, and that was quite another matter. This, combined with Rommel's command from the front, was enough to account for such a severe reverse.

Having brought up the subject of British tank radios, it is a good moment to recall the similar unpreparedness of the Americans. The U.S. Army seems not to have recognized the need for revolution in battlefield communications until it was demonstrated by Hitler's early successes. Indeed the "remaking" of U.S. Army communications for armored warfare did not start until the winter of 1940/41, at which time the Army had few tanks, none of them with radios. When it got going, however, the "remaking" was rapid. Experiments with cavalry radios were unsuccessful, but the tanks of the U.S. 1st Armored Division were equipped with police FM radios in time for their deployment to Africa in November 1942. By the end of that year a crash program at Bell Labs had produced the SCR 508, which proved superior to the German tank radios. The U.S. communications engineers had also dealt with other problems that were special to tanks—intercommunication inside the tank and the need to shield equipment from ignition noise. Tank crews wore crash helmets for protection; the intercom gear was simply built into the helmets.

A British offensive code-named Crusader started some 50 miles to the southeast of Tobruk, still held by the British, on November 18, 1941. The British tanks had superiority in numbers but were completely unsupported. In a series of cavalry-type charges on the morning of November 23 they tried to get at the German tanks, but found them supported by motorized infantry and artillery. They were shot to a standstill by the German antitank weapons. Out of 450 cruiser tanks the British Eighth Army lost at least 300. This disaster, Barnett says, was due to the cumulative and accelerating effects of twenty years of military decadence—the period of peace between World Wars I and II. The Eighth Army commander, General Sir Alan Cunningham, sent an urgent request to the new Commander in Chief in the theater, General Auchinleck, who flew in at once to handle what had become a crisis. Under Auchinleck's firm guidance the British recovered. He found out, possibly through Hut 6 Ultra, that Rommel's tanks were running out of supplies. He replaced Cunningham with General Sir Neil Ritchie. On the night of December 7/8, 1941, Rommel began to retire. On Christmas Eve the British were again in Benghazi.

The next phase was another disaster for the British. Between January 21 and February 4, 1942, Rommel drove the Eighth Army all the way back to Gazala, not far short of Tobruk (Figure 14.2). As David Kahn reveals in *The Codebreakers*, this part of the story started in Rome in August of 1941, when laxity of security precautions allowed an Italian, who had worked for the American Embassy for twenty years or more, to obtain or copy a key that enabled Italian agents to open a safe, remove and photograph the American Black Code and its attendant superencipherment tables, and then replace them unnoticed. This Black Code, so-called for the color of its binding, was used by American military attachés, and possibly even by American ambassadors. One American who used the code book and its superencipherment tables was Colonel Bonner Frank Fellers, the American military attaché in Cairo at the time. Once the Black Code and its superencipherment system were compromised, he unwittingly gave Rommel just about the most perfect intelligence

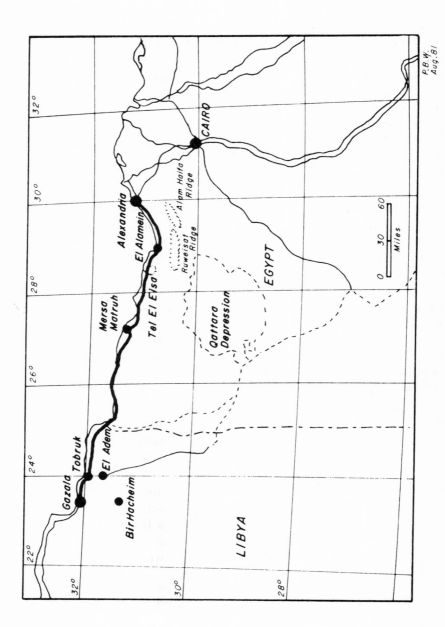

Figure 14.2 GAZALA to el ALAMEIN

any general could wish for by his frequent and meticulous reports to Washington.* Rommel knew the source of the Fellers intelligence and believed it. Ritchie was getting intelligence derived from Ultra but, not knowing the source, did not put very much trust in it. Moreover, Rommel's radio intelligence company under Captain Alfred Seeboehm was doing pretty well, thanks to poor British radio security.

Although Fellers and Seeboehm must have been of immense help, it is clear that Rommel's success was due in large measure to the continued British failure to match the German combined arms operations. Rommel, like Guderian in France, was with his forward troops, continually taking advantage of opportunities as they arose. At times the pursuit attained a speed of 15 miles an hour. Ritchie's communications failed to keep him in touch with what was going on.

In weaponry too, British thought at that time suffered from rigidity and departmentalism. The German 88-mm gun, designed as an antiaircraft weapon, was so dangerous that four of them could stop an armored brigade. The British had a magnificent 3.7-inch antiaircraft gun of even greater penetrative power, but it was not used as an antitank weapon in any of the desert battles. It was intended to shoot at aircraft. The army had been supplied with the twopounder to shoot at tanks. And that was that!

This is an example of the slow response of the British military authorities to new ideas. The Germans had used the 88-mm antiaircraft gun as an extremely effective weapon against the excellent British Matilda tanks during the Battle of France, as I well remember from German messages decoded by Hut 6 at the time.†

After his astonishing drive from Benghazi, Rommel needed time to reorganize before his next major offensive. From early February 1942 until May, the two armies rested. The senior British commanders used the lull to digest the lessons of the winter. During Crusader it had been learned that the Germans would not commit

* In his recent book, *Hitler's Spies*, Kahn says that the Italians did not give the Black Code to their Axis partner, but that the Germans cracked it analytically and were reading the Fellers messages by the fall of 1941.

† I have been told that the 88-mm was experimentally used for this purpose during the German involvement in the Spanish Civil War.

themselves to tank-against-tank battle of the kind the British had hoped for. In every phase of a battle they coordinated the action of their antitank guns, field artillery, and infantry with their tank maneuvers. Thus a cavalry-type attack by unsupported British tanks was bound to be disastrous.

But this was by no means the whole lesson that had to be learned, as Auchinleck clearly saw. He set about a complete reorganization of the British armored forces. His changes were intended to make the separate arms of the British service think and work together in the German manner. His efforts would bring success in the First Battle of Alamein, but before then the British were to suffer through the Gazala battles and those around Mersa Matrûh, which lay between Gazala and Alamein.

At the beginning of the Gazala battles of May 26 to June 14, 1942, Ritchie's defensive dispositions behind the minefields that ran from the sea at Gazala to the stronghold of Bir Hacheim still reflected an outmoded pattern of military thought, inappropriate for highly mobile desert warfare. He established a number of independent strongholds or "boxes" full of infantry and guns. His armor was separate. The troops near the sea, including those in Tobruk, were under the 13th Corps commander, General Gott. The troops in the southern area, including a Free French Brigade in Bir Hacheim, were under the 30th Corps commander, Lieutenant-General Norrie. Ritchie's headquarters was well to the rear.

Rommel was still getting the Fellers reports, which presumably gave him a clear picture of Ritchie's dispositions. Although his plan to swing around the southern end of the British defense line had been revealed by Hut 6 Ultra, and his movements had been observed by British armored patrols, Rommel was able to surprise and overrun the headquarters of the 7th Armored Division, part of Norrie's 30th Corps. By midmorning on May 27 the division was no longer a coherent fighting force, but neither Norrie nor Ritchie knew of the disaster; with the capture of division headquarters, there was no one to tell them.

When Norrie heard that Rommel was attacking, he ordered the 22nd Armored Brigade to drive southward to support the 4th Armored Brigade, not knowing that the 4th had already been shattered. Before the 22nd could move, Rommel was on them. News of the enemy advance in his rear finally reached General Gott in the northern sector.

The British response that followed was disorganized. Units from here and there came through the dust and heat haze. Heavy Grant tanks and fresh armored brigades joined in. With his ineffective communications, Ritchie's knowledge was twenty-four hours behind events, and he was unable to control his battle. Yet somehow by nightfall Rommel's battle, too, was slipping out of control. He was almost out of gasoline and far behind the British defenses. On the second day German armor was scattered all over the place, sitting ducks for want of gasoline, but the British two-pounder antitank gun could not damage them, and rigid doctrine forbade use of the magnificent 3.7-inch antiaircraft guns.

Rommel was in real trouble—wide open to a counterstroke. But Ritchie, sitting remote from the battle, could do nothing effective. He missed a great opportunity, for Rommel, by his personal leadership, was able to withdraw his panzers to the British side of the minefields in the center of the British defense line. He cleared a passage, and so obtained a greatly shortened supply route. Soon he was ready to resume the attack.

This time Rommel could not be held. In spite of a warning from Ultra, a massive British tank attack ran into his prepared defenses, and lost two hundred cruisers and sixty "I" tanks a little to the southwest of the El Adem "box." His radio intelligence company picked up clear radio signals that enabled him to surprise the El Adem box and clear the way for his advance on Tobruk, which surrendered on June 21, 1942.

After being driven from the Gazala line, Ritchie proposed to retire to Mersa Matrûh, inside the Egyptian frontier, where he intended to fight a final battle for Egypt. But Auchinleck had come to the conclusion that Ritchie was certain to be beaten. He decided to take command of the Eighth Army himself. In the few remaining hours he could not alter Ritchie's dispositions; nor could he eradicate the rigidity and orthodoxy of prewar British military doctrine, or the slow habits that had been a feature of British fighting since the capture of O'Connor eighteen months earlier. He did point out bluntly that the proudly separatist arms of the service were part of the same army, and told his commanders how he wanted them to support each other speedily to deal with German penetrations. He called for close control and coordination of battle groups by divisional commanders who must make their presence felt on the battlefield. But all this could not affect the battle of Mersa Matrûh.

British formations not actually under attack continued to be the inactive spectators of those that were. Rommel recklessly exposed himself to counterattacks on his flanks, but the counterattacks, though ordered by Auchinleck, did not materialize. Communications were totally inadequate.

Auchinleck had never wanted to fight at Mersa Matrûh; before the battle started, he sent Norrie and 30th Corps headquarters back to El Alamein to reorganize, and assigned the defense of Mersa Matrûh itself to the 10th Corps under General Holmes.

Some of the conclusions that can be drawn from Correlli Barnett's detailed account of Gazala and Mersa Matrûh are as follows: British communications were not only slow and unreliable; their use was not properly organized. A corps commander could, and did, withdraw his forces from the battle without the knowledge of a neighboring corps commander. Units were either not instructed or not equipped to listen to radio sources from which they could hear of impending threats. Information was passed up and down chains of command with little or no provision for alternative routing in case of failure of one link in the chain. There was no means by which the 8th Army commander could communicate directly with forward troops if and when he needed to. Moreover, thanks to ingrained habits of thought, it was no easy matter for Auchinleck, the theater commander, to get his troops to fight as a coordinated combined arms force. That he succeeded well enough to win the battle of First Alamein must be regarded as one of the great achievements of military history.

What makes this story so deeply disturbing is that our military thinking of today shows the same types of doctrinal inhibition and compartmentalization that were so disastrous for the British. We badly need to relearn the lesson and to face up to the twin problems of thinking out how our combat troops may be called upon to fight as a coordinated force of all arms, and of providing the necessary communications.

A TURNING POINT

Auchinleck's victory at El Alamein was a major turning point in many ways. It clearly shows the marked effect on the 8th Army of the new principles and practices that he introduced. It should be noted that, whether or not at his instigation, the Royal Air Force at last abandoned its concentration on distant strategic targets, and took part in the ground battle. It should also be noted that First Alamein was a turning point for Hut 6 Ultra and for clandestine activities in general.

During June 29 and 30, 1942, as the British and Germans raced each other to El Alamein, the RAF poured bombs on the German formations and slowed them down. Auchinleck went out to the coast road to meet his troops and begin to get to know them. The men impressed him and "The Auk" impressed the men. Then he established his headquarters in a place behind the Ruweisat ridge, where he would be within easy reach of his corps commanders. He issued his order of the day: "The enemy is stretching to his limit and thinks we are a broken army. . . . He hopes to take Egypt by bluff. Show him where he gets off."

Rommel launched an offensive on the morning of July 1, 1942. Auchinleck had been implementing the operational instructions that he had worked out before Mersa Matrûh. He extemporized battle groups that could move and hit. He regrouped all the artillery under his own command so that, for the first time in the desert since O'Connor, his troops were to defend and attack under cover of mass gunfire. He told his army to expect an attack at a very early hour on July 1.

Rommel's Afrika Korps, in its night approach, had trouble with terrain, and reached its starting points at about six A.M. instead of the planned three A.M. Then, as soon as it was light enough, the RAF contributed an air attack of unprecedented strength. When the panzer army finally got moving, expecting the usual easy morning's motoring, they immediately ran into heavy fire organized by Auchinleck. As they struggled forward the fire grew hotter. Another attack in the north around the El Alamein box did no better, the tanks being caught in fire from Auchinleck's prepared defenses. By midday the northern attack seemed to Rommel to be the more promising of the two, so he brought in his few reserves and went up in person to drive on the attack. But by late afternoon even Rommel was stuck, as his troops were shelled from all sides by Auchinleck's newly regrouped artillery. The initiative was beginning to pass from Rommel to Auchinleck.

I want to draw special attention to an action of the 9th Australian division. Auchinleck drew Rommel's attention away from the coast by a feigned withdrawal to the south of El Alamein. But during the night of July 9/10, massed guns of Auchinleck's artillery blasted Rommel's positions west of El Alamein. In the morning the Australians went in and scattered the Italians of the Sabratha Division. The hill of Tel el Eisa was captured, and on this hill was Rommel's radio intelligence company under Seeboehm. The defeat of the Italian Sabratha Division brought Rommel near disaster. He prevented catastrophe, but only by using German troops he needed for his offensive. Two days later Auchinleck routed the Italian Trieste Division, and again Rommel had to use German troops to avoid complete disaster. By July 17 the First Battle of Alamein was over. Auchinleck had won a historic victory. In the view of Correlli Barnett and many others, it was the military turning point, more significant even than Montgomery's subsequent British victories at Alam el Halfa and Second Alamein.

From the point of view of Hut 6, First Alamein was indeed the second major turning point of the war. I have found it hard to get the exact chronology from published accounts, but it would appear that in June 1942 the Americans put an end to the Fellers leak by changing the cipher system used for military attaché reports. This deprived Rommel of his primary source of intelligence and may account in part for his surprise at the reception Auchinleck had prepared for him at Alamein. Rommel's loss of the Fellers intelligence may also have helped Auchinleck pull off his surprise attack on the Italian Sabratha Division. Anyway, this attack resulted in the capture on July 10, 1942, of Seeboehm's radio intelligence outfit, whose location on Tel el Eisa had been discovered by the British Y-Service (radio intelligence). An Australian battalion recovered Seeboehm's records intact. They revealed a great deal about the help Rommel had received from the Fellers reports and about the success of Seeboehm's methods.* The British discovered that much of the foxiness of the "Desert Fox" was due to good German radio intelligence in the field and poor British radio security. Widespread reforms in radio security were imposed, and the

---

* There was also information about the abortive Kondor spy mission, the story of which has been told elsewhere.

British formed new companies to monitor the radio security procedures of their own troops.

So long as Rommel was getting superb intelligence from Fellers and from his experienced radio intelligence team, the steady stream of information from Hut 6 Ultra could not be fully effective. After these sources of intelligence had been denied Rommel, Ultra played an increasingly important role. Indeed, from the first battle of Alamein to the expulsion of the Germans from Africa it may be claimed that, with one exception, Ultra played the dominant role in intelligence. Winterbotham has told of the sinking of supply ships, and of the cover stories that concealed the fact that these sinkings resulted from the breaking of Enigma. Ultra helped Montgomery repulse Rommel's last attack on him, launched soon after the encounter with the Americans at Kasserine, which was the one case in which Ultra did not contribute. American radio security was poor, as British radio security had been not long before, but Rommel's was good. He ordered complete radio silence before his attack. Eisenhower's chief of intelligence, Brigadier E. R. Mockler-Ferryman, assumed that there could be no attack without warning from Ultra. Thus the very excellence of the service that was being provided by Hut 6 and Hut 3 contributed on this occasion to a costly defeat.*

Hut 6 was, of course, a clandestine activity—an important one, but by no means the only one to make a valuable contribution. As we look to the future we should perhaps regard it as no more than a highlight in an overall picture, other parts of which may prove of greater relevance today. In the 1980s our command organizations at home, and our commanders who may have to operate in the field, must worry about a lot more than the cryptographic security of their vital communications. More than ever before they must worry about vulnerability to forms of clandestine attack other than cryptanalysis. If they do not see that such matters as sabotage and spoofing are properly dealt with, who will? And who is going to see that the nation as a whole is not vulnerable to another clandestine weapon—propaganda in its many forms, instigated not only by our

* Note however that, as I have pointed out, the German radio nets that would be needed in the battle were almost certainly exercising, even though no Enigma traffic was being passed. Good radio intelligence could have given warning of the coming attack.

enemies but also by our own special interest groups who have little if any concern for national interest?

A very important form of clandestine activity that must be very much in the minds of our future commanders is use of a well-coordinated deception plan that forces the enemy to make errors and achieves surprise, the most precious ingredient in warfare.* Auchinleck's victory at First Alamein marked a turning point in the British use of deception schemes. This started in a small way as a result of the capture of Rommel's radio intelligence company, which made him very vulnerable to radio deception. When the new radio intelligence company arrived it had neither the ability nor the experience to distinguish truth from fiction. So the British were able to see to it that Rommel heard only the whispers they wanted him to hear. But radio deception was soon to be coordinated with many other means of conveying false information to the enemy, great care being taken to ensure that all such efforts would confirm and reinforce each other. This form of clandestine activity became a science, employing experts from many fields, including the magician Major Jasper Maskelyne. Who better than a conjuror to draw the enemy's attention away from what you do not want him to see?

The idea was applied in August 1942 and contributed to Rommel's defeat by Montgomery at Alam el Halfa, when he made his last attempt to break through to Cairo. It was applied on a larger scale in preparation for Montgomery's victory at Second Alamein. It was applied on a grand scale in preparation for the Allied invasion of Normandy. At the very least these coordinated deception plans considerably reduced the casualties involved in the ultimate achievement of victory. They are fascinating and complex stories, well worth studying for their military implications, but for my purpose I will do no more than mention a few facets that are related to Hut 6 or to communications.

THE GREAT DECEPTION

In *Bodyguard of Lies*, Cave Brown describes the origins of the coordinated plan of the high commands of America, Britain, and

---

* In the words of Liddell Hart, "Surprise is the supreme virtue of warfare, originality of mind the quality that breeds it."

Russia to mislead Hitler about Allied strategy and tactics. The extraordinary success of the plan (code-named Bodyguard) and the magnitude of its contribution to the invasion of Normandy (code-named Neptune) rested on the skillful combination of many clandestine activities. Among these were Hut 6 and Masterman's XX Committee with its controlled agents. By late 1943 Hut 6 Ultra was providing accurate information about the disposition of Hitler's forces—intelligence that helped shape the strategy and tactics of the invasion. At the same time Ultra was often able to reveal the German reactions to many of the deception activities, including those of Masterman's organization, thus making it possible to reinforce success (an old principle in overt combat applied here in a covert manner). Indeed Ultra intelligence was influencing the strategy and tactics of the deception operation.

Bodyguard included many regional plans, of which the one that interests us here was aimed, successfully, at persuading Hitler that the main Allied invasion of France would come through the Pas de Calais. The three dates, June 5, 6, and 7, 1944, on which tides and moonlight conditions would permit Neptune, happened to come in the middle of a period of bad weather. The Allies were able at the last minute to predict acceptable weather on June 6. The Germans believed that an invasion on June 6 was out of the question. In spite of this, however—and this is a point I want to emphasize—the ever-vigilant Luftwaffe radio intelligence service was not satisfied that all was normal. On the morning of June 5 it had detected massive wireless tuning in England—far heavier than anything intercepted before—and that always presaged aerial operations on the following night. During the night of June 5/6 it intercepted broadcasts from American weather intelligence flights over France, which suggested that, contrary to their normal practice, the Americans were about to undertake a nighttime operation.

The Luftwaffe duty officer was suspicious enough to scramble a few night fighters on air patrol. These were observed at 12:34 A.M. by the RAF Y service. It was the first sign of German reaction on D-Day. Luckily, thanks to the deception, the German patrol planes were vectored between Amiens in France and Arnhem in Holland. By that time the vast Neptune fleet had already entered the Bay of the Seine, but there the skies were empty. Allied radio security must have been good. But it had been a near thing. If the Germans had not been led to believe that the invasion would come through the Pas de Calais, the detection of massive tuning of radios might have had serious results. One must take into account all the ways in which an enemy could break down our radio security—not only the most obvious ones.

In the event, initial surprise was almost complete. The German army was not alerted until 2:11 A.M., when it was discovered that British and American paratroopers were landing. The sound of ships' engines was first heard at 2:35 A.M., by which time all units of the German 7th Army and 84 Corps were being rushed to their positions.

SABOTAGE

In our advanced planning of the communications on which the success of our military actions will depend, we need to pay far more attention than we do to the threat of sabotage. Although the means available to saboteurs today are far more alarming than those of World War II, we can still learn from the Normandy invasion, which provides striking examples of failure of communications due to sabotage at the outset of a campaign. Our military should be heeding those failures in any thinking about defense against a Soviet blitzkrieg.

As the invasion fleet approached the coast, resistance groups throughout France—having been alerted by the BBC—were preparing to execute the guerrilla and sabotage tasks that had been assigned to them. Their first task on D-Day was to disrupt German communications. All over the country, but particularly in the landing area, the lines went dead as "resistants" dug up and spiked trunk cables and pulled down overhead wires. Operators left their switchboards, electrical power circuits fused, and repeater stations exploded.

To give but one example, this sabotage affected Germany's 21 Panzer Division, which was stationed only a few miles from the area in which the British paratroopers were establishing their positions. The division's commander was ready to strike, but his standing orders permitted no private enterprise. He had been told that he was to make no move until he had heard from Rommel's headquarters. As a result of the breakdown of communications and the general confusion among the German high command, the 21 Panzer Division was kept out of the battle for twelve hours.

To coordinate the "maquis" (French resistance) with the invading forces, a large number of three-man special forces teams had undergone long, intensive training in clandestine warfare. Each team was composed of a Frenchman, an American, and a Britisher. Each was to be assigned an area in which it would make contact with, supply, organize, and control a local force of maquisards. About eighty of these three-man teams were deployed by air during Operation Neptune. One cannot help being intrigued by the simplicity of some of the tricks used by the maquisards to sabotage the movements of German armored divisions. They used cyclonite land mines that looked like cow droppings, planting them among actual cow droppings. They held up the line of march by placing upturned soup plates across the roads. At night these looked through a tank's periscope like the humps of buried land mines. There are many ways to delay a tank!

The successes achieved by the sabotage of German battlefield communications pretty obviously imply problems that might arise immediately in the event of an attack by conventional Warsaw Pact forces on West Germany. Considering that so many carefully trained three-man Allied teams could be deployed by air into German-occupied France before the Normandy landings, we must anticipate, and plan to deal with, considerable infiltration and well-planned attacks on NATO's communications, surveillance, and command facilities throughout West German territory, probably aided by already implanted agents. (The Russians put great emphasis on infiltration, and are masters of the art.) To me this makes it quite clear that it is dangerous to think only of defense along the front line (forward edge of the battle area, or FEBA, in U.S. military parlance). In West Germany NATO should see to it that there will be no undefended rear.

The failures in communications planning we have discussed had to do with exchanges of information between humans on a battlefield. Today's problem extends further still: to the communications needs of sophisticated, partly automated weapons systems. Before determining the potential military value of a nuclear missile installation or a super-high-performance aircraft, it is necessary to think hard about the communication that must precede the launching of the missiles or the vectoring of the aircraft to specified targets. What flow of information from place to place is needed for the decision-making? How must orders be transmitted to the missile sites, to aircraft controllers, and to the pilots? How long will the process take? And how easy would it be for an enemy, by some form of preplanned sabotage including electronic warfare, to cut enough of the essential communications links to prevent the missiles and the aircraft from being used when they are needed?

The Normandy D-Day landings clearly show how vulnerable command communications can be to simple forms of sabotage. Many other World War II incidents bear this out. Peenemünde is a particularly vivid illustration of the use of well-timed communications sabotage coordinated with a deception plan. By piecing together information from several sources, including Hut 6 Ultra, the British learned of the important scientific work on secret weapons at Peenemünde, on the Baltic. They planned a heavy bombing attack, code-named Hydra, for the night of August 17/18, 1943.* The Germans were allowed to learn that a heavy raid was coming across the North Sea, but were led to believe that it would be a raid on Berlin. That impression was created by a succession of small raids on Berlin, carried out by high-flying Mosquitoes† repeatedly following a course across the North Sea which took them near Peenemünde before they turned south toward their target. Night after night this maneuver set off air raid sirens at Peenemünde, and after a time the vigilance of the local defense relaxed. On August 17 the 8th U.S. Air Force exhausted the Luftwaffe in the most violent daytime aerial fighting of the war to that date. As the last of the American bombers were returning to England, the main British night attack force took off and crossed the North Sea to the region of Jutland at very low altitude, keeping under the horizon of the German radar screen. Just ahead of the three waves of the main force the usual small party of Mosquitoes set off for Berlin, where they were to drop marker flares, as if laying out the target for a large raid.

The deception worked. Nearing Peenemünde, the main British force rose to 7,000 feet for the attack, and the first RAF Pathfinders had no difficulty in marking the target with red flares. Called into

* See Cave Brown, *Bodyguard of Lies*, pp. 364–368.
† Not to be confused with the later Mosquitoes in Korea.

action by the Mosquito decoys, the Luftwaffe night fighters that might have intervened over Peenemünde were circling over Berlin some 100 miles away. A bit of sabotage in Holland further disabled the enemy's ability to respond. General Josef Kammhuber, Germany's leading air defense expert, had his headquarters at Arnhem-Deelen in Holland, and orders to his air divisions were transmitted over a teleprinter cable that fanned out from the Luftwaffe signals center there. Just as the raid on Peenemünde began, Kammhuber's cable was cut by saboteurs, and he found himself cut off from all means of directing his air defense forces.

Four thousand men were involved in this British raid, which was one of the war's most decisive air operations. The destruction was so great that Hitler ordered evacuation of all important activity and production from Peenemünde. The RAF did lose forty-one bombers, but the Luftwaffe reported afterward that, but for the deception and the ensuing chaos—aggravated no doubt by the cable cut—it would have shot down two hundred British aircraft on such a brilliantly clear night. Ingenious but simple means had won stunning success against a powerful, well-organized military machine.

PROPAGANDA

A further danger exists, that of allowing our national will to be eroded by subtle propaganda. This is related to the idea of winning without fighting. In *The Remaking of Modern Armies,* Liddell Hart talks about what he calls the Napoleonic fallacy: that the national object in war can only be gained by decisive battle and by destroying the main mass of the enemy's armed forces. He quotes Napoleon as saying "There is nothing I desire so much as a great battle." In contrast the more subtle 18th-century Marshal de Saxe is quoted as saying "I am not in favor of giving battle—I am even convinced that a clever general can wage war all his life without being compelled to do so."

Obscured in the mass of miscellaneous secret activities described in *A Man Called Intrepid* are several indications of ruses employed by Hitler as he prepared for the successive steps of his bid to dominate the world. By propaganda and covert activities he aimed to weaken his enemies so that his overt military battles, when they came, would be easily won. Like Marshal de Saxe he realized that many of his objectives could be gained without a fight. A clear and straight-forward picture of Hitler's activities in Britain and the Americas would be valuable today in suggesting areas in which continual future vigilance may be needed.

He found many supporters at all levels of society, some of them mere dupes, others concerned with promoting their own interests. In Britain he must have done pretty well with propaganda that influenced appeasement-minded citizens and politicians. One particularly bright young mathematician, whom I wanted to recruit for Hut 6, was not allowed to join us because he was a member of a pacifist organization that, although it had enrolled many public figures including dignitaries of the church, was known to be under German influence. We should know more about this sort of organization, and about the help Hitler was able to obtain from such individuals as Joseph P. Kennedy, the U.S. Ambassador to England; U.S. Senator Burton K. Wheeler; and John L. Lewis, president of both the United Mine Workers of America and the Congress of Industrial Organizations (CIO). The activities of German and American industries, such as I. E. Farben, International Telephone and Telegraph, and Standard Oil, should be included in the picture. It is said that Joseph Kennedy told his fellow Americans that the British would be defeated. It seems that many industrialists in America were only too happy to believe that Hitler would indeed become master of Europe, and would offer them preferential treatment in a huge market. Senator Wheeler was a supporter of the America First antiwar group, which was inspired by a massive German propaganda effort. He sold a million of his franked envelopes to America First, according to the Stevenson account, and 1,173,000 copies of Axis propaganda, supplied by German consulates and agencies, were mailed at the expense of the American taxpayer by twenty-four members of Congress.

These accusations suggest that a valuable picture has yet to be fully researched and painted. But the story must be told from the point of view of what Hitler was trying to do: We need to look for what others may be trying to do to us now and in the future.

In the late thirties it must have been hard for Americans to believe that Hitler really intended to annex South and North America, though it now seems certain that he did. Today it is still difficult for Americans to believe that the Soviet drive toward world domination can ever lead to a military threat to their own country, though perhaps we are more willing now to believe that we may be endangered by nonmilitary threats, if not by military ones.

Russia has traditionally been a land power, and its past military leaders have been concerned primarily with operations on the continents of Europe and Asia. Since World War II, however, the pattern of Soviet thought has changed. For the first time in history, Russia's politico-military leaders find their most powerful adversary on a different continent. In planning gradual isolation, encirclement, and general weakening of all their adversaries, they are striving for a balance among activities in many parts of the world. The coordinated effort aims at expanding Soviet influence and military potential in strategically important areas as favorable opportunities arise. On the one hand the Soviets are building up a powerful military machine designed for offensive action and capable of operating globally. On the other hand they may find it possible, by well-coordinated use of various subterfuges, so to weaken their adversaries' resolve and power to resist that they will be able, in successive stages, to expand their area of domination without having to fight a major war.

On the evidence of history, and particularly the history of World War II, we simply cannot afford to sit back in our comfortable chairs and suppose the attainment of the political objectives of nations to be purely a military matter. It is very definitely not so today; probably it never was. We do face grave military threats, but the nonmilitary threats may well be far more dangerous. Wars, whether hot or cold, will be won or lost by a combination of activities, some of them far removed from any battlefield, and many of them involving some form of communication directed at the minds of men. Any screen of secrecy that prevents our planners from anticipating future nonmilitary threats should be challenged. As for the military threats, we may well conclude that the conduct of war is very largely a matter of communicating true and false information, and of recognizing which is which.

TRAINING

A great many considerations need to be taken into account in the advanced planning of national defense measures and of the communications needed to make them effective. As has been pointed out, the development of increasingly sophisticated weapons systems is easily understood and glamorous. It appeals to our military command, to our armaments industry, to our politicians, and to the general public. But it is by no means the whole answer. Indeed von Mellenthin did not mention weapons in his analysis of the reasons for the quick success of the German blitzkrieg in May 1940.

We have been thinking of two matters that von Mellenthin stressed—a balanced force of all arms and command from the front. But ahead of these he rates the advantage of excellent training and communications, neither of which have the glamour of weaponry. I have a few comments to make about training, but will postpone most of my discussion of communications to the next chapter.

The problem of training personnel to respond effectively to any situation with which they may be faced on a future battlefield is an important facet of advanced planning that is too often neglected. The objective must be to provide latent capabilities at all echelons in all branches of the services. A dictionary meaning of "latent" is "present but not visible or active." Thus, latent capabilities are those that, though not in use at all times, can always be brought into play when they are needed.*

In view of the increasing complexity of warfare, a very important latent capability of each operational unit is that of prompt cooperation with other units when a commander at a higher echelon establishes a special task force to meet a new thrust or to exploit a new opportunity. The units of such a task force may not be accustomed to cooperating with one another. They will have dual responsibility—in the chain of command of their specialized activities and within the task force—but once the higher-echelon commander has spelled out the objectives of his special task force, and its internal command structure, the achievement of objectives will depend on direct cooperation among the units involved. These units will suddenly need information from other units with which they would not usually communicate. One of the objectives of a battlefield communications system, therefore, must be to make such

---

* Use of the word "latent" in connection with information and capabilities may be unfamiliar to the reader. Indeed I may well have introduced the idea myself in the course of my studies of tactical communications.

information "latent"—not present all the time but available when needed.

This idea of an interdisciplinary task force created to achieve a specified objective is essentially what Auchinleck had in mind in his establishment of closely coordinated battle groups. In today's business world it is known as matrix management.

Important tools of training are wargaming and exercises, aimed at preparing personnel at all echelons for the situations with which they may be faced. Guderian tells us that major German operations, such as his vital crossing of the Meuse near Sedan in 1940, were very thoroughly wargamed beforehand. The troops involved were trained and exercised for their roles, and it was found that the actual course of events would be close to the predictions of the wargaming oracle.

Guderian was concerned with the coordination in battle of tanks, self-propelled artillery, antitank weapons, motorized infantry, and air power. But the Soviet concept of blitzkrieg has gone a long way beyond that of Hitler's Germany, and there are many more combat elements, including those of electronic and chemical warfare, whose activities will need to be coordinated.

Quite recently I have studied a number of thick documents on which the execution of recent field exercises and war games has been based. The preparatory work is so immense and complex that exercises and war games cannot be performed frequently. And even such massive preparation fails to take important factors into account. In a recent major field exercise in West Germany, witnessed by a colleague, there was no attempt at all to simulate enemy jamming—yet even so the exercise ran into a lot of communications trouble arising from line-of-sight problems, poor management, and interference among radio nets.

Training for combat communications should be simple, focused on specific tasks, and accompanied by intensive exercising. A huge communications manual covering a wide range of possible situations would prove useless under combat conditions, for there is no time to find the correct response to an immediate situation in a large manual. The communications men in combat units need instead to be trained and exercised in simple procedures for handling the specific situations they are likely to face.

This idea of simple training aimed at specific tasks and accompanied by repeated exercises could prove very important on a battlefield. Indeed it seems to be a necessary application of the accepted U.S. Army doctrine that a commander is responsible for training his men. But this kind of training is a job, not for the commander at high echelons, but for the junior officer who will be on the spot. For in actual war the nature of a battlefield continually changes. Only those in close touch with combat operations will be able to recognize new tasks, improvise means of handling them, indoctrinate troops accordingly, and see that the new functions are exercised. If this idea is to work, moreover, the junior officers themselves must be well trained and exercised in this aspect of their responsibilities.

Not long ago—I would guess in the early 1970s—the Soviets set aside a whole year as "The Year of the Junior Officer." Since World War II, the level of intelligence and education in the ranks of their armies had been steadily improving. The year's primary aim was to indoctrinate junior officers in the task of training their troops to perform their battlefield functions. I do not recollect seeing an account of the results achieved by the Soviets, nor do I know how much attention they paid to communications functions. However, from anecdotes of a communications sergeant I know that the American junior officers of General Patton's army did not have the latent capability needed to improvise new combat communications procedures and provide the necessary training in the field. I do not know whether the situation is any better today. Yet it seems evident that combined arms operations will depend for their effectiveness on efficient handling of simple communications tasks by all combat units involved. We must identify, therefore, which simple facts about communications should be part of overall indoctrination, training, and exercising at all levels and in all services. And, in so doing, we must pay careful attention to the handling of intelligence and to matters of cryptographic security. We have seen that failure to pay such attention was disastrous for the security of the German Enigma.

THREE MILE ISLAND

I will close this chapter by talking about the spectacular disaster of March 1979 at the Three Mile Island nuclear power plant, because the causes of this disaster are very relevant to the military problems we must face today. If we are to remedy the faults in our overall defense posture, and in particular the glaring weaknesses of our tactical communications, we urgently need to conduct a wide search for applicable ideas, employing expertise from nonmilitary as well as military fields.

For example, as I will show later, we will do well to take advantage of academic studies in management theory and organizational communications, which have had a major impact in business and industry, where nonmilitary wars are being fought all the time. What I want to show now is that we have an extremely valuable source of ideas in the deliberations of the President's commission appointed to look into the disaster at Three Mile Island. Lectures on the subject by the commission's chairman, John G. Kemeny, given at Dartmouth College and at MIT, contain a great deal that is directly applicable to our military problems. For instance the study has led Kemeny to believe that the major problems of today are so complex that they can only be solved by interdisciplinary cooperation in planning, in operations, and in keeping a lookout for the winds of change. We can no longer expect, he says, to muddle through if and when we are faced by further technological developments and new threats. We must pay far more attention than we do to "people problems."

The Three Mile Island disaster, the worst accident in the history of commercial nuclear power generation, occurred on March 28, 1979. Two weeks later President Carter established a twelve-member commission to conduct a comprehensive study and investigation of the accident. The members of the commission represented the greatest possible diversity the White House could create. Each of them had some degree of relevant expertise, but none of them was an expert on all the subjects they had to investigate. Initially they were led to believe that the accident was all the fault of the operators, but they soon discovered that this was not so. To a man, the operators and their supervisors testified that they were simply never prepared for anything like the situation they had faced. At that point the commission, which was concentrating on the equipment, began to focus even more on other matters. In the end their major conclusion was that the real problem was not the equipment but the people. They found "people problems" in more different places than they would ever have guessed at the outset. The greatest fault in the equipment was the poor design of the control room, which was the principal interface with the operator. Kemeny states that the design was thirty years out of date. Otherwise the basic equipment was found to be extremely good.

In accordance with Nuclear Regulatory Commission (NRC) regulations, operators were only required to be trained for an accident in which one thing went wrong. In this accident three things went wrong simultaneously. What happened is of considerable interest.

During routine maintenance, a minor mishap caused a pump to be turned off, which stopped the flow of water into the steam generator.* As a result the nuclear reactor was not being properly cooled; but this was automatically detected, and two safety devices functioned properly. A relief valve at the top of the pressurizer lifted to release pressure, and control rods dropped, causing the nuclear chain reaction to stop. So far, ten seconds after the mishap, things seemed under control. Then three more serious mishaps occurred.

First, an emergency supply of water was automatically turned on, but failed to reach its destination, the steam generator. After eight minutes of frantic search, an operator discovered that some manually controlled valves that should have been open had been left closed. Second, a light in the control room showed that an electric signal had been sent to close the relief valve on the pressurizer, even though this valve had in fact stuck open. Had the operators known of this open valve immediately, they could have solved the problem by closing a second valve from the control room. But it was two hours and twenty minutes before the sticking of the valve was discovered, and by that time tens of thousands of gallons of water needed for cooling had been lost.

Even with the valve stuck open, everything would have been brought under control automatically by the main safety system, which came on by itself two minutes after the initial mishap; but a third thing went wrong. The safety system, using two pumps, was capable of injecting a thousand gallons of water a minute, which would have been more than enough. But the operators turned off one of the pumps and cut the other back so that the rate of water

---

* It will not be necessary for the reader to understand the functions of the steam generator, pressurizer, and other system components.

injection was reduced to less than one hundred gallons a minute. This turned a minor incident into a major accident.

Why did the operators do this? To find out, the commission studied the selection and training of operators. They found that the operator school taught button-pushing; it did not teach the fundamentals of nuclear power. A key training device was a computer that was supposed to simulate what could happen in the control room, but the commission found that the computer program was incapable of reproducing the conditions that actually occurred. Thus the operators and supervisors were proven correct in claiming that they had not been prepared for what happened.

But they could have been! By searching a mass of documents, the commission learned of an earlier accident, in September 1977, at the Davis-Besse nuclear plant. A somewhat different initial mishap caused the pressure-operated relief valve to open; the reactor operated correctly, and the chain reaction stopped. But the valve did not close and, when the emergency water system came on, the operators turned it off. However, at Davis-Besse it took the operators only twenty minutes, instead of two hours and twenty minutes, to discover that the relief valve was stuck open. When they closed it, there was no longer a need for the emergency water supply that they had turned off. Little harm had been done; but the conditions at Davis-Besse were far less dangerous, in that it was operating at 10 percent power and was a newly fueled plant, requiring less heat to be removed than would otherwise be the case.

Someone investigating the incident for Babcock and Wilcox Company, manufacturers of the steam supply system, was worried that the operators could have turned off the emergency water supply when all the recorded evidence showed that water was disappearing from the system. He found that the operators had not been watching the water pressure in the core. They were looking at the pressurizer, in which the level of water kept rising—from which they deduced, wrongly, that they had too much water in the system.

The investigator went to one of the top nuclear engineers, a Mr. Dunn, who realized what must have happened and wrote a memorandum pointing out that under certain conditions of malfunction the pressurizer can be full, with water escaping from the top, while the core could be almost empty. It was a possibility that had never been considered before. Seriously concerned, Dunn was saying that operators must be warned that in certain circumstances evidence from the pressurizer can be totally misleading. They must be taught to watch the core as well as the pressurizer, and to keep the emergency water pouring in, because, if the Davis-Besse accident had happened at full power, it could have left the core seriously uncovered and resulted in major core damage. This is precisely what happened at Three Mile Island thirteen months after Dunn wrote his memorandum. If his recommendations had been acted on during this period the major disaster need not have occurred.

In spite of Dunn's efforts, the training division at Babcock and Wilcox was not willing to change existing doctrine without approval from another division that was concerned with the overall system. The other division, however, was busy with other matters. It seems clear from Kemeny's account that the Babcock and Wilcox division responsible for training did not have the detailed understanding of systems operation that would have enabled them to see the importance of what Dunn had discovered, or, indeed, to develop adequate training in security measures. As a result of delays, caused in part by a misunderstanding in verbal person-to-person communication between the heads of the two divisions involved, the necessary instructions to operators did not get out until too weeks after the accident at Three Mile Island. Dunn had very nearly succeeded, but not quite.

Two other chances of avoiding the Three Mile Island disaster were missed through what can be categorized as gross failures in human communication. An inspector, quite low in the hierarchy of the Nuclear Regulatory Commission, became worried about the implications of the Davis-Besse incident in September 1977. He kept going to his superiors, but got nowhere. Finally he went to see two of the five commissioners of the NRC, telling them about the problem. They took him very seriously and called for an investigation. But this was on March 21, 1979—only seven days before Three Mile Island. The third chance was provided by an engineer associated with the Tennessee Valley Authority, which has similar equipment. Purely on theoretical grounds, this engineer became worried about similar possibilities and issued a number of warnings, one of which concerned the kind of problem that caused operator misunderstanding at Davis-Besse and at Three Mile Island. These warnings were sent to the TVA, to Babcock and Wilcox, and to the Nuclear Regulatory Commission, and for all kinds of reasons none of them ever did anything about it. Three failures of human communication at the receiving end!

When the commission studied the part played by the Nuclear Regulatory Commission, they found that there too the section responsible for operator training was very weak. The requirements for licensing a new plant were too lax. But the greatest weakness was found in the arrangements for enforcing the NRC's rules and regulations. The so-called "inspection" of plants was an inspection of paperwork. The Three Mile Island plant was checked by an NRC inspector a few months before the accident, but he never looked at a single piece of equipment.

The President's commission looked at the response of the NRC to the accident, and found it utterly confused. There was a lack of communication, and many resulting actions made matters worse. The famous hydrogen bubble was an example. It was well known to experts in the field that, under some conditions of overheating, a large amount of hydrogen could be created. It was also known to scientists, though not apparently to the NRC, that the hydrogen generated at Three Mile Island could not possibly explode. So the NRC, in its ignorance, spread a warning about a possible hydrogen explosion to the press, and thereby created a completely unnecessary scare.

The commission came to the overall conclusion that the NRC was an agency hypnotized by equipment. It had a firm belief that equipment can be made fail-safe, and as a result the NRC totally ignored the human element in nuclear power. All the individual members of the President's commission promised not to speak until October 30, 1979, when their recommendations were due to be made public. These included a completely new approach to operator training, graduation on fundamentals before on-the-job training, modernization of the control room, more attention to procedures, planning for overall response to emergencies, location of plants in remote areas, insistence that states have emergency plans, and better public education. The commission concluded that it had not found any problem that was not curable or that led to the conclusion that nuclear power is too dangerous to exist as a viable energy source.

Someone, however, gave premature leaks that distorted the press coverage. The public was given a false account of the commission's deliberations, concentrating upon what kind of moratorium on new construction permits should be enforced. When the report came out, therefore, everyone wanted to know about the moratorium, an issue that had by then been blown totally out of proportion, and the most important recommendations went largely unnoticed. The biggest story, on new construction permits, never got proper media coverage: a unanimous recommendation that neither a construction permit nor an operating license should be issued until three separate requirements are met: first, that new safety requirements, recommended by the commission and others, have been implemented; second, that the applicant meet a much higher qualification for running a nuclear power plant, including having an acceptable operator-training program; and third, that the construction permits and operating licenses be made conditional on review and approval of state and local emergency plans.

Kemeny himself thinks that, if recommendations like those of the commission are implemented during the next few years, nuclear power can be one of the energy alternatives available to humanity. He is equally convinced that there should be a permanent oversight committee watching over what is being done both by a reformed Nuclear Regulatory Commission and by the nuclear industry. This watchdog committee, like the President's commission, should be composed of diverse members. It should report at least annually to the President and Congress.

In his lecture at MIT, after discussing the work of the commission, John G. Kemeny went on to discuss the changes in American democracy that are needed for survival in an age that is increasingly governed by technology. His ideas on this matter are similar to those of John A. Morse, who claims that we have reached a point at which technology drives the world. This depressing fact of life in our times has to be taken into account in our advanced planning. Kemeny is telling us that we must not be fooled by the technology salesmen, who exaggerate the capabilities of their products. Two of the principal reasons for the Three Mile Island disaster were a mistaken belief that equipment could be made fail-safe, and dependence on a computer program to simulate trouble that might occur. Both led to poor training of operators. The same symptoms show up in our military thinking, and affect not only the operators of equipment but the command function as well. For the salesmen have been maintaining that their equipment will do all that is needed, and that computers can tell commanders what to do in battle. We can only hope that a major military disaster will not be needed to prove the technology salesmen wrong.

Kemeny also stressed the need for interdisciplinary teams to work on the major problems of today, many of which are far more complex than Three Mile Island. Each member of such a team will have to expand his own field of expertise in order to contribute to the solution of the problem. His colleagues and superiors in his own field cannot have the necessary outside knowledge for all the problems in which a contribution from their expertise may be needed. So teamwork must not be inhibited by directives from the specialized communities that are represented.

These ideas on interdisciplinary cooperation translate readily into military situations. Let us suppose that at some future date a military task force is created in battle to handle some new situation. Achievement of objectives by such a task force will depend on intimate teamwork among units drawn from different specialized activities. Each such unit must acquire a detailed understanding of the current status and intentions of the other units with which it must cooperate. Superiors up the various chains of command cannot possibly keep in close touch with all the details of combat operations. Their contribution must have been made ahead of time by anticipating problems and ensuring that a subordinate, assigned to the task force, will have the necessary capabilities.

These ideas are very reminiscent of Hut 6, where success depended on uninhibited collaboration at the operating level between outside activities—Hut 3, the intercept stations, and the bombe installations—and internal activities—the Watch, the Intercept Control Room, Central Party, the Registration Room, and the Decoding Room. It must be noted, however, that, apart from our initial intercept facilities, we were an entirely new organization created to handle unprecedented wartime problems. Thus we were not inhibited by rigid doctrine developed in peacetime.

Another similarity between the Three Mile Island disaster and the Hut 6 story, this time with the German side, is that, as a result of poor interdisciplinary cooperation, the operators at the nuclear power station were not given an overall understanding of nuclear phenomena, and there was no interdisciplinary committee to keep an eye on what was going on. I have a feeling that the disaster in the security of Germany's Enigma traffic may have been due to similar failures.

I have cited many of the technical reasons for this disaster under the title "comedy of errors," and have suggested that, if the Germans had brought in people from other walks of life to attack the security measures developed by their cryptographers, they might have thought of the bombe. But perhaps the underlying cause was failure to achieve interdisciplinary cooperation, first in planning and training and then in the watchdog function. If experts in Enigma system design, in communications, and in military operations had gotten together, disaster might have been avoided. The Enigma system designers could have been given a clearer picture of how their equipment would be used. The officers who used the Enigma, the signals personnel, and the cipher clerks might all have been trained to avoid the errors that contributed to the disaster. An interdisciplinary watchdog committee might well have spotted weaknesses as they arose. This thought supports my contention that, to deal with today's problems, experts in the many relevant fields of activity—military and clandestine, offensive and defensive—must work together and learn from one another. The problems are too complex for any other approach.

15

Communications for Combat and Command

INTRODUCTION

It is said that, in the 1930s, when Leon Blum was Premier of France, Charles de Gaulle warned him about the risk of military disaster. Blum replied that this was nonsense, since France was spending more on defense than ever before. Yes, said de Gaulle; and it is what you are spending it for that concerns me.

Today the Soviet drive toward world domination poses many types of threat in many parts of the world. The ghastly prospect of nuclear war is on everyone's mind, but in Europe we and our NATO allies are also threatened by a non-nuclear attack for which the Soviets have made very thorough preparations. Our military, in deciding how to spend defense funds, have put too much emphasis on technological achievement in weapons systems and too little on the people who must maintain and operate the equipment—too much on providing sophisticated capabilities for commanders and too little on the needs of the combat units that will do the actual fighting. Success on a future battlefield will depend in large measure on how effectively the actions of the many diverse combat elements can be directed and coordinated, particularly in response to an unexpected threat or a new opportunity. This in turn will depend on the availability of adaptable means of communication that can handle information at the speeds called for by ever-

255

advancing technology. We have no such communications today—and what use is any ultra-advanced weapon, or superbly armed combat unit, without a means of communication to bring it into play at the right time with the right objective?

After World War II, the planning of battlefield communications gradually deteriorated into little more than methods of applying telephone-system thinking and switchboard technology to provide a rigid structure of point-to-point linkages. This is evidenced by the prevailing emphasis on determining "needlines" in answer to the question "Who will want to talk to whom?" The flexible inter-element connectivity that the Germans provided for their blitzkrieg by using interlocking common-user radio nets could have served as a model for our own future planning, but it was forgotten. Perhaps one should say that it was buried as a result of over-prolonged secrecy imposed on anything to do with Hut 6.

In recent years, however, both in the military and in the non-military spheres, progress has been made in the application of newly available digital technology, such as distributed data processing and data-by-the-packet. One of the most revolutionary battlefield communications systems under development today is at present known as the Joint Tactical Information Distribution System (JTIDS—pronounced Jaytids). It can claim to be a truly remarkable engineering development, taking full advantage of today's available technology; but it is more than that. It stems from serious attempts to foresee the communications needs of combat forces on potential future battlefields in different parts of the world. No comparable attempts have been made since the 1930s, when Germany was planning the battlefield communications systems needed to support its concept of wide-ranging blitzkrieg.

The development of JTIDS equipment is now supported by the U.S. Army, Navy, and Air Force. Proposed applications differ, but successful demonstrations have already proved that the system can indeed offer revolutionary capabilities. However, the equipment in its present form has been aimed at a few specific applications for which funding was forthcoming. Study of a wider range of applications is now being funded, but the rate of progress needs to be greatly accelerated. Our present means of tactical communication would certainly break down in actual battle. They are totally inadequate to deal with the problems of tomorrow. The only solution in sight lies in the development of ideas that were put forward more than ten years ago. The problems have grown more complex since that time, and will be worse still by the time that new capabilities of tactical communication can become a reality. Consequently a new and intensive round of conceptual study is needed. This must be based on an uninhibited review of military considerations. To be effective it will need contributions from many fields of expertise. And, because time may be running out, our national security calls for prompt action.

RESPONSIBILITIES OF COMMANDERS

In this chapter I will be largely concerned with the inadequacy of our present capabilities for communicating on a battlefield and with the sensational improvements that are offered by the application of available digital technology. I will start with two contrasting attitudes to a commander's duties in regard to communications.

During World War II, dignitaries visiting Bletchley Park would sometimes talk to us about what was going on in the war. On one such occasion the speaker was talking about a commander's responsibilities in battle. He asserted that a commander must make his contribution before the battle starts. He must do everything possible to give his subordinate commanders and combat troops the best possible chance of success in advance, for once battle is joined events will pass out of his control. I suppose he wanted to tell us that the Ultra intelligence we were providing was a great help in carrying out this pre-battle function in the African desert. Knowledge of enemy strength, dispositions, and intentions could help the commander foresee the course of events, lay his plans, issue his orders accordingly, and so give his army that "best possible chance."

Looking back, we can recognize this idea that the commander would lose control during battle as part of the outmoded thinking that characterized British operations in the desert at the time of the Gazala battles. Many years later I was to hear a very different story from my colleague, John Clapper, who had been a U.S. Signals Officer during the war and a member of the staff of the U.S. Army Command and General Staff College at Fort Leavenworth, Kansas, after the war. I will repeat what he said in the form in which I copied it down at the time. Although some of the phrases may be regarded as military jargon, their meaning is clear.

Clapper told me that the need to delegate decision-making responsibility during battle is well recognized in the operations of ground forces. Before battle an army task force commander must have defined his battle objectives and methods to achieve them. He must have issued guidance, orders, directives, and information requirements to all command echelons. He must issue standard operating procedures (SOPs) that clearly state what information is to be acquired, what items are to be included in messages, who is to receive messages of each category, and what the recipients are to do with the information they receive. During battle he must use preplanned tactical reconnaissance and communication to obtain information about the enemy and about his own forces. As necessary, he must redefine his objectives and methods. Again using preplanned communication, he must ensure that new directives and guidance will reach all command echelons accurately and in time. Only by meeting both his preparatory and his battle responsibilities can the task force commander ensure that in the heat of battle the junior commanders at all levels will have the best possible chance of using their local initiative effectively.

Note that in this second assessment the commander does not give up hope for exerting his influence after the battle starts, but that the means by which he does so depend largely on his having thought out ahead of time how he wants information to be acquired and distributed on the battlefield, what he wants each recipient to do with the information he receives, and what means of communication are to be used. A second set of communications procedures is to be preplanned for issuing new instructions during battle.

The second statement very clearly defines an important part of the commander's responsibilities, and presents a challenge to the designers and users of future battlefield communications systems, which must provide the capabilities that the future commanders will need. Yet this definition, though it may be recognized in operations, is contrary to official U.S. Army doctrine, as set out in the July 1976 edition of Field Manual FM 100-5, which is as follows:

In the division of responsibilities on the battlefield, Generals commanding corps and division *concentrate the forces.*

Colonels and Lieutenant Colonels of brigades and battalions *control and direct the battle.*

Captains and their companies, troops and batteries *fight the battle.*

There is no mention of responsibility for organizing information flow.

A few anecdotes, taken from very different environments, will show how communications problems of commanders have been tackled successfully in the past. I believe they suggest ideas that will be helpful in our advanced planning. I will start with another story from John Clapper, who gave me the definition of a commander's responsibilities in battle. It shows that a commander and his staff must be able to come up with on-the-spot improvisations suited to the situations in which they find themselves. It also illustrates the importance of careful planning of information flow with due regard to terrain in order to overcome the line-of-sight problems to which most of our communications are subject.

My colleague was signals officer of one of Patton's divisions during the Battle of the Bulge. His division was to attack the German southern flank through hilly country. His division commander, who appreciated the value of communications more than most, took him along to the planning conference. So, knowing exactly what would be needed from reconnaissance patrols, Clapper studied his contour maps and laid his plans. He told each patrol exactly what they were to discover and report. He told them how to report in very short messages, to reduce the chance that they would be heard by enemy radio intelligence. And he told them where to report from, so that they would be within line-of-sight of one of his carefully placed listening posts. It worked like a charm. The division commander received the information he wanted about enemy dispositions. The radio reports were not picked up by the enemy. Complete surprise was achieved, and the attack was highly successful.

In the hope of obtaining guidance for the future, let us also consider a few examples from the more distant past in which communications were well planned by commanders and attention was paid to terrain. I have spoken of Albert James Myer, the pioneer of U.S. Army signaling and inventor of wig-wag. Although Myer himself fought on the Union side in the American Civil War, and rose to the rank of General, many of his assistants and trainees fought on the Confederate side. One of them, a Lieutenant Alexander, was assigned to General Beauregard as signals officer during the Battle of Bull Run. When a strong Union force under General McDowell had turned Beauregard's flank and was closing in for a knockout blow, Alexander, well placed on a hill to the rear, saw McDowell's force as it emerged from cover and signaled Colonel Evans, "Look out for your left, your position is turned." This short wig-wag signal virtually turned the tide of battle. It reached Bee, Hampton, and Jackson, who promptly maneuvered their forces to aid Evans. Their quickly coordinated efforts stopped McDowell. This was the time when Jackson stood "like a stone wall" until Johnstone, who had also received Alexander's signal, arrived with fresh troops and the battle was turned into a great Confederate victory. Note that the wig-wag system and a well-organized signals unit made it possible for one vital tactical message to be conveyed very rapidly to five front-line commanders who were thereby enabled to coordinate their actions against a surprise attack.

The American Civil War was fought from 1861 to 1865. Two decades later, on April 12, 1886, General Nelson A. Miles of the U.S. Army was put in command of the Department of Arizona. For many years his predecessor had failed to subjugate the Apache Indians under the leadership of Geronimo. General Myer had drawn Miles' attention to the heliograph, a recently developed optical signaling method used by the British in India. Its simple principle, familiar even to children today, is that a carefully positioned mirror can reflect sunlight to a chosen point at a considerable distance. If a mirror is positioned in this way, with a drive mechanism to compensate for the movement of the sun, messages can be transmitted in Morse code to the distant point by masking the mirror at intervals, so that the reflected sunlight is transmitted in dots and dashes. The clear dry air of Arizona and New Mexico, combined with the almost continual sunlight, provided ideal conditions for signaling by heliograph. Furthermore, this system would not be vulnerable like telegraph lines to sabotage, at which the Apaches had become skilled.

In short order a network of observation and communications points was established, using carefully selected locations on mountain ranges. Guided by this communications network, the U.S. Army, in spite of the rugged terrain, was able to trail the elusive Apaches. By September 4, 1886, less than five months after General Miles' assignment to Arizona, Geronimo and the remainder of the Apaches had surrendered.

This success story of a blitzkrieg based on speed of communications contains several interesting features. It was of course concerned with small-scale operations in unusual terrain. But, if we take global threats seriously, we too may find it necessary to conduct small-scale operations in which the nature of the terrain will be an extremely important factor. We also may find that sabotage of our communications, and other tricks that can be played on us even by an unsophisticated enemy, may be disastrous. We should remember how this theater commander saw that his problem could be solved by new technology particularly well suited to the characteristics of the environment in which he had to operate.

Another example of speedy on-the-spot improvisation to meet the particular situation with which a commander found himself faced is an even earlier form of blitzkrieg based on speed of communications, developed by the French under General Bugeaud in Algeria in the late 1830s. Bugeaud developed "flying columns" of troops that could move rapidly to any part of the country without support from any established strongpoints or lines of communications. As in Arizona, the country was mountainous and the air clear. General Bugeaud hit on the same idea of using signaling stations on the mountain ranges to communicate rapidly with his flying columns wherever they might be. The type of heliograph used by General Miles had not yet been invented (it was developed from a device invented in India by Captain E. E. Begbie in 1873), but General Bugeaud obtained excellent results from semaphore signaling. Again we should remember that we may find it necessary in some small-scale conflict to employ the old concept of flying columns, and that this will probably call for improvisation of a suitable means of communication.

One wonders whether General Miles, and perhaps Hitler's planners too, may have been inspired by study of General Bugeaud's combination of flying columns and a countrywide signaling network. We do know for certain that in 1959 another French general took full advantage of this episode of military history. In January of that year General Challe of the French Air Force was appointed Commander in Chief of the French forces in Algiers. He immediately set to work to build a super-mobile force of twenty thousand men. Using Bugeaud's maps, he installed VHF radio repeaters where the old semaphore stations had been located. By this means all of Algeria north of the Sahara was served by a voice radio net. All military aircraft carried radio repeaters, so that any soldier on the ground with a "walkie-talkie" could talk directly to any command post via the radio net whenever an aircraft was in his vicinity. Thus General Challe was able to coordinate all his mobile ground units and all his air resources quickly and effectively.

The successes of Generals Bugeaud and Challe reinforce the lessons drawn from the story of General Miles. But the General Challe story also contains the important idea that every operational aircraft can very easily be made to act as a communications relay.

EARLY CONCEPTS USING DIGITAL PACKETS

I have noted that a U.S. Air Force "master plan" for an advanced air control capability, completed at MITRE in April 1966, contained a new concept, known as AEGIS, for handling position reports from some 120 friendly aircraft. Each individual aircraft was to determine its position in a common grid by a scheme involving triangulation. The reports were to be in the form of short coded digital messages, now called "packets." The positions of all subscribing aircraft would be shown on screen displays at the command center and in each aircraft. Using AEGIS ideas and the recent possibility of laser ranging, I contributed an ATAST concept that would enable an airborne forward air controller to report the position of an enemy ground target as well as his own. The target locations could then appear on the screen display of an attacking pilot. These two early conceptual ideas, both exploiting digital packet technology, have been considerably improved and extended. Their feasibility has been demonstrated, and their value is fully recognized by many pilots, but after fifteen years the necessary hardware is still under development.

Later, in 1966, I worked out a concept, aimed at combined arms operations, that involved a high-capacity common-user radio repeater net dedicated to the handling of short formatted operational messages as digital packets. I called these packets Unit Digital Messages (UDMs) in recognition of their close similarity to the Unit Records of punched-card terminology. Information-retrieval technology, already under development, was to enable each subscriber to select just the messages he wanted, while rejecting the mass of messages that he did not want. Each UDM was to contain a set of descriptive codes for this purpose, called the "selection indicator" of the UDM.

The concept of a receiver-oriented UDM system for battlefield use arose from studies of military history that I had undertaken in an attempt to develop an insight into the real nature of combat in the various categories of limited war that I had been analyzing. I had found that the planning of communications, even for a single battle, had often been sadly neglected. Over and over again information available to some combat unit had failed to reach other units to which it would have been of great value. I had found vivid examples of this in the naval battles of Midway and Leyte Gulf, and in many episodes from Korea, a war for which we were singularly ill prepared. Moreover, I had become convinced from talks with experienced signals people that the really important tactical messages on a battlefield need not be long—indeed tend to be short—and that many of them could be reduced to a sequence of coded symbols in standard format, much as items of information are handled in punched-card systems. Such UDMs offered many advantages, among them that message assembly in format would ensure that no necessary item would be omitted; there was little danger that a message would be misinterpreted; and communication between combat elements speaking different languages would be facilitated.

The UDM concept of 1966 led to a more ambitious concept of a general-purpose battlefield communications system that could handle teletype, digital data, digitized voice, and digitized pictures as well as UDMs.

In June 1968 I set out my tentative ideas in a working paper on "cyclic information systems" (CIS). The inverted horseshoe diagram of Figure 15.1 was presented, I believe for the first time, to

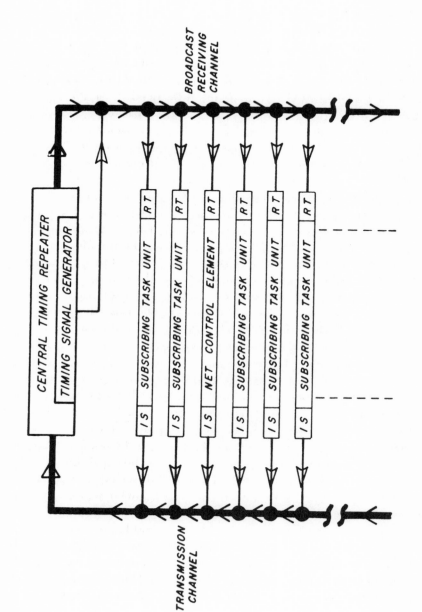

Figure 15.1 The HORSESHOE Diagram

illustrate the basic principles.* The diagram shows five of many thousands of force elements, or "task units," that could be subscribers to a net, and the single Net Control Element (NCE). I was concerned with the functions and responsibilities of each task unit as an information source (IS) and as a receiving terminal (RT). The IS boxes in the diagram indicate the equipment needed for message preparation and transmission in the form of digital packets. The RT boxes indicate equipment needed for reception of packets, for applying test criteria to the selection indicator of each packet to determine whether it is wanted or not, and for handling selected messages. All the IS boxes transmit on the same radio frequency (or channel) to a central timing repeater (CTR), which we will assume to be on an aircraft or other high-altitude platform. The CTR retransmits each packet on a broadcast channel using a second frequency. It also puts numbered timing signals on the broadcast receiving channel; these are picked up by all RT boxes. The intervals between the timing signals are the time slots on the receiving channel into which packets must be fitted. Using the received timing signals and an internal clock, the IS box of each subscribing task unit calculates the exact time at which it must transmit a packet on the transmission channel so that it will be repeated in an assigned time slot on the receiving channel.

The subscribers shown in the diagram who can communicate directly with the CTR are called first-stage subscribers. Other task units who are prevented by distance or terrain obstacles from communicating directly with the CTR may operate in the net as second-stage subscribers with the assistance of a first-stage subscriber. Their IS and RT boxes need not have all the capabilities of the first stage. There may also be third-stage subscribers, such as forward elements with even simpler equipment, who will obtain access to the net with assistance from second-stage subscribers.

My CIS paper aroused quite a lot of interest, and led to engineering design and partial development of a demonstration system. The demonstration was designed to show how the RT boxes of a number of subscribers could select those that were wanted from among the messages continually flowing on the broadcast receiving channel.

---

* Since about 1970 virtually the same diagram has been used repeatedly in descriptions of packet communications systems.

Selection criteria were quite complex, but the experimental RT boxes handled them without difficulty. Trouble arose, however, with the magnetic tape equipment that was to simulate the broadcast receiving channel by pouring a prerecorded stream of packets into the RT boxes. It proved quite impossible to obtain reliable performance from the only magnetic tape equipment available to the project, and the demonstration had to be canceled. This was a great blow to all concerned, because they were really excited about the concept, feeling that they had something completely new and very worthwhile to demonstrate.

While others were working on the CIS demonstration, I went on looking into various aspects of the overall problem. To determine what characteristics the system should have, I did a lot more reading of military history and studied the forward-looking writings of military scientists. I looked into the problems of exchanging information between nets with different areas of coverage. And I thought a good deal about how a net could be managed by its net control element in accordance with the overall wishes of the commander in the theater of operations and with the changing needs on the battlefield. By late 1970 I had written a two-hundred-page document setting out my analysis of military considerations, system characteristics called for by these considerations, principles of system operation, and methods of net management. The title was *Selective Access to Tactical Information*, SATI for short—a more suitable name than "cyclic information systems."*

I was due to retire from MITRE at age sixty-five in June 1971, so it was agreed that without delay I should go to Washington to obtain reactions to SATI, and to discover among people and organizations any sign of interest, support, funding, or even development work under contract. Armed with my document, I set off in mid-November 1970 on my first SATI sortie to Washington. There, in three days, I had discussions with five organizations. The last of my ports of call was the Joint Services Office in the Pentagon, where I talked to a colonel who was quick to grasp all the important SATI ideas. He was enthusiastic, felt that I had made a good start with

---

* The document, M70-97, prepared under U.S. Air Force contract F19(628)71-C-0365, Project 603C, was approved for public release. A greatly shortened version appeared in the February and March 1971 issues of *Signal*.

the other people I had seen, and asked for several copies of my document. He intended to arouse interest in other quarters and to have a meeting set up for my next visit.

When I met him in Washington again in January 1971, however, the picture seemed a little less bright. The colonel told me that he had discussed SATI with several people in the Pentagon. He and everyone else felt that my analysis of military considerations was fine and that the resulting SATI concept was interesting. They also felt, however, that my approach to a battlefield information system was dauntingly broad and that, because it rested on a doctrine of command responsibility for organization of information flow, it required a revolution in thinking. In the colonel's words, the general conclusion was that "they didn't know what the hell to do about it." I was told that in the Pentagon of those days the word "command" meant "computer," while the word "communications" meant "TRI-TAC," a program then aimed at developing a telephone switchboard that could handle the traffic of all three services. The idea of command responsibility for communications was revolutionary, contrary to doctrine, and therefore unacceptable. And that was that!

DEVELOPMENT OF JTIDs

Much of the UDM, CIS, and SATI thinking on how best to meet the communications requirements of combined arms operations is still valid, but it was aimed at environments that could have been expected in limited wars outside Europe in the 1960s. At that time it was considered that war in Europe would go nuclear at once. By 1970, however, the possibility of conventional warfare in Europe had become the focus of our military thinking. The AEGIS study of 1965 had been followed by a series of projects with different names, one of which had just obtained USAF funding for the development of experimental hardware. This was the beginning of what we now know as JTIDS. The far greater threat from enemy weapons and electronic warfare systems in a European environment led to a new approach to the design of a high-capacity common-user radio net handling digital packets. A valuable relative navigation capability emerged from this new approach. The leaders of this MITRE project studied the overall problem of battlefield communications, but the development of equipment and the important study of what formatted messages will be needed had to be oriented toward a few specific applications.

In the early days of conceptual thinking—the mid-1960s—it was realized that a great deal of positional information could be carried on a high-capacity radio net in the form of various categories of UDMs. For example, the pilot of an aircraft assigned to a ground attack mission would be able to call up a geographical display showing the positional data of special interest to him at each stage of the mission from takeoff to return to base. The data, entered on the net by a variety of sources, would include positions of friendly aircraft, enemy aircraft, targets, friendly antiaircraft defenses, enemy antiaircraft defenses, terrain obstacles, waypoints, friendly airfields, and so on. Such a net, serving a battle zone, would carry a mass of UDMs, but by using selection indicators and the positions contained in the messages, the pilot's equipment would display only wanted information in a chosen sector of the zone. Fifteen years ago it seemed clear that available technology could provide this capability, and moreover, that the effectiveness of fighter aircraft could thereby be greatly increased.

The first Air Force funding for experimental verification of feasibility came in the fall of 1969. By scrounging existing items of equipment, MITRE personnel produced successful demonstrations in New England. USAF funding for engineering development began in 1972. Demonstrations were given in Europe in 1973 in which aircraft tracks over Albania, picked up by AWACS* aircraft over Italy, were displayed in a command center in West Germany. But this engineering development project was tied to the AWACS program, its purpose being the distribution of information concerning aircraft positions observed by AWACS and ground-based surveillance centers.

Unfortunately, the AWACs application did not fully utilize the capabilities that JTIDs has to offer. It called for transmissions from one terminal to many terminals, essentially in a broadcast mode. It did not call for the high-capacity many-to-many connectivity that is one of the principal features of JTIDS. For example, if a

---

* Airborne Warning and Control System

combined-arms task group has to be formed to achieve some particular objective, it is possible in JTIDS conceptual thinking to arrange for each task unit of the group to receive all messages relevant to group activity from all the other task units. An individual task unit need not know the identities of all the other task units that may need his messages. Provided that each task unit has been told what information to include in reports, and what selection indicators to use, the information can get to all the places where it is needed.

The possibility of providing a comprehensive display for a fighter pilot was perceived in the conceptual thinking of the mid-1960s, and was a prime objective of the JTIDs team. But the JTIDs equipment for the AWACs program was designed for use on the ground or in a large aircraft. It was not suitable for use in a fighter aircraft.

In early 1973 a cockpit simulator in MITRE was fitted with display equipment to demonstrate types of presentation that would be valuable to a fighter pilot. In 1977 the USAF called on MITRE to write specifications for equipment for use in fighters then under development. In the meantime a contractor working for the U.S. Navy had designed experimental equipment suitable for fighters. In the late 1970s this compact equipment formed the basis of a program aimed at JTIDS pods that could be attached externally to existing fighters. The Army had been developing a position location and navigation system for ground elements in an area of combat, and were studying the applications of JTIDS to Army problems. Up to 1979 progress had been made at a disappointingly slow pace, but in this year the U.S. Army became seriously interested in capabilities offered by JTIDS for more effective coordination of ground and air forces, particularly in the area of air defense. In 1979, however, and again in 1980, the USAF wanted to stop the development of JTIDS terminals for fighter aircraft, thereby threatening other developments aimed at facilitating the coordination of air and surface elements.

Many U.S. Air Force pilots, particularly those with experience of communications foulups in Vietnam, have been enthusiastic about the type of geographical display that could be provided. This is only one of many military advantages that could be gained by developing a general-purpose battlefield communications system. But problems have changed radically since the early thinking was done.

Although the need to be prepared for a massive blitzkrieg in West Germany may be foremost in our minds, it is very necessary to pay attention also to the many types of military action that may be necessary in other parts of the world—a matter that has been neglected since the 1960s. A study with so many facets calls for contributions from many fields of expertise—in fact, for an interdisciplinary effort. It has taken more than a decade to get from the first USAF funding to where we are now. Can we afford to continue at a snail's pace?

POTENTIAL VALUE OF JTIDs

From my very brief account of the battle of Gazala it will, I believe, be evident that a high-capacity many-to-many communication system such as JTIDs could have made all the difference to the British 8th Army. If every unit had been able to transmit reports on a single net, available to all other units, Rommel's moves would have been known everywhere, and the rapid organization of countermeasures would have been greatly facilitated. A study of the more detailed account in *The Desert Generals* will show much more clearly just what JTIDs could have done. I propose, here, to illustrate the potential value of JTIDs by discussing how it could have helped the U.S. Air Force in Vietnam.

When the Vietnam war escalated, the U.S. Air Force introduced its most sophisticated aircraft and its cumbersome Command and Control (C^2) Systems. A few anecdotes will suffice to indicate that, whereas in the south we were just grossly inefficient, in the north we allowed our planes to be shot down unnecessarily. I will show that the situation could have been very different if the digital communications system, JTIDs, now being developed, had been available to the commanders and pilots of those days.

The following stories were told to me by a pilot, Kenneth Kronlund, who flew F-4s in Vietnam—magnificent aircraft with varied capabilities, but largely wasted because of C^2 system foulups. Ken Kronlund went to Vietnam as a major, having flown aircraft for the U.S. Air Force since 1952. After his tour of duty in Vietnam, he was assigned, in 1968, to the Electronic Systems Division of the Air Force Systems Command to work on Research and Development Programs related to C^2 systems. He found himself involved in the supervision of two MITRE programs, one of which was a forerunner of JTIDs. At this point he began to think seriously about what had gone wrong in Vietnam and why. He soon became enthusiastic about the thinking in MITRE and elsewhere about what recently available digital communications could do for our C^2 systems and for our fighter pilots. As project supervisor, he was able to make a major personal contribution to the present JTIDs program.

Our F-4s usually flew in flights of two or four aircraft. Before each mission the flight leader would be briefed. He would be told the mission identification number, the purpose of the mission, and how the mission was to be executed from takeoff to return to base. Usually the mission would involve coordination with other aircraft and with ground-based elements. The flight leader was told how this was to be achieved. He was given the callsigns and frequencies that he would need.*

The initial briefing for a mission could take one of three standard forms. First, in the case of preplanned missions, the details of which had been worked out in advance, the pilot would get his briefing well ahead of time, and would be able to study the problems he would be likely to encounter. Secondly, there were the "scramble missions" intended to provide quick response to a need or an opportunity. Pilots and aircraft assigned to such missions would wait on the ground for "scramble" orders, calling for immediate takeoff. In this case, the pilot would get his initial instructions, or briefing, by radio in the cockpit of his aircraft. Thirdly, to achieve faster response, aircraft could be held in readiness in the air, on Combat Air Patrol (CAP), in which case, also, they would get their briefing by radio.

As he studied the notes that he had made at the time, Ken Kronlund was disturbed to find that, out of some sixty-five F-4 missions that he had flown, only about five had gone as originally briefed. He had "war stories" to tell about his attacks on ground targets, but he found that not one of his positive combat achievements had been

---

* Ken's talk about callsigns and frequencies takes me right back to my early days in the Bletchley Park school in September 1939. Many things have changed, but some persist.

included in an initial mission briefing. They had occurred only because he was redirected or had acted on his own initiative to take advantage of some unexpected opportunity. So, instead of telling "war stories," Ken found himself telling what he calls his "non-war stories" to illustrate the failings of the established C^2 systems and the urgent need for change.

It was not easy to pin down the exact cause of each foulup, but a basic reason for most of them was some form of fragmentation. The C^2 system was compartmentalized and lacked the flexibility needed for the on-the-spot improvisation at the combat level—so essential in actual battle. Each mission would involve people in different hierarchies, any one of whom, by failing to perform some function properly and without delay, could prevent the mission from doing anything of value. The lack of a common navigation grid was a form of fragmentation. Furthermore, the available means of communication, which followed the fragmentation of command and control, failed to provide the immediate connectivity so badly needed in battle for the coordination of different types of combat elements who would not normally need to communicate with each other. Communications capabilities tended to provide for one-to-one links between individual elements, and for one-to-many links between a command element and its subordinates. Voice radio nets, each operating on one frequency, could provide few-to-few communications for small groups of elements, but there was no provision for the widespread many-to-many links so essential nowadays to the coordination of diverse combat elements who must work together, sometimes on their own initiative, to deal with newly apparent threats and opportunities.

I will recount a few of Ken Kronlund's non-war stories, not all of which are related to his own missions, but let us first consider the number of different radio frequencies that the leader of an F-4 flight would have to use, remembering that he could operate effectively on one frequency at a time.*

At the start of a mission six different frequencies would be needed to talk to the other pilot(s) of the flight, to the Tactical Unit Operations Center (TUOC) associated with his airfield (which, in Ken's

---

* Actually an F-4 pilot would have a GIB (Guy in Back) who could be operating on a second frequency, but many of our military planes are single-seaters.

case, was at Da Nang), to the airfield taxi control, to the tower controlling takeoff, to the center controlling departure from the immediate vicinity of the airfield, and to a radar monitoring his progress on the first stage of his route. All this was commonplace to an experienced pilot; but, if the mission involved coordination with some other element, for example an Airborne Forward Air Controller (AFAC), he would need other assigned frequencies. He might also need to talk to the Direct Air Support Center (DASC) to which the AFAC was assigned, or to the Airborne Battlefield Command and Control Center (ABCCC), if not to other elements of the fragmented C^2 system—including, of course, the TUOC to which he himself was subordinate.

The success of his mission might well depend on whether one of these many elements sent him information that he needed when he needed it. And this in turn would depend on whether the element knew his callsign and the radio frequency on which he was operating, for without this information they would not be able to communicate with him. So long as his mission was going as briefed, the elements involved should have known how to contact him. But any diversion to another task would probably cause him to operate on a new frequency, which would not be known to elements needing to make contact with him. Moreover, Ken himself might want to make contact with other fighters looking for targets of opportunity in order to enlist their support in attacking a target that he had discovered. To do this, he would need to know what friendly fighters were in his vicinity, their callsigns, and the frequencies on which they were currently operating.

These problems of having to use different frequencies for different purposes would not have arisen if the potential capabilities of JTIDs had been available. All traffic would have passed on one high-capacity net, available to all elements, both for transmission and for reception. Messages could have been put on the net by any subscribing element, and other subscribing elements could pick off whatever was important to them. The receiving equipment of each element would automatically examine the selection indicators to determine which digital packets should be accepted. System design would ensure that each subscriber would know when a message in which he should be interested was arriving.

Ken Kronlund would often be briefed to establish contact with an

Airborne Forward Air Controller in some remote place, only to find on arrival that the AFAC might have been there at some earlier time, perhaps an hour or two or even a day or two ago, but certainly wasn't there now. This could have been prevented by JTIDs because the AFAC's JTIDs terminal would be automatically determining his position in the common grid and reporting it on the common-user net. Both the control center handling Ken's mission and Ken himself could have known where the AFAC was at all times.

On one occasion he was to provide cover for a defoliation mission in the Khe-Sanh area, involving rendezvous with an AFAC and the aircraft equipped for defoliation—both much slower than him. On arrival at the designated place he found no activity. He contacted every conceivable element in the C^2 system (his TUOC, various DASCs, radars, etc.) for information and instructions, without success. He requested a mission over North Vietnam. Finally, running out of gas, he returned to base only to find that the defoliation mission had been diverted to another area, and no one had told him. With JTIDs, Ken would have been able to select from the common-user net all messages related to the mission, including the designation of a new target area and position reports from the other participating aircraft.

The reason for the refusal to assign him a target in North Vietnam is almost unbelievable. Coordination among aircraft over North Vietnam was so bad that no two missions were allowed to be flown in the same general area at the same time for fear that they might attack each other. When he made his request another mission was in progress, so he couldn't go. Moreover there was no adequate coordination between the Air Force and the Navy, which was also sending planes to North Vietnam, so it was necessary to allocate zones and times.

Again JTIDs could have helped, in that the current position of each friendly aircraft over North Vietnam would have appeared on the cockpit display of every other friendly aircraft in the vicinity.

On one occasion Ken was sent to North Vietnam to attack a mobile command post shown on a reconnaissance photograph, but he noticed that the photograph was a month old. Even JTIDs could not have prevented this type of C^2 system foulup. More attention to people problems might have done so.

An AFAC, also, had communications problems. If he was in contact with an army unit under enemy attack and wanted to call for air support, he might be able to get through to the nearest Direct Air Support Center (DASC), which could scramble a fighter mission. Often, however, the AFAC would have to call the Airborne Battlefield Command and Control Center (ABCCC), which would pass his request to the 7th Air Force headquarters, which would relay it to a DASC—a process that could well lead to delay. In any case the AFAC's request, transmitted in the clear, could be picked up by the attacking enemy, who would know that an air attack was to be expected but could not arrive in less than a certain time— perhaps twenty-five to thirty minutes.

In this case JTIDs could have helped in two ways. First, the AFAC's request, carried on the common-user net, would have been picked up immediately by a DASC that could scramble aircraft, by any aircraft on CAP that could provide faster response, and by any C^2 center whose approval was needed. Second, the JTIDs signals could only be picked up and interpreted by highly sophisticated equipment. In the somewhat peculiar environment of Vietnam, JTIDs, with its ability to make information available anywhere, could have helped in a third problem—that of coordinating air support activities with the South Vietnamese Province Chief in the area of operations.

Another of Ken's "non-war" stories concerns an attack on a ground target that was to be designated by an AFAC who had spotted it. Ken's F-4 had an accurate inertial navigation system, which gave him his position in Geo Ref coordinates (a system that does not take the curvature of the earth into account, as does positioning by latitude and longitude, but is nonetheless very satisfactory for use in pretty large areas). Both Ken and the AFAC pilot, however, used the range and azimuth system known as TACAN. When told an AFAC's position in TACAN coordinates, Ken would be able to rendezvous to within 10 miles, which was good enough to establish radio communications. On this particular occasion the AFAC was in the valley that contained his target. Ken in his F-4 came in at a fairly high altitude, so his communications with the AFAC were not blocked by the hills. At this point, however, because TACAN would be of no use in the valley, the AFAC began to use terrain features as a means of guidance.

He described his valley, in which there was a stream that took a turn to the left, and instructed Ken to follow the turn and look for a target with certain characteristics. Ken dropped into a valley that answered the AFAC's description, followed the stream's turn to the left, but could see no target. Finding that he had lost radio contact with the AFAC, he climbed to altitude, made radio contact again, and found that the AFAC was in the next valley, which happened to have a similar stream. A frustrating waste of time, particularly because opportunities of attacking ground targets were apt to be fleeting. Again JTIDs could have helped, if the AFAC in his valley had functioned as a subscriber to the JTIDs net, so that his position would have appeared on Ken's cockpit display.

Over North Vietnam our Air Force pilots had to contend with enemy surface-to-air missiles (SAMs) and MIG intercept aircraft. Under these circumstances, the lack of communications security could, and did, result in our planes' being shot down. Our aircraft formations operating over North Vietnam talked in the clear and used fixed callsigns. The callsign indicated the unit, which might be a flight of F-4s or a flight of F-105s. Thus the enemy, by listening to our radio transmissions, could learn a great deal. For example, they might know from callsigns that the aircraft of an incoming flight were F-4s. They would also know whether the F-4s were specialized for air combat or for bombing. In either case they would keep their MIGs out of the way and alert their SAMs. On the other hand they might know that the approaching aircraft were the less dangerous F-105s, in which case they would send in their MIGs, which would have a good chance of downing our planes. Sometimes we would fox the enemy by sending in F-4 flights using the callsigns of F-105 units, in which case MIGs would get shot down. In JTIDs planning, there will be built-in cryptographic security both for aircraft identity and for message content.

Lack of security was by no means the only way in which the inadequacy of our communications systems could cause our planes to be shot down. Lack of connectivity between combat and combat-support units could do it. On one occasion a radar controller north of Da Nang spotted two aircraft near Vinh, in North Vietnam. He could tell that they were friendly, but he did not know who they were. The controller could also see on his radar screen that some enemy MIGs were moving into position to attack.

All he could do was to send a repeated message on the frequency of the "guard channel," monitored by all aircraft, saying "You two aircraft flying near Vinh are threatened by MIGs." But sending such a message without giving the callsign of the intended recipient was comparable to using a hospital paging system to call an urgently needed doctor to the emergency ward without giving the doctor's name. The two friendly aircraft were interceptors, flying F-106s, and looking for targets of opportunity. The lead pilot, after some delay, did realize that the radar controller was trying to talk to him, but at that moment his companion was shot down. What went wrong was not simply that the warning message did not get through. The lead pilot of the pair of interceptors heard the message, but did not realize in time that it was addressed to him. If he had heard his callsign, he would have taken notice, but this piece of information, which must have been available elsewhere, had not been made known to the radar controller covering the area in which the interceptors were flying. If JTIDs had been available, the radar controller would have entered the positions of the MIGs on the common user net, and they would have appeared immediately as hostiles on the cockpit display of the two friendly aircraft.

Over North Vietnam our pilots developed methods of knowing the positions of enemy SAMs and dodging them. But in that environment there were not all that many SAM sites. In the event of a Warsaw Pact attack in Europe, the situation would be far worse. It would be a great help to our pilots if all known locations of enemy air defenses could be put on the net so that those of concern to each pilot would appear on his display. In JTIDs thinking, a pilot will be able to vary the coverage of his display, so that he can survey the hazards in the target area as well as along possible routes of approach and departure. If our SAMs are also subscribers to JTIDs, any of our aircraft in their areas of coverage will appear on their displays as friendlies and the chance of fratricide will be considerably reduced. In general, the many-to-many features of JTIDs connectivity could be of immense importance. Information of potential value to pilots would be transmitted on the net by many different elements, including, for example, the weather service, and would be immediately available to all. Each pilot on mission would be able to obtain selective access to what he needs, without being bothered with information he does not need. Studies have shown that widespread use of JTIDs would result in a spectacular improvement in the effectiveness of our fighter aircraft and in their chance of survival in a high-intensity environment. As I have indicated, the U.S. Army is very interested in JTIDs not only for its own use, but also as a means of achieving more effective coordination of ground and air forces in combined arms operations. In view of all this, it is hard to understand why progress has been, and still is, so slow.

16

Secrecy, Security, and Survival

In the story of Hut 6 we see many examples of the need for and misuse of secrecy. The security of German Enigma traffic was broken down by Hut 6, which enabled Hut 3 to produce valuable intelligence. But it was important to maintain secrecy about the source of that Ultra intelligence, and this secrecy often had an adverse effect on the survival of Allied forces. A striking case in point is the Germans' success in taking Crete by airborne assault in May 1941 in spite of the fact that Ultra had revealed every detail of their plans. An inquiry showed that the island need not have been lost if the defending commanders had paid attention to what they were being told. Not knowing the source, however, they had been discounting Ultra messages. Was this a case of excessive secrecy? As we have seen, similar questions arose in connection with the desert battles. On many occasions the Eighth Army suffered serious losses because its commander, not knowing the source of Ultra intelligence, did not accept what he was told about Rommel's intentions. Yet, as far as I know, there has been no study in depth of the organization and methodology developed for the handling and use of Hut 6 decodes and Ultra intelligence.

At the beginning of World War II, I doubt anyone had the faintest idea of the volume and variety of messages that would be decoded by Hut 6. Existing cryptanalytic and intelligence handling capabilities were quite inadequate. New methodology, new organizations, new interrelationships, and new rules of communications had to be developed. The very newness of the problem resulted in utilization of very able people from different walks of life whose thinking was not inhibited by outmoded doctrine. But one cannot believe that everything was done perfectly. Surely it would be extremely valuable if an interdisciplinary group, similar to the President's commission on Three Mile Island, could report on what was done well, what could have been done better, and what recommendations for the future can be deduced. And I can see no reason at all for continued secrecy about the handling of Ultra in World War II, though there may be a real need for secrecy about recommendations for our future handling of intelligence problems.

I would guess that an investigation would give very good marks to the methodology developed in Hut 3 for extracting the maximum amount of intelligence from even the smallest details of Enigma decodes studied over a long period. But I suspect that a commission would discover many faults in using this intelligence that could help us in advanced planning. For example, during the Battle of Britain I heard of an RAF duty officer who expressed puzzlement about some chap who phoned him most evenings to say where German air attacks were coming. He never did anything about it, because he didn't know who the chap was. But the extraordinary thing, he said, was that this "chap" was always right. It was in fact Ultra intelligence. Evidently no one had thought of telling the duty officer that he could trust, and act on, those reports.

Of course, Hut 6 Ultra, though an important contributor to World War II intelligence, was only part of a total picture of which I know very little. Yet, from what I do know, I am convinced that careful study of the obstacles to, and errors in, the use of intelligence in World War II could be of immense importance in our planning for the future.

ADAPTABILITY IN BATTLE

It is evident that many considerations must be taken into account in the advanced planning of the communications capabilities on which the effectiveness of our national defense measures will depend. Let me mention a few considerations that are particularly relevant to our plans for achieving communications security on the battlefield without imposing regulations that will adversely affect the fighting ability of our combat troops.

On a battlefield we need to find means of providing survivable and secure communications for two distinct purposes—for communications up and down the chains of command of the many specialized branches of the services, and also for direct communications among the elements assigned to a combat task force with designated objectives. Attention has been focused far too much on the former purpose, far too little on the latter. The crying need for quick adaptability of both types of communication has been largely ignored. The outmoded communications systems that are still in use today would give our forces little chance against the fast and furious blitzkrieg for which the Soviets have been planning, training, and exercising. Yet our military doctrine takes little account of this. Our main multi-channel system of tactical communications cannot be set up or modified until a time-consuming "needline" analysis has been carried out.* When a subscriber or relay moves, it cannot operate in the system. Even our forward area radio nets, which offer good connectivity for a limited number of subscribers, are regarded as primarily a means of passing messages up and down the many chains of command, not of providing the immediate internal communications needed for cooperation among the diverse elements of a task force assigned to deal with a critical situation.

Even in planning for the survivability and security of chain-of-command communications, no account is taken of the fact that, as a result of enemy action, it may become necessary to change our command structure in a hurry. This is illustrated by the Battle of the Bulge, when the German penetration split the American forces in two. It became imperative that two American Armies, the First and the Ninth, be temporarily shifted to the operational control of the British 21st Army Group. At the same time two American Tactical Air Commands, IX and XXIX TACs, operating to the

---

* The design of a commercial telephone network that is to serve a group of customers is based on an analysis of who will want to talk to whom—in other words, what *lines* of communication will be *needed?* For each such "needline" the expected traffic load and urgency will be considered. Unfortunately this commercially oriented thinking has been applied to tactical military communications.

north of the German penetration, had their direct lines of communication to U.S. Ninth Air Force cut or compromised; these TACs were temporarily transferred to the operational control of the British Second TAF, which was the air partner of the 21st Army Group. A Soviet penetration against today's NATO forces would almost certainly have a similar effect, making it necessary to change the structure of the chain-of-command communications and the associated security procedures.

To see the need for adaptability of lateral communications among advanced combat elements, let us consider what would happen if the Soviets were to choose, as the main line of a major thrust, the boundary between zones assigned to two allied corps. On either side of this boundary there will be divisions, brigades, battalions, companies, platoons, and squads belonging to the two corps, together with artillery and other elements. At all levels there will be a sudden need for close cooperation between elements of the two corps on either side of the boundary. The necessary coordination of combat elements cannot possibly be provided by chain-of-command communications traveling up one side of the boundary, across from corps to corps, and then down the other side. It will be essential to create a special task force composed of elements from both corps, and to provide direct communications among the diverse elements involved, including Air Force units. There will be no time to fuss with needlines. The necessary communications capabilities and security measures must be latent—not in use all the time, but available at very short notice when needed.

The danger of our insistence on an analysis of needlines is illustrated by an anecdote from the Battle of France. Guderian, in his personal account, makes it clear that he took advantage of his studies of French doctrinal rigidity:

> We did not imagine that General Frère would advance against us as long as we kept on moving ourselves. According to the basic French formula, he would wait until he had exact information about his enemy's position before doing anything. So we had to keep him guessing. This could best be done by continuing to push on.

Guderian did indeed push on, and General Frère made no effective countermove. Let us imagine a Soviet version of Guderian. He would know the basic American formula that a needline analysis for a static situation would have to be completed before the U.S. Army could put its mainline direct-dialing telephone system in operation. All the Soviet Guderian would need to do would be to keep the situation fluid.

Indeed, our peacetime thinking on tactical communications has tended to ignore the fundamental objectives of rapid adaptability to unforeseen situations. And this, I am afraid, has been true of our thinking on the cryptographic protection of our battlefield communications.

CRYPTOLOGY HAS GONE PUBLIC

Advanced planning of military communications and associated security measures in the 1980s can hardly fail to be affected by the remarkable developments that have occurred in the nonmilitary sphere. These developments have occurred in three areas: organizational communications, common-user digital networks, and cryptology. In the 1950s and 1960s a rapidly growing number of professionals specializing in organizational communications appeared in several colleges, universities, businesses, industries, and other groups throughout the United States. A spate of attempts to develop a theory of organization had led to awareness of the importance of human communication within organizations. As early as 1938 the Harvard University Press published the now classic Lowell Institute Lectures by one of the greatest organizers of his day, Chester I. Barnard, who declared that "the first function of the executive is to develop and maintain a system of communication."* This dictum was accepted by the professionals, who analyzed the many difficulties that arise in human communication and tried to devise means of increasing the efficiency of organizations by improving their internal communications. It was some time before the new ideas caught on, but by 1970 a number of academic institutions were offering degrees in organizational communication, and the stu-

* The lectures were published under the title *The Functions of the Executive*. The quotation is from page 226. Note the contrast between Barnard's dictum of 1938 and the Pentagon dictum of 1970 that the idea of command responsibility for communications was revolutionary, contrary to doctrine, and therefore unacceptable.

dents who had these degrees were in great demand in business and industry. Since then the number of degree courses offered in management theory and organizational communications, based in part on possibilities offered by new digital technology, has greatly increased, as has the demand for people who hold these degrees.

Many of the ideas that have arisen in recent studies of management and communication in business and industry apply to military force coordination as well. An important set of ideas concerns the characteristic orientation of different types of organization toward power, role, task, or person. During peacetime the military organization as a whole tends to be role-oriented, aspiring to be as rational and orderly as possible. There is strong emphasis on hierarchy and status. Procedures involved in instituting change are cumbersome, and there is sometimes a tendency to place procedural correctness before task effectiveness. Nonmilitary examples of such role-oriented organizations include many banks, insurance companies, public utilities, and social service organizations. In wartime, by contrast, the military organization in a theater of operations must become task-oriented in a hurry. In a task-oriented business organization, structure, functions, and activities are evaluated in terms of contribution to business objectives, and nothing is permitted to get in the way of doing the job. Structure is shaped and changed to meet the requirements of task or function, and the response to change is rapid and flexible. Businesses sometimes form "task groups" to cope with specific problems, transferring individuals from several specialized branches or departments to work as a team until the task is achieved and the personnel return to their specialized activities.

The year 1970 seems also to have marked a turning point in nonmilitary interest in common-user networks employing advanced digital communications technology. In the previous year, under the sponsorship of the U.S. Defense Advanced Research Projects Agency, a communications network named ARPANET was designed to employ packet switching as a means of linking a wide variety of digital computer capabilities scattered around the United States and extending to Hawaii, Norway, and England. In 1970 the ALOHA system, implemented at the University of Hawaii, broke new ground by introducing the idea of "contention." Outlying computer terminals transmitted to a central computer via a common 2,400-bits-per-second radio channel. There was a separate return channel from the central computer. Each terminal would transmit a packet on the inbound channel whenever it had data available, and would wait for acknowledgment from the computer. If two or more terminals happened to transmit packets whose arrival at the computer overlapped, the collision would be detected by the computer and no acknowledgments would be sent. Each of the transmitting terminals would then try again after a certain time interval, made random to avoid repeated collisions.

This procedure was a lot simpler than the time-slot assignments I had envisioned in my 1968 paper on cyclic information systems for military use. But ALOHA's use of contention is only practical when the packet transmissions from each terminal are infrequent or "bursty"—that is, occurring in bursts interspersed by periods of inactivity. The original ALOHA was wasteful, but other contention schemes were soon suggested to obtain higher efficiency by reducing the time during which the circuit was put out of action by collision.

During the 1970s, interest in common-user packet networks boomed. In May 1979 a symposium on local area communications networks, cosponsored by the National Bureau of Standards and the MITRE Corporation, was held in Boston. A wide range of applications, operating systems, developmental programs, available technologies, and leading-edge research projects was discussed. That symposium was followed by a flood of conferences on packet-communications networks and related matters. It had become one of the hottest areas of research and development. Hopefully this is a sign that an upsurge of serious interest in using packet technology for military communications is approaching, if not already here.

Several speakers at the Boston symposium agreed that it is no longer advisable to rely on "users" of equipment to state their future requirements, since they do not know what could be done for them by new technology that is just around the corner. They tend to ask for improvements in the capabilities they already have, rather than for revolutionary capabilities that they might have. On the other hand the "suppliers"—scientists, engineers, and manufacturers who can make new technology available—tend to be motivated by achievement of spectacular advances in their fields of specialization, and are likely to be only partially aware of the problems to which their achievements might be applied—in the military case, by commanders and combat elements in the heat of battle. Thus there has been a growing need for contributions from the middle ground, where generalists and applications engineers, working in well-balanced teams, strive to maintain a broad view of the problem areas and the technological possibilities. Since new capabilities create new problems, however, it is only too easy for these teams of intermediaries to lose their grasp of the overall situation if they fail to review all its aspects at reasonably short intervals. To sum up, the "top-down" approach to planning and direction of research and development (user states his requirements) does not work any more. Nor does the "bottom-up" approach (industry develops advanced equipment). The approach must work from the middle outward.

Even before the 1970s, digital data communications technology was increasingly being applied on a common-user basis, and a need to guarantee privacy for individual users was becoming apparent. Before the late 1960s almost the only use of encryption was for national security purposes. Since then the revolution in communications technology has been rapid. But at the same time new electronic technology has been making it possible, and more and more inexpensive, to intercept common-user digital data and voice transmissions, particularly those passed on microwave links. Thus individual users have come to need cryptographic means of protecting their traffic from people who could misuse or interfere with it, including commercial competitors and criminals. Suddenly the need for cryptographic technology has burst its old boundaries. The rapid development of widespread public interest in the entire field is evidenced by the establishment in 1977 of *Cryptologia*, a new quarterly journal devoted to all aspects of cryptology. Indeed by that time cryptology had gone public.

In 1972, in response to the expanding need for cryptography, the National Bureau of Standards started development of a means of encryption that could be adopted as a standard and manufactured in sufficient quantities to carry an acceptably low price tag. The result was what is now called the "Data Encryption Standard" (DES). I happen to dislike the block-encryption philosophy that underlies the DES—but that is irrelevant so long as the system will do the job for which it was designed.

In 1975 a most remarkable breakthrough in cryptography was achieved by two electrical engineers at Stanford University, Martin E. Hellman and Whitfield Diffie.* They introduced the idea of a system in which encoding and decoding are performed with different keys—one public and the other private. This is completely different from the system characteristics on which the World War II achievements of Hut 6 were based, and makes it clear that we are living in a completely different cryptological age. However, in the first account I read of the Hellman-Diffie ideas I found this statement: "In principle these new ciphers can be broken, but only by computer programs that run for millions of years." This assurance implies that cryptanalysis would have to depend on computers that can only examine one possibility at a time. I am uneasy because I suspect that this might conceivably not be the case.

I believe the cryptographers of today would do well to study why our World War II bombes were so effective. The German cryptographic experts may have reckoned that their vast numbers of stecker combinations would have to be examined one by one. In actual fact, as I have shown, the stecker combinations were virtually useless. An electromechanical machine that had been tailored to the problem was able to examine all two hundred trillion stecker possibilities in around one millisecond. Admittedly I have not studied the new cryptographic principles, and I have no reason for supposing that some newcomer to the game might be lucky enough to hit on a method of attack that would avoid the necessity of trying the possibilities one by one. But it seems worth pointing out that the bombe's function was to examine each of around one million possible combinations of wheel order and initial wheel settings. For each such combination it could throw out those for which a solution of the stecker problem was impossible. This left only a reasonable number of combinations requiring cryptanalytical investigation. Remember also that our original method of breaking, the stacking of the Jeffreys sheets, made it possible to examine 26 × 26 or 676 possibilities simultaneously, and without bothering about the stecker combinations.

One of the new-style cryptanalysts showed me an article in the

---

* The Hellman-Diffie ideas triggered great interest. Important contributions were soon made by Ronald L. Rivest, Associate Professor of Computer Science at MIT, and others.

New York Times of November 18, 1979, reporting a "Mathematic Problem-Solving Discovery" by an obscure Soviet mathematician. I doubt whether this particular discovery is relevant to the new methods of cryptography, but my overall uneasiness is somewhat confirmed by this statement:

> The Russian discovery offers a way by which the number of steps in a solution can be dramatically reduced. It also offers the mathematician a way of learning quickly whether a problem has a solution or not, without having to complete the entire immense computation that may be required.

SECURITY PROCEDURES

If the problems of cryptanalysis have "gone public," so have those of communications security, and indeed of security in general. In the industrial sector one has to worry about what competitors and criminals may be able to do. In the military sector one has to worry about clandestine capabilities as well as those of an enemy's regular armed forces. The governmental sector, too, has problems of communications security, including preventing leaks to the media that are deemed damaging to the national interest.

In the 1970s, and particularly in the second half of the decade, there was a revolution in the technology of communication, and in the recognition of what communication is all about. But what we have seen so far is only the tip of the iceberg. We must expect major developments in the 1980s, and they are sure to introduce new security problems. The new problems must be foreseen and faced. This is no time to perpetuate outmoded doctrine—no time to give dictatorial powers to any one community. It is a time to bring together innovative thinking from many fields of expertise.

The present phase of JTIDS equipment development is aimed at the relatively simple military problems for the solution of which funding could be obtained. Cryptographic measures have been designed accordingly. Far more flexible capabilities will be needed, however, when systems in the JTIDS category are applied to the overall requirements of combined arms operations in the 1980s and 1990s—by which time technology will have taken several leaps forward. Patching up deficiencies in cryptographic systems as the problems grow more complex is fundamentally unsound. The objective should be to plan now for the communications systems of the future, and to provide maximum flexibility for unpredictable twists in the security problems.

In my own experience, one of the more worrying aspects of the present security arrangements is that far too much detailed information about the design and proposed methods of use of JTIDS equipment has been published, or described in open briefings that could have been recorded. It should have been made known long ago that Hut 6 Ultra would never have gotten off the ground if we had not learned from the Poles, in the nick of time, the details both of the German military version of the commercial Enigma machine, and of the operating procedures that were in use. The Germans tried to protect their secrets. Why give ours away?

Moreover, it has become more and more evident that the most difficult problems in security are not purely cryptographic. We must not forget the probability of sabotage attempts on a global scale. The cryptographic protection of the JTIDS system, and of its more widely used successors, will call for creation and distribution of a vast amount of cryptographic material, offering many lucrative targets for use of the new weapons of sabotage, possibly with the help of implanted agents. There is also the possibility that cryptographic secrets may be obtained by agents, as well as the more obvious danger of compromise by capture on the battlefield.

Considerable attention must be paid to the procedural rules that must be observed by all users and operators, and to the monitoring of their performance. The history of cryptology is full of cases in which a cipher system has been betrayed by carelessness or downright failure to obey operating instructions. This danger is aggravated by the fact that, in actual war, communications equipment is likely to be used for purposes that were not foreseen in the planning. Moreover the exact nature of future security problems is scenario-dependent, meaning that in system planning it is extremely important to study the scenarios that could materialize in the various potential trouble spots of the world.

Indeed the overall problem of achieving security for the type of communications facilities that will be best suited to combined arms operations in the 1980s and 1990s is extremely complex. But the problem should not be shirked. It calls for an interdisciplinary attack with full support from military thinkers as well as from experts in several specialized fields. And there must be strict secrecy, for, while we must attempt to anticipate all the tricks that might be used against us, we do not want to reveal whatever security measures we may be planning. In fact, in planning security measures, two fundamental objectives must be to keep the enemy in the dark as long as possible, and to be several steps ahead of him by planning systems so that they can be modified as necessary. Our planners should have been allowed to study how the Germans, following good cryptographic principles, did in fact introduce modifications in their Enigma machine and in their operating procedures. They added two new wheels not long before their invasion of Poland. They made a major change in operating procedures when they invaded France and the Netherlands. And they made several more changes later on.

Advanced planning of the kind we are discussing could be greatly helped by reforms in the present system of handling the security of day-to-day work. Picture a man who works for a government agency or military service, and who is responsible for deciding whether a particular item in a paper he is writing is to be classified secret, and what arrangements, if any, are to be made for downgrading its level of classification at some later date. His common sense may suggest that the information need not be classified secret at all, but he knows that if he is found guilty of a breach of security he may lose his job, or at least his prospects of promotion. A black mark of any kind on his record is something he desperately wants to avoid. From the human point of view one can hardly blame him if he decides to play it safe, slaps on a secret classification, and insists that there be no automatic downgrading of the classification level after stated periods of time. A decision on secrecy is by no means a simple problem. But it should *not* be determined by considerations of personal risk. It calls instead for a broad overall view and a specialist's knowledge.

Current security procedures have an unfortunate side effect. A lengthy document, say of two hundred pages, containing information that could be valuable to many workers, is only too often classified secret because a few items appearing on a few pages are considered to deserve that classification. The result is that the whole document has to be subjected to the full security procedure. It must be stored in a locked cabinet and even its unclassified pages are frequently subject to restrictions on copying. This makes it unnecessarily difficult for researchers to obtain access to and quote from unclassified information of potential importance. One would think that a paper of this type could be issued in two parts—an unclassified major portion made available to all interested workers and a classified appendix made available under full security regulations to people qualified to know the few secret items.

There is also another side effect that is far from trivial. If some of the applications of a system of security regulations seem to be ridiculous, people may lose faith in the system as a whole, and it may become much harder than it need be to achieve strict obedience to regulations when it really matters. Indeed a general lack of respect for security procedures may produce more leaks of classified information than would otherwise occur.

In the advanced planning of systems that may develop from JTIDS, and particularly as concerns their cryptological aspects, very strict secrecy on many matters will be needed over long periods, but not forever. In many cases a time will come when a particular secret—for example, the cause of a system failure—should be made known because it will be helpful in advanced planning and in making people in general as aware as possible of what concerns their survival. With this in mind it would be well to provide for periodic review by competent authorities to determine when the release of secret information would be more beneficial than damaging—by no means an easy matter to resolve.

THE HUT 6 EXPERIENCE

In our thinking about future security measures we can draw lessons from the Hut 6 experience. Study of our records and those of the Central Party could be of real value in the advanced planning task of the early 1980s. Tom Belden, when he was lecturing at MITRE on the subject of crisis management, remarked that historical examples may give a truer picture of weaknesses than can be obtained from exercises, which tend to be artificial if not downright rigged. This remark has far deeper implications than I realized at the time. It applies also to scenarios. If we are to develop communications that will meet the needs of combat forces on future battlefields, we must think out many realistic scenarios, picturing situations that may arise. Of course our scenarios of future conflicts will try to take account of trends in military thinking and capabilities, but, as Belden suggests, our dreamed-up scenarios may tend to be artificial or rigged. Why not think of wars of the past as scenarios against which our advanced planning of communication can be tested? In this book I have been doing that in a negative way—examining past failures that must not be repeated—but a positive approach is also possible.

In thinking about communications systems that will meet the needs of future battlefields we must try to form a realistic picture of the messages that should flow through those systems. What information should the messages contain? Who will need what messages? How can one ensure that each combat element gets what it needs, and is not overloaded with information that it cannot absorb? One also has to worry about matters of internal security. Who is authorized to receive what messages, and how does this affect the arrangements for distributing cryptographic keys and other material? Answering questions such as these is, believe me, by no means easy. But, following up on Belden's remark, why not find out what we can learn from the tactical messages that were passed, how they were distributed, and how internal security was handled in a real war?

I believe the Central Party that became part of the Hut 6 organization at Bletchley Park had more detailed knowledge of the entire communications system that handled Enigma traffic than anyone in Germany. It followed the movements, changes in control, retransmissions, the handling of different keys, and of course the chitchat that appeared in the logs. Leading members of the Central Party, given access to their old records, could no doubt piece together a very complete picture of a communications system that grew out of the realities of a wide-ranging war.

The Hut 6 decodes are another mine of still valuable information. Our breaking of Enigma keys was so extensive that the decodes would permit analysis of the types of messages that needed to be sent, the patterns of distribution, and the reasons for using so many different keys. Such an analysis, based on the firm foundation of real warfare, could provide a valuable background picture for our work on scenarios of future conflicts.

Here then—assuming that the wartime records of the Central Party, Hut 6, and Hut 3 have been preserved—we have a store of information meaningful to our advanced planning for future military communications and security procedures. This store, it seems to me, urgently needs to be opened up and studied. We cannot know precisely what we may bring to light; but we can be certain it will help us. If we do our studies well—and can manage to put the results to proper use—the spirits of Alastair Denniston and Edward Travis may well have reason to rejoice.

Appendix

The Bombe with
a Diagonal Board

THE DOUBLE-ENDED SCRAMBLER

The principle of the bombe that was to be used by Hut 6 occurred to me in the School at Bletchley Park in November 1939, before the war was three months old. That the idea came so early was indeed fortunate, because many months of engineering design and development were needed to go from a blue-sky concept to a working machine that came into operation late in 1940.

I will discuss the concept as it stood at the end of 1939 and the main features of the design, but let me first remind the reader that an Enigma machine had a keyboard, a lampboard, and a steckerboard, as well as a scrambler unit. The scrambler consisted only of in-out terminals, three moving wheels, and a fixed turn-around wheel, or *umkehrwalze*. When I talk about a scrambler, I mean just that.

Let us first consider the very simple purpose of what I have called a double-ended scrambler. In the German Enigma the scrambler had only one set of twenty-six in-out terminals, which were connected by a twenty-six-way cable to the lower sockets of the steckerboard. Thus electric current entering the scrambler at one of its in-out terminals would return to another terminal of the same set, and would go back to the steckerboard along a wire of the same twenty-six-way cable. For reasons that will become evident in a moment, in order to perform the tests we had in mind Turing and I wanted the return current to come out at a second set of terminals. This second set would be connected, by a twenty-six-way cable, to in-out terminals of another scrambler for the purpose of making logical deductions.*

At the time I don't think I worried too much about how this would be done, once I had satisfied myself that it could be done. It may have occurred to me that the fixed commutator at the right of a scrambler, the moving wheels, and the fixed *umkehrwalze* on the left could all have two concentric circles of twenty-six terminals, instead of one circle. In each of the three moving wheels the internal connections between the right-hand and left-hand terminals of the outer circle would be as in a standard single-ended scrambler; the two inner circles of terminals would be cross-connected in exactly the same manner. In the *umkehrwalze* each terminal of the outer ring would be connected to a terminal of the inner ring. Thus a single interconnection between terminals X and Y of a single *umkehrwalze* ring would be replaced by two connections: X of the outer ring to Y of the inner ring and Y of the outer ring to X of the inner ring. This arrangement would have the effect Turing and I desired. There would be two sets of twenty-six in-out terminals, each of which could be connected by twenty-six-way cable to another scrambler. Current entering at any letter of either set would go through the wheels to the *umkehrwalze* and return to a letter of the other set. The letter substitution so obtained would be the same as that of the single-ended scrambler.

To proceed further I need a simple way of representing what I am talking about. Unfortunately I cannot remember how I drew the original diagram I showed to Turing and later on to Keen. Several years after the war I asked to see it at GCHQ, and did in fact see it, but I understand that since then it has been lost or destroyed. However, Figures A.1, A.2, and A.3 will serve the purpose rather better.

Figure A.1 introduces a diagrammatic representation of a double-ended scrambler. At the top, in (a), I have replaced the permanent connections between the single-ended scrambler and steckerboard of an Enigma machine by pluggable connections. One

---

* Not for the purpose of lighting a lamp under the Enigma lampboard.

of two terminal jacks has twenty-six pin terminals that can be plugged into the sockets of the scrambler's in-out terminals. This jack, shown in Figure A.1(a), is connected by a twenty-six-way connector cable to another jack, not shown, whose twenty-six pin terminals can be plugged into the sockets of the in-out steckerboard terminals shown in Figure 3.6, which are connected to keyboard and lampboard. The scrambler itself is represented by a rectangular box, indicating its in-out terminals and internal structure of moving wheels and fixed *umkehrwalze*.

Figure A.1 (b) represents the double-ended scrambler I am talking about, with its two sets of in-out terminals, each of which can be connected by a twenty-six-way terminal jack and connector cable to any selected set of female sockets. Note that the two sets of in-out terminals are interchangeable in that, if current entering at the upper P terminal comes out at the lower Q terminal, then current entering at the lower P terminal would come out at the upper Q terminal. In Figure A.1 (c), I show the *condensed* representation of a double-ended scrambler (b) that I will use in Figures A.2 and A.3 to illustrate the principles of the bombes, both Turing's and mine. The twenty-six-terminal jacks are represented by single lines. The box between them represents the double-ended scrambler with its two sets of in-out terminals.

TEST LOGIC OF A TURING BOMBE

Back in Figure 4.4 (*q.v.*), I postulated a "crib," which produced three diagrams of letter pairings involved in the encoding. The basic idea of the bombes, both Turing's and mine, was to interconnect a battery of scramblers in accordance with some such diagram. Initially the scramblers are set at the relative positions indicated in the diagrams. Then the whole battery moves in synchronism through all $26 \times 26 \times 26 = 17,576$ positions of each scrambler. In each position a test is applied that determines whether that position is a "drop" requiring further analysis.

Let us first see how a Turing bombe would have been applied to the first diagram of Figure 4.4, which is reproduced as part of Figure A.2. The top scrambler unit in Figure A.2 is to be set initially at position 10 in the crib sequence, in which letter P is the encode of letter I. As I have just explained, single lines represent

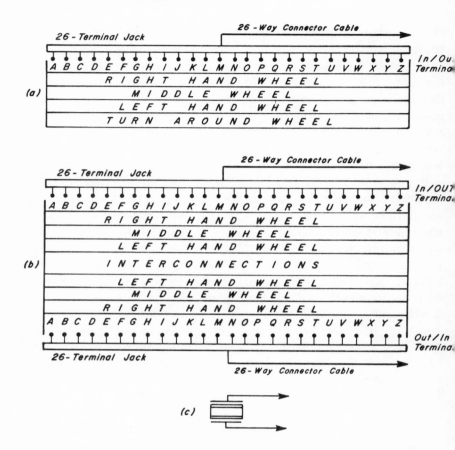

Figure A.1 Diagrams Of Scrambler Units
(a) Single-Ended Scrambler Unit
(b) Double-Ended Scrambler Unit
(c) Condensed Representation for Bombe Diagrams

twenty-six-way connections between alphabet jacks associated with the in-out or out-in terminals of the double-ended scramblers.

The overall logic of the bombes is a form of *reductio ad absurdum:* make an initial assumption, draw logical deductions, and prove that the initial assumption is wrong.* For each position of the battery of scramblers we assume that we have the correct wheel order and wheel positions. We then try to solve the problem of the stecker connections. If we can prove that there is no solution to this problem, we will have disproved the assumption.

The test register of Figure A.2 is a set of twenty-six terminals connected by twenty-six-way cables to four sets of in-out or out-in terminals of scramblers in positions 10, 8, 22, and 13. In each case the letter that is encoded through the whole Enigma, including steckerboard as well as scrambler, is I. Current input at terminal A of the test register is an electrical form of the assumption I/A (letter I is steckered to letter A). Let us follow the current through one loop. Current enters the scrambler in position 10 at the assumed stecker of I, so it emerges at the stecker of P. This provides an input to the scrambler in position 5, whose output must be the stecker of E. This goes into the scrambler at position 8 and emerges as the deduced stecker of I, which goes back to the test register. If the current comes back to any terminal other than A, we have a contradiction, proving that the initial assumption, I/A, was wrong.

There are two other loops along which current can get back to the test register. One goes through the scramblers in positions 10, 6, and 22. The other goes through the scramblers in positions 13, 3, 15, 21, and 13 again. For each such closed loop the chance that the current will return to terminal A of the test register is 1 in 26.

Suppose that, having selected a wheel order, we set nine scramblers of the bombe to initial relative positions that could correspond to the actual positions 3, 5, 6, 8, 10, 13, 15, 21, and 22 of the crib, and that we interconnect the scramblers and the test register in accordance with Figure A.2. Suppose that we then run the whole battery of scramblers in synchronism through the 26 × 26 ×

---

* A classical example of *reductio ad absurdum* is a proof of the theorem in plane geometry that two lines perpendicular to the same line at different points A and B cannot meet. To demonstrate this, we assume that the two lines meet at a point C. We then have a triangle ABC in which angles CAB and CBA are right angles, and angle ACB, though small, is not of zero magnitude. But this is absurd, because we know that the three angles of a triangle add up to exactly two right angles. Therefore the assumption is false.

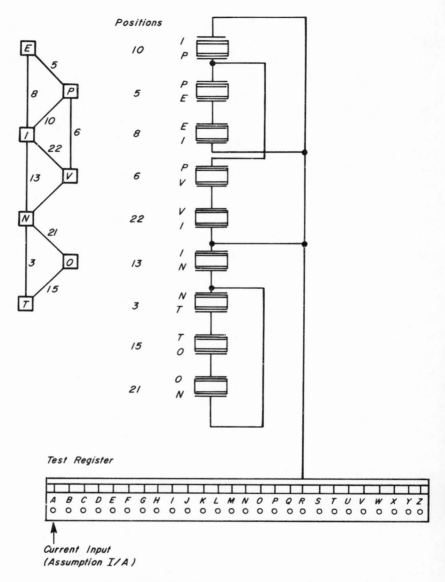

Figure A.2 Application of Turing Bombe

26 possible positions and, in each position, test whether current gets back to any terminal of the test register other than A. Having three closed loops, for each of which the chance of current's returning to A is 1 in 26, we would expect only one drop per wheel order.

Fortunately we do not have to repeat the test run with current inputs at other terminals of the test register, because, whenever current gets back to the test register at a terminal other than A, it will go through the loops again. Indeed with three loops feeding back, the reader will not find it hard to believe that, in most positions of the bombe, the test register will "fill up"—in other words, current will reach all its twenty-six terminals.

Note, however, that if the true stecker of I is some letter other than A—say, P—then, when the scramblers of the bombe are in their correct positions, and we are trying the correct wheel order, current put in at P, representing the assumption I/P, would not come back to the test register at any other terminal. Consequently current from terminal A could not reach terminal P.

Thus, in order to detect a "drop," the bombe needs to look for one of only two situations: a case in which current does not get back to any test register terminal other than A, or one in which there is some terminal other than A to which current does not get back. In the vast majority of positions the test register will fill up.

When a particular wheel order is being run, each "drop" will tell us that, for some set of positions of the scramblers, the bombe has been unable to reject the possibility that we have hit on the correct wheel order and wheel positions. More work will be needed to determine whether we have a false drop.

PRINCIPLE OF THE DIAGONAL BOARD

Let us now consider how my version of the bombe would be applied to the second diagram of Figure 4.4, which uses positions 1, 3, 5, 6, 8, 10, 11, 12, and 13 of the crib. The right-hand portion of Figure A.3 shows a diagonal board, which is simply a 26 × 26 matrix of terminals. It acquired its name because, for example, the terminal in row E and column A is connected diagonally to the terminal in row A and column E. The cross-connection is no more than an electrical equivalent of the fact that, if E is steckered to A, then A must be steckered to E. I believe that the name "diagonal board" was introduced by Doc Keen.

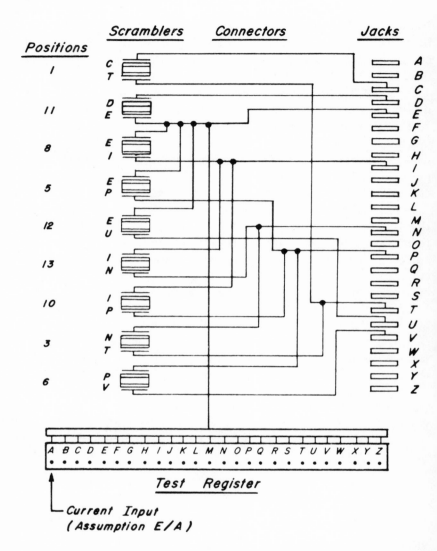

Figure A.3 Bombe with Diagonal Board
Left Hand Side
Connections between Scramblers,
Jacks, and Test Register

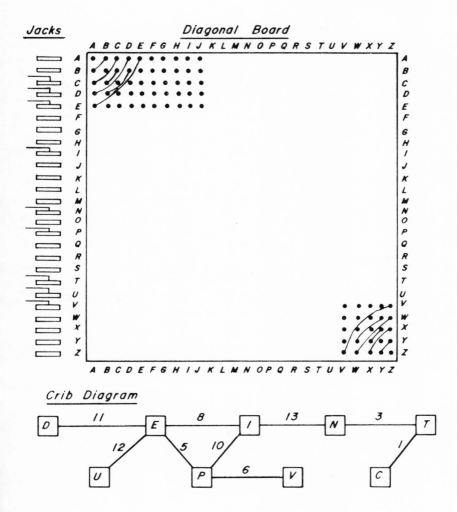

Jacks　　　　　　*Diagonal Board*

Crib Diagram

Right Hand Side
Diagonal Board with Jacks
Crib Diagram

The terminals of each row of the diagonal board are also connected to a twenty-six-terminal female jack shown to the left of the row. These same jacks appear also in the left-hand portion of Figure A.3, which shows how twenty-six-way cables connect them with a set of double-ended scramblers and a test register.

As in Figure A.2, the test register is associated with a letter, in this case E, and current input at terminal A is equivalent to the assumption E/A. My new idea, which made so much difference, was simply to connect the test register and the scramblers to the diagonal board, in the manner shown in Figure A.3. The point was that, if the input current could reach the terminal of the diagonal board in row X and column Y, then that X is steckered to Y must be a logical deduction from the assumption that E is steckered to A. Furthermore the current would be connected diagonally to the terminal in row Y and column X (meaning Y is steckered to X), and would have a chance of getting back into the scramblers via the twenty-six-terminal jack associated with row Y. As I said, Turing, though initially incredulous, was quick to appreciate the importance of this new twist in Enigma theory, which greatly reduced the number of bombe runs that would be needed to ensure success in breaking an Enigma key by means of a crib. I had no difficulty in explaining the idea to Doc Keen at BTM, and once he got it, he was really with it. I do not remember any reaction from Dilly Knox, but I shall never forget the facial expression of a representative of the U.S. Navy when the validity and importance of the idea dawned on him.

Looking at Figure A.3 a little more closely, it will be seen that five different twenty-six-way cables, from the test register and from the four scramblers, in positions 11, 8, 5, and 12, had to be connected with the twenty-six-way female jack of row E of the diagonal board. The problem of making these connections was easily fixed by providing sets of "commoned" female jacks that would interconnect twenty-six-way cables plugged into them. For example, if a set of six commoned female jacks was available, the five male terminals of the twenty-six-way cables from the four scramblers and the test register could be plugged in, and a single cable could connect them all to row E of the diagonal board.*

---

* Similarly three cables had to go to row I, three to row P and two each to rows N and T. This could be handled by using other sets of commoned female jacks.

The input current from terminal A of the test register goes to this "commoning board" and proceeds to terminal E/A of the diagonal board. This is connected to terminal A/E, which does us no good because row A of the diagonal board is not connected to a scrambler. At the same time, however, the input current is getting to scramblers in positions 11, 8, 5, and 12, giving deduced steckers for the letters D, I, P, and U. The deduced steckers for I and P feed into scramblers in positions 13, 10, 10 (from the other end), and 6, giving deduced steckers for N, P, I, and V. We thus have eight immediately deduced steckers: two each for P and I; one each for D, U, N, and V. These eight deductions result in electric current's energizing terminals in rows P, I, D, U, N, V of the diagonal board. The diagonal connections will energize terminals in other rows, which may feed back into the scramblers and produce further deductions. Since nine of the twenty-six rows of the diagonal board are so connected, there is a good chance that further deductions will be made. Furthermore, since each scrambler unit is connected to one or more of the other eight, any single deduction flowing back from the diagonal board is likely to have an effect comparable to that of the input assumption E/A. The first round of deductions, which is roughly equivalent to what the Turing bombe could produce, could lead to a return flow from eight rows of the diagonal board, each of which has a 9-out-of-26 chance of reentering the scrambler interconnections. Furthermore, each such reentry can produce another round of reentries.

VALUE OF THE DIAGONAL BOARD

Why was this idea so important, and what can it teach us today? Well, let me say at once that my two ideas were by no means the complete answer to the often-asked question of "How did we do it?" As I stated at the beginning, my ideas did no more than reduce—by enormous factors—the number of possibilities that had to be examined by the wizards. The methodology was worked out by others, and I was never personally involved. I think I can see how it could have been done, but I will not go into details. I might so easily be wrong. Perhaps some of the surviving wizards may provide a true account of what they did, pointing out any errors in detail that I may have made in this book. However, although my memory of my unrecorded thinking of forty years ago may not be completely accurate, my two ideas, the first of which had already been thought of by others, did in fact reduce the task of the wizards to manageable proportions.

I have stated that in the use of the diagrams of Figures A.2 and A.3 the scramblers of the bombe would be set to the relative positions indicated in the crib diagrams of Figure 4.4. But we must worry about the fact that a turnover of the middle wheel will occur somewhere in each sequence of twenty-six encipherments of the crib letters, and we have no means of knowing where. Thus, to apply Turing's bombe in the manner indicated in Figure A.2 we would like to assume that no turnover will occur in the nineteen consecutive transitions between the positions in the scrambler cycle that we have arbitrarily numbered 3 through 22. Then, in the initial setup of the scramblers for the bombe run, we could put all left-hand and middle wheels to the same settings. Thus, if we use ring settings ZZZ as a standard, we could set all left-hand and middle wheels to AA.

But, to assume no turnover in nineteen consecutive positions out of 26 would have given only a 7 in 26 chance of success. The positions involved were 3, 5, 6, 8, 10, 13, 15, 21, and 22, for which the appropriate letter settings of the right-hand wheel are C, E, F, H, J, M, O, U, and V. The biggest gap is between positions 15 and 21. If we assume that the turnover occurs in this gap, we can set the starting positions of the left-hand and middle wheels for positions 21 and 22 to AB instead of AA. But a second run on this assumption would add only another 6 in 26 chance, to give a total of 13 in 26, or 1 in 2. Not too good; and even then we would be risking the possibility that a left-hand wheel turnover might accompany the middle-wheel turnover. To allow for all turnover possibilities would require a lot of bombe runs.

In contrast to this, the diagonal board idea makes it possible to obtain a usable diagram of scrambler interconnections from a much shorter section of the crib. Thus in Figure 4.4, showing diagrams derived from a crib, the second and third diagrams, both of which are made feasible by the diagonal board, depend on positions 1 to 13 and 14 to 26. We can confidently assume that there will be no turnover in one of these two stretches. For each of these two assumptions we can set all left-hand and middle wheels to the same positions, AA, for the start of a bombe run. Between them these two bombe runs will cover all turnover possibilities. A big gain.

ENGINEERING DESIGN OF THE BOMBE

Doc Keen of the British Tabulating Machine Company (BTM), the designer of our bombes, adopted a configuration for a double-ended scrambler that used rotating "drums" rather than wheels. The general idea is illustrated in Figure A.4. A flat template, (a), contains three commutators, each of which has four concentric rings of twenty-six terminals with a hole at the center for a shaft. Three drums can be mounted on and driven by the three shafts, as is indicated in Figure A.4 (b). Each drum has four concentric rings of terminals making contact with the terminals of a commutator. Wiring inside a drum interconnects the two outer rings. Separate wiring interconnects the two inner rings. These interconnections are the equivalent of those between the right- and left-hand rings of terminals on an Enigma wheel.

Keen obtained the desired effect of a double-ended scrambler by fixed wiring at the back of the template. A set of twenty-six in-out terminals was connected with the outer ring of the top commutator on the template, which would be connected through the top drum with the second ring of the top commutator. This ring was connected, behind the template, to the outer ring of the middle commutator, which would be connected through the middle drum to the second ring of the middle commutator. Similarly the second ring of the middle commutator was connected, behind the template, to the outer ring of the bottom commutator, and the bottom drum would provide connections with the second ring of the bottom commutator. This ring was connected by the equivalent of the *umkehrwalze* cross-connections to the third ring of the lower commutator and thence through the two inner rings of terminals on the drums and commutators to a set of twenty-six out-in terminals associated with the innermost ring of the top commutator. Finally a battery of twelve double-ended scramblers was mounted on a frame, as indicated in Figure A.4 (c).

To obtain reliable electric contact and fast mechanical motion, Keen mounted wire brushes, rather than spring-loaded pin terminals, on his shaft-driven drums. These brushes were standard on

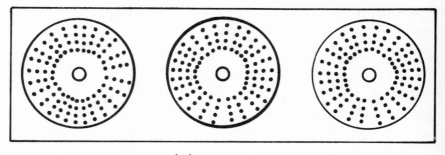

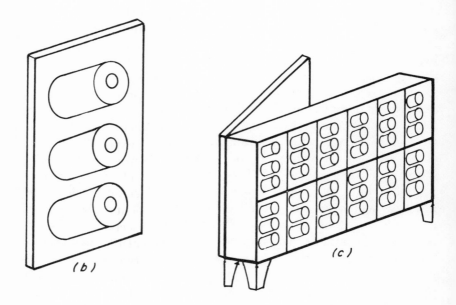

Figure A.4 Keen's Design of the Bombe

(a) Template
(b) Drums on a Template
(c) A Bombe

BTM punched-card equipment, so they were already being manufactured in large quantities. The use of brushes meant that the drums could rotate in one direction only.

One big advantage of Keen's configuration, as opposed to a wheel-type scrambler, was that the shafts on which the drums were mounted could be driven by a mechanism on the other side of the templates. In each of Keen's scramblers the top, middle, and bottom drums correspond to the right-hand, middle, and left-hand wheels of an Enigma scrambler unit. All the top drums were driven together in synchronism. Similarly the middle drums were all driven together, as were the bottom drums. As far as I remember, each drum was about 5 inches across; the bombe, mounted on casters, was somewhat over 4 feet long. A door at the back served as the frame for a diagonal board, testing device, and other electrical circuitry. It was connected by an enormous cable to the in-out and out-in terminals of the twelve scramblers. With the door open the drive mechanism could be reached.

Keen's first step was to design and build two prototype bombes, with ten scramblers each. He made use of standard BTM brush-sensing technology and well-known electromagnetic relay switching, but even the prototypes were essentially experimental machines. Indeed the bombe was totally different from any machine that Doc Keen or anyone else had ever designed. He and his principal assistants paid many visits to the prototypes after they were installed, to correct faults, to try out improvements, and to learn from the technical experience of the two engineers in charge of maintenance, both of whom were experienced in the operation and maintenance of standard BTM equipment. The two prototype machines were soon followed by twelve-scrambler production models. The organization for operating the bombes, and the way they were used by the Hut 6 watch, are discussed in Chapter 8.

ACKNOWLEDGMENTS

In this book I pay belated tribute to many individuals and organizations who played essential roles in the story of Hut 6. I describe several postwar experiences that, combined with my memories of Hut 6, have proved valuable in my work on problems of today. In the Bibliography I have included several writings not mentioned in the text that I have found particularly helpful. Yet many more acknowledgments are needed. I owe so much to so many.

First I want to acknowledge that the success of the activity that I initiated at Bletchley Park owed a great deal more than has yet been recognized to F. W. Winterbotham, the author of *The Ultra Secret*. I never met him, but I can now see that the full implementation of my plan for Hut 6, the fruitful partnership that developed between Hut 6 and the intelligence organization known as Hut 3, and the exploitation of Ultra intelligence on the battlefields of World War II were all due in large measure to two of his personal contributions. First, as a result of his prewar experience in the British Secret Service, Winterbotham was instrumental in arranging that the exploitation of our breakthrough would be handled as an interservice venture under Foreign Office management. Second, his expansion of specialized Secret Service communications and his organization of Special Liaison Units in the field were of critical importance.

Next, I would like to acknowledge the great debt that I owe to the Governing Body—the Master and Fellows—of Sidney Sussex College, Cambridge. They allowed me to leave my college duties at the outbreak of war. They augmented my foreign office salary by continuing my fellowship stipend throughout the war, even though I was doing absolutely nothing for the college. And they wished me well when, at war's end, I did not feel that I could return to my academic life.

The war had given me the opportunity to start doing what I have been trying to do ever since; to absorb new ideas from experts in many fields and to find ways of combining them with other ideas, old and new, to solve some worthwhile problem. I want to acknowledge the help that I have received from all these experts, and the enjoyment I have derived from my contacts with them. I can mention but a few.

When I emigrated to America in 1948, I was extremely fortunate to find a position on the staff of Project Whirlwind at MIT. This was, in my view, the most enterprising of the many pioneering computer projects in that, from its inception towards the end of the war, it was aimed at problems of real-time physical control in which computation was only a means to an end. On joining the project in the summer of 1948 I found a wealth of fascinating ideas that were new to me, and it was my job, as head of Applications Research, to think about what could be done with them. I owe a great debt to the project leader, Jay Forrester, and two of his principal assistants, Bob Everett and Norm Taylor, for drawing me into their highly innovative thinking.

In 1951 I left MIT for eleven years in industry. I first worked on computer applications for Engineering Research Associates and Remington Rand in the U.S. and for Ferranti in the U.K. I then had contacts with Ferranti research establishments in England, Scotland, Canada, and America. From 1959 to 1962 I worked for the Itek Corporation. I will mention only two of the many debts that I incurred during this period. While I was personal assistant to the manager of the Ferranti computer department, we were exploring ways of combining the resources of Ferranti and Powers Samas Accounting Machines. This enabled me to work closely with the head of the Commercial Research Branch of Powers Samas, a Mr. Whitwell, to whom I am particularly grateful for all he taught me about principles and practice in the punched-card world. Secondly, at the end of my period in industry, I had the great pleasure and stimulation of leading an engineering group at Itek. The members were Brian O'Brien, Heinz Zeutschel, Don Oliver, and Dick Malin.

I was on the staff of the MITRE Corporation from 1962 to my retirement in 1971. Since then I have been a consultant, working on a variety of projects. A major part of my work has been supported by contracts between the U.S. Air Force Electronics Systems Division and MITRE. During these nineteen years I have incurred many more debts to colleagues. It has been extremely exhilarating to have had contact with many fresh young minds, and I would like to make special mention of Lou Williams and Larry Hill. But, in connection with the development and realization of this book, my greatest MITRE debts are to B. J. Workman and Bob Coltman.

In summer 1971 I was assigned to work on a project headed by Workman, concerned with the need for speed of communications on a battlefield. Our collaboration was to continue for seven years. It was at Workman's suggestion that I made contact with IISS and RUSI during a vacation in England, a contact that was to prove very valuable. Together we searched military literature for clues to problems of the future. We were much concerned with the development of scenarios depicting what may be expected to happen on a future battlefield. A tireless student of military affairs and a prolific producer of ideas, Workman was extremely good at impromptu presentations, but was so involved in making further progress that he could hardly spare the time to refine and consolidate what he had already achieved. Refinement and consolidation were my roles, then, in what proved to be an extremely happy and productive working relationship.

The President of MITRE, Bob Everett, is an old friend from the days of Project Whirlwind. He has provided encouragement and strong practical support for the writing of this book. In summer 1976 he arranged that Bob Coltman, with whom I had worked on MITRE projects, could help me with my book. We had no idea that this help would continue until the fall of 1980, when a "definitive draft" was handed to Bruce Lee, Senior Editor of the General Books Division of the McGraw-Hill Book Company, another person to whom I owe a major debt of gratitude.

Bob Coltman is a MITRE writer-editor. A few readers may perhaps have heard his published recordings of folk songs. We worked hard together, in perfect harmony, and this was very important to me because the nature of the book was changing. By 1976 my work for MITRE had already shown me that the story of Hut 6 and other clandestine activities of World War II contains much that is of value today. But in summer 1978, when my collaboration with Workman came to an end, the focus of my work switched to the security of the communications system on which we were working. Later, at the end of 1980, the focus switched again to the utilization of electronic intelligence gathering systems on future battlefields. These two new areas of interest led, of course, to contacts with still more colleagues, to whom I am most grateful. They also led to a fuller appreciation of the value today of the Hut 6 story of World War II. Bob Coltman's steady collaboration in revision after revision was a tremendous help in creating what is now Part Four, and in improving the earlier parts.

In April 1978 McGraw-Hill had undertaken to publish my book, and I had the first of many enjoyable and stimulating meetings with Bruce Lee.

He was extremely sympathetic to my interest in lessons for the future and asked if I could extend this aspect of the book by writing a chapter on the present situation in communications. He wanted me to emphasize the applied history and advanced planning features. The new draft that resulted from this meeting was read towards the end of 1978 by a young writer, Neill Rosenfeld, who had been asked by Bruce to produce a lot of questions. The resulting comments, written informally as he read the draft, were very helpful. But, when I had finished answering Neill's questions, I realized that a great deal of improvement was needed, and set to work on another draft. By that time, however, the focus of my MITRE work had already changed and I had thought more about lessons from World War II. With help from Bob Coltman and Bruce Lee, the principal themes were clarified and a better organized draft was submitted in November 1980. After another writer had suggested further improvements, Bruce Lee took personal charge of the final stages of editing. Under his guidance the structure of the book was greatly improved. I have a happy memory of the last few days of work in his office, when we were tying up the loose ends.

During the final stages, Kristina Lindbergh of McGraw-Hill made a major contribution. She managed to keep track of all the material that I sent to Bruce, and kept on getting me out of difficulties by digging out something of which I did not have a copy. I am also very grateful to Philip White of MITRE, who drew all the illustrations.

In conclusion, I want to say a very special word of thanks to Bobbie Statkus, head of MITRE's Word Processing Department. For more than four years she did a magnificent job, working closely with Bob Coltman and battling imperturbably with revision after revision. She did most of the work herself, and had to cope with two installations of new equipment, which made it difficult to use previously recorded text. The quality of the drafts she produced was spectacular.

Bibliography

Books and Articles

BARAN, PAUL, *On Distributed Communications*, The RAND Corporation, Memorandum RM-3420-PR, August 1964. (Research sponsored by the United States Air Force under Project Rand—Contract No. AF49 [638]-700.)

BARNETT, CORRELLI, *The Desert Generals*, New York, Viking Press, 1961.

BAXTER, WILLIAM P., *The Soviet Threat from the Sky*, ARMY, April 1981.

BECKER, C., *The Luftwaffe War Diaries*, New York, Ballantine Books, 1969.

BELDEN, THOMAS G., *Crisis Conferencing and the Pueblo Case*, Institute for Defense Analysis (IDA). Systems Evaluation Division, February 1970.

CANBY, STEVEN, "NATO: More Shadow than Substance," *Foreign Policy Quarterly No. 8:* National Affairs, Inc., 1972.

CANBY, STEVEN, "The Wasteful Ways of NATO," *IISS Survival*, January/February 1973.

CAVE BROWN, ANTHONY, *Bodyguard of Lies*, New York, Harper & Row, 1975.

CLIFFE, TREVOR, *Military Technology and the European Balance*, IISS Adelphi Paper Number Eighty-Nine, 1972.

CONCEPTS DIVISION, AEROSPACE STUDIES INSTITUTE, AIR UNIVERSITY, *Guerrilla Warfare and Air Power in Algeria, 1954–1960*, Air University, Maxwell Air Force Base, Alabama, March 1965.

DIFFIE, WHITFIELD, and HELLMAN, MARTIN E., "New Directions in Cryptography," *IEEE Transactions on Information Theory*, November 1976.

DIFFIE, WHITFIELD, and HELLMAN, MARTIN E., "Privacy and Authentication: An Introduction to Cryptography," *Proceedings of the IEEE*, Vol. 67, No. 3, March 1979.

DONNELLY, C. L., "The Soviet Desant Concept," *RUSI Journal*, December 1971.

ERICKSON, JOHN, *Soviet Military Power*, London, Royal United Services Institute (RUSI), 1971.

ERICKSON, JOHN, "Shield-72: Warsaw Pact Military Exercises," *RUSI Journal*, December 1972.

FALLOWS, JAMES, "America's High-Tech Weaponry," *The Atlantic Monthly*, May 1981.

FEHRENBACH, T. R., *This Kind of War; A Study in Unpreparedness*, New York, Macmillan, 1963.

FITZGERALD, PENELOPE, *The Knox Brothers*, New York, Macmillan, 1977.

FUTRELL, R. F., *The United States Air Force in Korea*, New York, Arno, 1971.

FUTRELL, R. F., *Ideas, Concepts, Doctrines: A History of Basic Thinking in the United States Air Force, 1907–1964*, Air University, Alabama, 1970.

GARLÍNSKI, JÓZEF, *The Enigma War*, New York, Scribner, 1980.

GARTHOFF, R. L., *Soviet Military Doctrine*, Glencoe, Illinois, Free Press, 1953.

GARTHOFF, R. L., *The Soviet Image of Future War*, Washington Public Affairs Press, 1959.

GUDERIAN, HEINZ, *Panzer Leader*, New York, Dutton, 1952.

HAMMETT, JACK C., JR., *Tactical Communications—A Precious Resource*, U.S. Army War College, June 1979.

HUNT, KENNETH, *The Alliance and Europe: Part II: Defence with Fewer Men*, IISS Adelphi Paper Number Ninety-Eight, 1973.

IEEE—INSTITUTE OF ELECTRICAL AND ELECTRONICS ENGINEERS, Publications: *Proceedings, Spectrum*, etc.

IEEE COMMUNICATIONS SOCIETY MAGAZINE: Special Issue on Communications Privacy, Vol. 16, No. 6, November 1978.

IEEE PROCEEDINGS, Special Issue on Packet Communication Networks, Vol. 66, No. 10, November 1978.

IISS—INTERNATIONAL INSTITUTE FOR STRATEGIC STUDIES, Publications: Adelphi Papers, *Survival, The Military Balance*, and *Strategic Survey*.

JONES, REG. V., *The Wizard War*, New York, Coward, McCann, & Geoghegan, 1978.

KAHN, DAVID, *The Codebreakers*, New York, Macmillan, 1967.

KAHN, DAVID, *Hitler's Spies*, New York, Macmillan, 1978.

KAHN, DAVID, "The Ultra Conference," *Cryptologia*, January 1979.

KAHN, DAVID, "Cryptology Goes Public," *Foreign Affairs*, Fall 1979.

KAHN, ROBERT E., GRONEMEYER, STEVEN A., BURCHFIEL, JERRY, and KUNZELMAN, RONALD C., "Advances in Packet Radio Technology," *IEEE Proceedings*, Vol. 60, No. 11, November 1978.

KEMENY, JOHN G., "An Extremely Small Malfunction (at Three Mile Island) and Then Something Terrible Happened," *Dartmouth Alumni Magazine*, December 1979.

KEMENY, JOHN G., "Saving American Democracy: The Lessons of Three Mile Island," *Technology Review*, June–July 1980.

LEWIN, RONALD, *ULTRA Goes to War*, New York, McGraw-Hill, 1978.

LIDDELL HART, BASIL HENRY, *The Remaking of Modern Armies*, Boston, Little, Brown, 1928.

LIDDELL HART, BASIL HENRY, *The German Generals Talk*, New York, William Morrow, 1948.

LIND, WILLIAM S., "Some Doctrinal Questions for the United States Army," *Military Review*, March 1977.

LUTTWAK, EDWARD N., "The American Style of Warfare and the Military Balance," *IISS Survival*, March/April 1979.

LUTTWAK, EDWARD N., "Towards Rearming America," *IISS Survival*, January/February 1981.

MASTERMAN, JOHN C., *The Double Cross System*, Yale University Press, 1972.

MELLENTHIN, F. W. von, *Panzer Battles*, Norman, University of Oklahoma Press, 1958.

MORSE, JOHN H., "Advanced Technology in Modern War," A Lecture given at RUSI on November 26, 1975, *RUSI Journal*, June 1976.

PARKER, C. F., "Signals in the Sun," *Arizona Highways*, June 1967.

PRESIDENT'S COMMISSION, JOHN G. KEMENY, CHAIRMAN, *The Accident at Three Mile Island*, U.S. Government Printing Office, October 1979.

RANDELL, BRIAN, *Report on Colossus*, Computing Laboratory, Newcastle University, England, 1976.

REDMOND, KENT C., and SMITH, THOMAS M., "Lessons from 'PROJECT Whirlwind,'" *IEEE Spectrum*, October 1977.

RIDGWAY, MATTHEW B., *The Korean War*, New York, Doubleday, 1967.

ROBERTS, LAWRENCE G., "Data by the Packet," Computer Report III, *IEEE Spectrum*, Computer Special, February 1974.

RUSI: Royal United Services Institute for Defence Studies (Whitehall, London, England), Regular Publication: *The RUSI Quarterly Journal*.

STENGERS, JEAN, "La Guerre des Messages Codés (1930–1945)," *L'Histoire*, No. 31, February 1981.

STEVENSON, WILLIAM, *A Man Called Intrepid*, New York, Harcourt, Brace, Jovanovich, 1976.

U.S. ARMY AIR FORCE, *Condensed Analysis of the Ninth Air Force in the European Theater of Operations*, with a Foreword by General Hoyt S. Vandenberg, 1946.

U.S. ARMY COMMAND AND GENERAL STAFF COLLEGE, "Readiness for the Little War," *Military Review*, April–May 1957 editions.

WEYLAND, OTTO P., "The Air Campaign in Korea," *Air University Quarterly Review*, Fall 1953.

WINTERBOTHAM, FREDERICK W., *The ULTRA Secret*, New York, Harper & Row, 1974.

WOODS, DAVID L., *A History of Tactical Communications Techniques*, Martin Company, Orlando, Florida, 1965.

Index